DUNFEY FAMILY TREE

Mary
1922–1989

John "Jack"
1/7/1924

William "Bud"
1925–1991

Walter
1932-1989

Gerald "Jerry"
5/23/1935

Eleanor
11/6/1938

"This spirited and spiritual journey of the Dunfey family is shared in loving, often humorous stories that reach from a mill town in America to townships in South Africa. Thank God for parents who inspired their twelve children to make a difference in our world."

 —**Archbishop Emeritus Desmond** and **Mrs. Leah Tutu**

"The Dunfey family have been faithful, long-term voices for children. I am so grateful Eleanor Dunfey has chosen to share these stories and her family's inspiring legacy."

 —**Marian Wright Edelman**, president, Children's Defense Fund

"I loved the book! It's an uplifting story of the Dunfey family's values, their respect for their individual differences and their determination to work together constructively in life and in business. As one of the woo'd executives, I saw those same merits build a great company, and more importantly, make our country and the world better."

 —**Jim Stamas**, former chief administrative officer, Omni Hotels, and founding dean, Boston University's School of Hospitality

"This is first and foremost a family memoir, told with love and good humor. But it is so much more. The Dunfey family story is a quintessential American story (and a good bit an Irish story) of hard work, social mobility, and success. It is a sprawling tale, not only because the Dunfeys were a sprawling clan, but because this first family of New Hampshire Democratic politics connected with almost every important political figure in 20th C. American politics, and also touched down in places like apartheid era South Africa, Northern Ireland during the 'Troubles,' and Castro-ruled-Cuba. Anyplace in which people suffered injustice. It is a story of self-made fortune, faith, and especially family. And oh, what a family. The world needs more Dunfeys and it was a balm in these troubled times, to visit with them on the pages of this lovingly told remembrance."

 —**Paul LeBlanc**, president, Southern New Hampshire University

"If you want to learn how to achieve in business, faith, social justice, and politics as lived through the lives of one family, then this is the book for you. From the mills of Lowell, Massachusetts to the shores of New Hampshire, Northern Ireland and South Africa, it shows how the values instilled by the Dunfey parents to their twelve incredibly different children transformed people's lives as local and global citizens.

    —**Monica McWilliams**, Founder of Women's Coalition Party, Northern Ireland, signatory to the Belfast Good Friday Peace Agreement, and global advocate for human rights

"Irish emigrant roots, long hours in the cotton mills, endless days in the first small shop—to an international group of hotels. But always each family member and worker was first. *Counter Culture* is a riveting read. It shows that it is possible to have a hugely successful business and yet to infuse this with an absolute commitment to the dignity of the poor man next door and worldwide. This uniquely rounded tale could only have been written by a family member. We are all in the debt of Eleanor Dunfey."

    —**Frank Lewis**, founder & chairman, Storied Kerry/Ciarr ai Scealach; producer/presenter, The Saturday Supplement, Radio Kerry'

"At first you think this is a book about business, buildings, and balance sheets. And then you begin to realize that this saga is also about the power and responsibilities that come whenever church, politics and social responsibilities are willingly embraced with eyes and hearts wide open. But ultimately you understand that the story Eleanor Dunfey shares is really just a love story. It's a love story about a resilient, optimistic, hard-working family with its share of ups and downs, great successes, great struggles, and their share of tears and plenty of laughter, too. And most of all, it's a love story about a family with a mission, thriving, surviving, making things happen, all the while looking out for each other, and then graciously, naturally, seemingly without effort, gathering others around the table."

    —**Paul Boynton**, author, *Begin with Yes*

COUNTER CULTURE

Clams, Convents, and a Circle of Global Citizens

by

Eleanor Dunfey-Freiburger

Peter E. Randall Publisher

Portsmouth, New Hampshire

2019

ISBN: 978-1-942155-15-7
Library of Congress Control Number: 2018960493

Published by Peter E. Randall Publisher
Portsmouth, New Hampshire 03801
www.perpublisher.com

Book design: Martha de Lyra Barker

Front cover photograph captions:
LeRoy W. Dunfey proud owner of Dunfey's Luncheonette. Left to right: Bud Dunfey
and Pat Paterson. Inset: Catherine "Kate" and her drummer fiancé Roy, circa 1914

Back cover photograph captions:
Top: Behind the counter in the first Dunfey's Luncheonette, Lowell, Massachusetts
Left to right: Paul, Walter, Jack, Dick, Bob, our father, LeRoy; Eileen, Jerry, circa 1940s

Lower left: Family reunion at St. Patrick's School, Lowell. Left to right; Back row:
Roy, Jerry, Jack, Walter, Eleanor, Paul, Dick, Bob, Bud. Front row: our father, LeRoy;
Kay (Sr. Francesca); Eileen (Sr. Julie Francesca); Mary (Sr. Ann Francesca), our mother,
Catherine. June 14, 1952

Lower right: In front of newly purchased Parker House, Boston, Massachusetts
Left to right: Bob, Jack, our mother, Catherine; Walter, Jerry, Bud, circa 1969

Back endleaf photograph caption:
Two adjacent hamlets outside of Dingle, County Kerry, Ireland, left to right:
Bailagisha, the birthplace of my grandmother, Mary O'Connor
Ballyferriter, the Manning homestead, birthplace of my grandfather, James
Kate and Eleanor Dunfey at the O'Connor homestead, Bailagisha, circa 1970s

Dedication

To my parents, Kate and Roy,
who gave each of us twelve children
time to love and space to grow
from looms to a kitchen table and counters,
from classrooms and boardrooms,
to a circle of global citizens…

To Jim,
for making what seemed impossible—possible,
our unexpected fifty-year journey together

To Joel and Lanny; Maria and Max,
for the growing years with two loving children
and to more growing years with two extraordinary couples

To Simon, Sophia, Willem, Emily, and Jackson
for being my five unique ways of
saying "yes" to the future

"For all that has been—Thanks. For all that will be—Yes."

—*Dag Hammarskjöld,*
Second United Nations Secretary General,
1953–1961

Contents

Preface

"That story would have more plots than St. Patrick's cemetery!"
—*Rick Dunfey*

Countless plots, for sure.

As the youngest of twelve, I have been given treasures, not of brick and mortar, antiques or jewels, but of lasting gems—stories, woven memories, some pieced and patched, some of whole cloth my siblings have sworn are true. I have often been told: "You should write a memoir, Eleanor!" Each time I smiled, assented, and promptly filed the suggestion in the overflowing file of "someday—maybe." I shrank from the enormity of even finding the right voice for such a saga. Whose memoir would this be, anyway? Just where did my own river of recollections begin and end, and where did it channel into my eleven siblings' ebb and flow? Beyond the improbable feat of sorting fact from fiction, how could I possibly do justice to any one of our lives, much less those of all twelve and our parents?

My nephew, Rick, clearly anticipated my challenge. "That story would have more plots than St. Patrick's cemetery!" he cracked, referring to the Lowell, Massachusetts, burial ground where many of our forebears are laid to rest.

He was right. I've never had an inclination to write some kind of "tell all" tale. Even if I did, I couldn't possibly convey the context and variables of all the plot lines that have shaped our family life. But now I begin this saga in gratitude to my parents and siblings. I want to give back what has been so generously given to me. The "plots" are many and, like St. Patrick's, are sacred ground to me.

I tell my parents' story as the youngest child of these two resilient, humble people. Their life lessons shaped us—around the table, over the counter, and across the world. Cobbled together in this book are direct reminiscences from my mother's unpublished recollections, *Not Cheaper by the Dozen: A Mother's Priceless Memories*, as well as contributions from siblings, including a book of poems by my sister Kay (#4), *Give Me Wings*. The vivid memories of Jack (#5) and Eileen (#9) also feature prominently. I culled the greatest store of recollections from Jerry (#11), which, thankfully, had been indelibly forged in his memory. Without his willingness to dig deep into his reservoir of memories and take the time to share them, I could not have embarked on this hundred-year journey.

My mother lived thirty years longer than my father. She adapted—holding fast to her spiritual convictions while embracing the unpredictable stages in each of her twelve children's lives. "After all," she reflected during the historic cultural upheaval of the sixties and seventies, "I have four daughters who are nuns; I've got to be ready for four times the change." Actually, Catherine Dunfey chose to be ready for *twelve* times the change. This is a story of some of those ages and stages.

From Ireland to "God's Holy Acre"—
The Paddy Camps

> They came to build the canals. They stayed to build a city, eventually evolving from canal diggers and mill workers to police officers, firefighters, business leaders and politicians.
>
> —*David D. McKean,* Lowells Irish
> The History Press 2016

In the spring of 1822, thirty Irish immigrant laborers, carrying shovels and hired by boss Hugh Cummiskey, trudged the twenty-seven miles from Charlestown to Lowell, Massachusetts. McKean adds, it was "a location identified as having the water power necessary to power the cotton looms that would bring wealth to the financial backers and turn America from an agrarian into an industrial nation."

Kirk Boott, manager of the Merrimack Manufacturing Company, had realized he needed a workforce to dig what would become the five miles of canals powering the mills that built the city. Cummiskey's Irish laborers needed jobs. McKean reports:

> And so enter the Irish with their numbers multiplying to more than meet the need…Work gangs grouped by "the old country's 'county' identifications" formed clusters of huts and crude dwellings…The Yankees began calling this mix of shanties and huts the "Paddy Camps." They thought the Irish had come temporarily to work on the project, but the Irish had come to stay.

Once completed, the canal underlay the infrastructure for what was to become the first planned industrial city in the country. The Middlesex Canal eventually powered forty mills.

Many men lost their lives in the building of America's Industrial Revolution. These first laborers who emigrated from Ireland arrived starved and impoverished, rough and rowdy customers. They and their families remained starved by scanty wages. Laborers received no provision for food or housing, and most had no formal education. Those who managed to scrape out an existence settled in the "Paddy Camps," an outlaw settlement that lacked governing authority. The unruly bunch were Catholics, but there wasn't even a church. It is rumored that Kirk Boott's Irish maid, Mrs. Winters, tipped off her boss that trouble would continue to brew as long as there was no church for the Irish settlers. "Get a priest," she advised, according to Jennifer Myers in her account, "Built on the Backs of the Irish" in the *Lowell Sun*.

A call for help went out to the archdiocese of Boston. In 1831, hoping that the Church might strike some God-fearing into the laborers and help to quell the rising river of violence, the company donated an acre of land to build a Catholic church. "The Acre," as it came to be called, is short for God's Holy Acre. When St. Patrick's Church was completed, its towering spire stretching skyward marked the permanent settlement of the Irish in Lowell. The Church would take charge of its members, but like so many other political, civic, and religious institutions, it generally excluded other ethnic groups, most notably the French-Canadian Catholics, who built their own parish compound, St. Jean Baptiste, a few blocks over on Salem Street. Spired silos pointing heavenward—Irish, French, Greek, Polish, or German—claimed most street corners in burgeoning cities, each hoping to corner a direct line to God.

Jennifer Myers adds that Rev. Timothy O'Brien was a proponent of education and identified an order of nuns to start a girls' school. In 1852, five members of the teaching order of the Sisters of Notre Dame de Namur arrived in Lowell from Cincinnati, Ohio. Xaverian Brothers soon followed to staff the boys' school. Dunfeys and Keefes bolstered enrollment: my eight brothers and three sisters, our four Keefe cousins, and a couple of Acre kids who would end up associated with our family throughout their careers attended St. Pat's. In keeping with accepted cultural norms, they had more than a little "God-fearing" struck into them, as well. The Acre's reputation as the Wild West of the East slowly ameliorated. St. Patrick's Church and the parish school became the immigrants' center of life, while the mills imposed order on the work day. By 1850, Lowell's population exceeded 30,000 and the mills employed 10,000 workers, producing 50,000 miles of cloth annually.

My Irish forbears—Elizabeth "Eliza" Powers Dunfey and Matthew Dunfey, Mary O'Connor Manning and James Manning—emigrated from rural villages in Waterford and Kerry Counties, Ireland, to Lowell. Eliza and Matthew were among the second wave of Irish immigration to the States, part of the Famine Irish who arrived in Massachusetts in 1851. Mary and James were part of the third wave of Irish immigrants, arriving in Lowell in the mid-1880s.

Lowell was America's largest industrial hub. It supported entrepreneurial enterprises that grew into industries and drew more Irish, along with thousands of others: Greeks, whose section was dubbed "Acre-Acropolis," Germans, French-Canadians, Poles, Lebanese, and more. Immigrants worked at the Lowell Machine Shop, Hood's Sarsaparilla Laboratory, the Jewett Vinegar Factory, and Massachusetts Mohair Plush. The soft drink Moxie was invented in Lowell, and it was the first city in America to have telephone numbers. Lowell became a melting pot of new Americans.

CHAPTER I

1901

Death at Sea

My maternal grandfather, James Manning, an Irish immigrant, survived the arduous journey to America in the early 1880s, but died just twenty years later on his way back to Ballyferriter, Dingle, County Kerry, Ireland in 1901.

From the *Lowell Sun*:

Buried At Sea
Died on board the Ultonia *while on his way to Ireland*

Denis Murphy, local agent of the Cunard line of steamships, received a cablegram this morning from the office of Cunard Line Co. in Queenstown (Cobh), stating that James Manning, resident of 66 Suffolk Street in this city [Lowell, Massachusetts] who sailed Aug. 3rd, 1901, on board the *Ultonia*, died and was buried at sea after the boat was five days out from Boston. With him was his little five-year-old son who was then left without anyone to care for him but the officers of the boat took him in charge and upon arrival in Queenstown, he was turned over to the steam ship company. In the cablegram that was received in this city [Lowell, Massachusetts] today, it inquires what shall be done with the little boy.

My mother was three weeks away from her seventh birthday when news of her father's death reached the second-floor flat above Donahue's barroom in Lowell's Acre. That was the home where my grandmother, Mary O'Connor Manning, and her husband, James, were raising their four daughters and one son: Mamie, Kate (my mother), Jack, Annie, and Josie, all born between 1892 and 1900.

Adding to my grandmother's heartache and hardship was the fact that five-year-old Jack, on board ship with his father, would arrive in Ireland alone.

After James Manning's death and burial at sea, Cunard Lines notified his relatives in County Kerry. They "collected" Jack, who remained in Ballyferriter from August 1901 until April 1902. During those months, my mother recalls addressing letters from her mother to Irish relatives, pleading that they "send my Jack back to me." Finally, my grandmother's youngest sister, fifteen-year-old Ellie O'Connor, was chosen to escort six-year-old Jack back to the States. It was an occasion of great joy. His four sisters soon nicknamed Jack "Irish" because of the brogue (the name given to the Irish accent) he had picked up. My teenage Aunt Ellie acquired a job as housekeeper for Mr. Chase, the Lowell City Library director, and made friends with many of the other greenhorns fresh off the boats.

By 1901, generations of Lowell mill girls had been at work for more than seventy-five years. Like the poor but aspiring women before her, my maternal grandmother, Mary, had come to America at the age of fifteen, drawn there in 1865 by the promise of honest work, the hope of advancement, and, perhaps, the possibility of reconnecting with James, also from Ballyferriter. Family lore conjectures that Mary and James may have been "seeing each other" back in the old country, but being second cousins, they would not have been permitted to marry.

Like so many before her, my grandmother took her place in the Lowell textile mills, her days measured by the whistle and the bell. Suddenly finding herself a single mother of five children under nine, she barely had time to mourn the death of her husband. She must work. She must make ends meet. My mother's memoir depicts the daily struggle of her mother as sole provider for her family:

> Our home was a tenement over a barroom. My mother, Mary Manning, now a young widow, was working in the mill supporting five of us children. She also took on another job—washing and ironing all the altar cloths and vestments for St. Patrick's Church. Those were the days of starching and there must be no wrinkles, whatsoever! The long altar cloths, therefore, had to be rolled and sent back in long boxes when finished. Delivering those cloths in perfect condition was my job.

Mary O'Connor Manning worked in the mills for many years, as did my mother and her older sister, my Aunt Mamie. My grandmother's days were defined by the loom, the laundry, and eventually, a welcome move from the mill to the Lowell City Library's cleaning duties. But her life was far from dull. In the corporate town that historians recognize as the epicenter of the industrial revolution, "gaiety" was a necessary corrective to the drudgery of spindle and wheel. When my mother talked about my grandmother's ingenuity on those long-gone Saturday nights, she revealed Mary Manning's resilience and resourcefulness:

She would hire a fiddler most every Saturday night for an Irish
dance in our kitchen–admission, twenty-five cents—all the girls
from the boarding houses would come to jig the night away to
the delight of us kids.

A year after her brother Jack returned from Ireland, my mother was sent by
my grandmother Manning to live with a "rich aunt." Elizabeth Gallagher
was married to my grandfather's cousin Patrick, owner of "Manning's
Place," a grocery store and a tenement on Salem Street. In her self-deprecating way, my mother writes about those days:

I suppose that I was sent to live with them because they did not
have any children, and also as a help to my mother who was now
trying to support five children. This was quite a change for me
and I was spoiled...given lovely clothes, dancing lessons, sent to
the Bartlett School, meeting all new rich playmates. I must have
been seen as the "poor little rich girl" you read about.

She doesn't remember that any of her family members came to visit, even
though they lived only a few blocks away. When she did see them, "it was
only for about fifteen or twenty minutes." She would be directed by her
aunt "not to let the children spoil or muss my dress."

After the death of Elizabeth's husband, Patrick Manning, my grandmother, possibly seeing that young Kate was being spoiled, brought my
mother back to their flat. Elizabeth was heartbroken and would send for
young Kate, sit her on her lap and cry. My mother recalls in her memoir
that she "hugged me until I could barely breathe. I was confused by the
fuss and so glad to be back at home out of the smothering reach of a permanent adoption." I remember, years later, my dad singing popular ballads.
I wonder what went through my mother's mind when she heard the one
from 1906 about a young mother who had lost her baby girl. The woman
frequently sees a beautiful neighborhood child and sings, "Won't you come
over to my house...I'll give you playthings, a dolly or two...I'll put your
hair in a curl; If you'll come over to my house and play that you're my little
girl." Sad ballads were the top hits in my father's repertoire.

An early separation of my father from his parents had also been a possibility. As a baby, LeRoy Dunfey (better known as simply "Roy") was
almost given up for adoption. A cousin and her sea captain husband, a
childless couple, pleaded to take him. There was discussion but my grandparents could not part with him. We have no further details of the story.
He was the second of four children and the first son, which may have had

some bearing on the decision. Although my father's given name is listed in birth records as William Dunphy, his full name, William LeRoy Dunphy, appears in the 1900 census of Lowell residents. Since the spelling of surnames was not standardized before the end of the nineteenth century, it is unsurprising that family records list the traditional Irish spelling, Dunphy (similar to Murphy). As far as we can ascertain, all Dunfeys are related, and some Dunphys may be, as well.

Eleanor Smythe Dunfey (for whom I am named) was born in Nova Scotia in 1865. My grandfather, Nick, born in Cambridge, Massachusetts, in 1860, worked 1870–1880 as a mill worker in Lowell. At some point, he was associated with liquor shops both in Lowell and in New York's Manhattan, where he and his wife moved with their one-year-old daughter, Myrtle, six months before my father was born on December 13, 1891. My grandparents had two more children, Richard (Richie) and Leila. That just may be where my Grandmother Eleanor got her idea of the perfect family: two boys and two girls, which she would refer to a few years later in speaking with my mother. From the few accounts passed on in family lore, my grandfather, Nick, was a warm and friendly chap who may, for a time, have owned the liquor enterprise in Manhattan, but whose moves from Lowell to Manhattan and back to Lowell mark him more as an "Irish scamp" than as a businessman. Whatever the true story, we do know that my father, at age twelve, began working in the mills alongside his father. Both were mule spinners, a skill that required great strength and agility. My father remained until 1915.

My uncle, "Irish" Jack Manning, Lowell Massachusetts, circa 1903, at age seven. This photograph was sent to the County Kerry relatives who had cared for him for almost a year after he arrived alone from America aboard Cunard Lines in 1901.

The Manning homestead in Ballyferriter, near Dingle. This is the home and these are the relatives who cared for "Young Jack" for almost a year. 1981.

Letter sent from cousin Tom Manning returning Jack's photograph. 70 years later, to my mother in Lowell in 1972.

My maternal grandfather, James Manning, ca. 1890, died on board the *Ultonia* in 1901, returning to Ireland. My maternal grandmother, Mary O'Connor Manning, ca. 1890. She was widowed when my grandfather, James, died at sea, leaving her with five children to raise.

CHAPTER 2

1913–1915

Before and After "Labor" Day

"The two-week summer holiday of 1913 at Salisbury Beach with the Violet Club Girls," my mother writes, "was to be a breathless time for which each of us girls saved twenty-five cents a week for the whole year, to rent a cottage." That's where my mother met my father.

The Violet Club Girls were happy about their location. A group of young men from the Lowell Chicksaw Club had moved into the cottage next door. There was immediate contact followed by dancing, roller skating, beaching, and bowling. It wasn't until the last day of the vacation that my father approached Kate for an actual date. After that, he wasted little time, surely a sign of his good judgment. On Labor Day, LeRoy Dunfey proposed to Kate Manning in a canoe on Lake Mascuppic, a few miles up the Merrimack River from the Lowell Mills where each of them worked. Years later, when we would plead with our mother of twelve to write her autobiography, she loved to quip: "Oh, I don't need a book to tell my life; I can write it in one sentence: I was engaged to your father on Labor Day and was in labor ever after."

Showing evidence of her own "good judgment," she accepted his proposal on condition they wait a year. One reason for this delay was that Kate had had another suitor, Jack Sullivan, who had already given her an engagement ring. She had told him she wasn't ready to accept a ring, but he had insisted she take it, so there the diamond was—hidden in her lunch pail. She had shown it off only to a few girlfriends at the mill. She definitely would not show it to her mother. Kate was beside herself trying to figure out what to do about the situation. She didn't want to hurt Jack Sullivan's feelings. He was a great guy, but she knew in her heart that Roy Dunfey was the man she wanted to marry.

For better or for worse, the rumor mill was alive and well. Jack Sullivan heard that Kate had gone on a date with Roy Dunfey and showed up at Kate's door, asking if the rumor was true. Hearing her honest, embarrassed response, he demanded the ring's return, a demand that removed the weighty predicament from her life, lightening her heavy heart—and her secret hiding place, the lunch pail.

The mills: "College of knowledge"

It had not been easy for these immigrants to move from agrarian to urban life, to journey from a known country into the unknown. It was a time when swelling immigrant waves crashed on formerly small farming communities like Lowell, and the real people who made up those waves were often treated with derision and suspicion. Starting at the bottom of the economic and social ladders, families bore the costs of numerous upheavals. This was true for my parents and for so many other ethnic minorities. They chose to deal with that reality by working hard.

My mother's memoir echoes sentiments published in the mid-nineteenth-century journal, the *Lowell Offering*. One of the essays of unknown authorship, "A Week in the Mills," concludes: "Few would wish to spend a whole life in a factory, but few are discontented who do thus seek a subsistence for a term of months or years."

From the beginning of her memoir, which she started hand writing at age seventy-eight, Kate Dunfey reflects realistic optimism that characterized her entire life. Even in the later, prosperous years when she received an honorary degree from Merrimack College along with Boston Pops conductor Arthur Fieldler, she mused that she earned her education at the Boott Mill—her "College of Knowledge" along the banks of the Merrimack River:

> At the age of 14, I also became a mill girl earning seven dollars a week. I remained a mill worker until I married at the age of 21. No, it was not horrible! My teenage years were happy, happy ones. Working hard all day from 6:30 a.m. 'til 6:00 p.m. and dancing every night until 11:30 or midnight at Associate Hall to the Miner's Union Singing Orchestra.

I am certain that our family story would not have unfolded as it did, had my mother not left school in the seventh grade to work in the mills to help support her family, a sacrifice modeled on her mother's sacrifices and those of so many of her contemporaries. She chose to focus on the hijinks and humor, the real and raw life-learning, the spiritual ties, and family bonds weaving a mood of hopefulness that envisioned brighter days ahead. She would meet Roy Dunfey and termed it "a happy fate" to discover that the handsome mill-worker-by-day was a drummer and leader of his own orchestra by night. They soon realized they shared the same life learning and outlook.

Most of what we do know about my father's early years comes from my mother's memoir, which focuses primarily on their life together after 1913:

> When I was 19 and he was 22, Roy came courting on a bicycle
> from the Pawtucketville section of the city to Fletcher Street in
> the Acre section where I lived. I enjoyed Roy because he was a
> talker and, by nature, I am a listener—a good combination!

My mother also recalls loving to dance with the drummer. She could not help but be impressed with the hard working, outgoing leader of "Dunfey's Orchestra." Besides laboring all day at the Suffolk Mills, he and his orchestra were booked three to four nights a week. My mother respected my father's entrepreneurial spirit and was impressed that he had escaped the mills in 1915 for a much better job at the John Hancock Insurance Company, while still moonlighting with his orchestra for a goodly sum.

1915: "Fate, Date, Kate, and oh how we did propagate"
—Catherine Dunfey, Memoir

With delight and conciseness, my mother describes in her memoir what did happen: "Fate, Kate, a date—and oh how we did propagate!" On November 24, 1915—a blowing and chilly Thanksgiving Eve sprung straight out of the Irish imagination—the lovely bride, Kate Manning, made her way down the crooked stairs from the Manning flat above Donahue's Bar at the corner of Fletcher and Broadway. Three such bars anchored the Acre section of Lowell, but the dank watering holes did not distract or dismay the bride. She saw only the soaring spire of St. Patrick's Church two blocks away.

My mother was proud of the wedding dress she had made, a copy of one she had seen in the window of the Gilday Shop downtown. She never could have afforded a store-bought dress on a mill girl's pittance, so she had sewed long and hard on that gown. Along with twenty-four other couples, Catherine and LeRoy Dunfey were married in the rectory of St. Patrick's parish. The priest blessed all their marriages in a brief ceremony, because these couples could not afford a church wedding. This slight toward the young mill workers did not faze them a bit. My maternal grandmother, Mary O'Connor Manning, ensured the joy of the occasion by doing all the cooking for my parents' reception, which continued through the "wee hours" and probably spilled down the stairs to Donahue's Bar.

Kate and Roy slipped out of the celebration to meet up with the other newly married couples at the Boston & Lowell Railroad Station. From there, the "Honeymoon Express," as it was dubbed, would take them to Boston for a long weekend getaway. Spirits were high and practical jokes were plentiful. Some grooms hid in the station, making it look as though their brides had been left at the tracks. Others, in response to cheering friends, swooped in and lifted their new spouses onto the train or pretended they were choosing different partners as they all began their journey to Boston and new lives together.

My father would forever after tease my mother that they had spent most of their three-day honeymoon in convents. He was right. Two of my mother's sisters and her aunt were Sisters of Notre Dame, a religious teaching order with a number of schools in the Boston area. On the first day of their honeymoon, the newlyweds visited my mother's older sister Mamie, where they were served Thanksgiving dinner. The following day, my Aunt Annie was on the list. Then, Aunt Ellie welcomed them to her convent. Ellie was my grandmother's youngest sister, the one who had emigrated from Ballyferriter to Lowell all those years ago, at age fifteen, to bring "Irish Jack" home to his family.

Some might dub Kate's delight with her marriage as youthful naïveté. For my mother, however, it was reality:

> We were a happy bride and groom as we returned to Lowell to our own little tenement consisting of five rooms in a nine-tenement block at 138 Cross Street, quite close to my mother. How proud we were to have furnished our own place with the fabulous wages we were earning: $12 a week for Roy and $7 for me.

That attitude endured.

In the "family way"

My mother gave birth to the first five of their twelve children in that small Acre flat. She delivered four daughters and eight sons over the next twenty-two years, and also welcomed a few waifs, orphans, and strangers along the way. Our parents' propagation was not unique, especially considering our Irish-Catholic roots in Lowell's Acre at the turn of the twentieth century. Growing up in that era, my parents knew no such thing as the nuclear family. "Family" meant whoever needed a meal and a place to sleep, no matter how straitened one's own circumstances might be. While my grandmother Mary Manning cared for her five children, for example, she also took in her partially blind younger sister, my great aunt Josie, who later returned to the family homestead in the hamlet of Baile Eaglaise (pronounced Ba-ág-ish-a) in Ireland.

Besides looking after (a common Irish phrase for taking care of) relatives, my grandmother also reached out to a needy teenage orphan, John Heslin, who became a member of the family, and then to the young Rose

Langlois, taking her home as well. My mother's nonchalant reference to such a practice shows its normalcy. It was a custom to bring children from an orphanage to the church and after Mass, with the hope that parishioners would choose a child to take home for the short- or long-term. Meanwhile, in an apartment that seemed to grow smaller each year, my parents were birthing their own babies, with the third expected in March, 1920.

August, 1913.
Mary O'Connor Manning and
my mother, Kate, in 1913.

Mill workers from 6 a.m. to 6 p.m.; members of Violet Club (ladies) and Chicksaw Club (men) on weeknights, weekends and one-week's vacation, here socializing at Salisbury Beach.

Engaged to Roy Dunfey on Labor Day, 1913, at Mascuppic Lake. Kate enjoyed describing the rest of her life: "I met your father on Labor Day and was in labor ever after!" I am their 12th child.

Always ready to pose on their Sunday afternoon dates with their Violet and Chicksaw club friends were Roy and Kate, second and third from left.

Thanksgiving Eve, November 24, 1915, Catherine [Kate] Manning and LeRoy [Roy] Dunfey were married in St. Patick's parish rectory along with 24 other couples. Only the rich had church nuptials.

Kate and Roy Dunfey's first apartment, a tiny one in the middle of a nine-tenement block at 138 Cross Street, Lowell, Massachusetts. They furnished it with their fabulous mill worker weekly wages: $12. for Roy and $7. for Kate.

The third job—the first Dunfey store 1920

LeRoy Dunfey
circa 1920

The third child—Kay
the first Dunfey girl.

CHAPTER 3

1920

Counter Culture: First Girl, First Store

"Over that counter, all twelve children learned about the world from their dad."

—*Catherine Dunfey*, Memoir

My mother soon faced her first test of confidence in her husband's entrepreneurial skills:

> Roy was now entertaining the idea of going into business for himself. His work with John Hancock Insurance and his orchestra engagements were bringing in a salary to keep us comfortable. I was pregnant with my third child and not too anxious to see Roy make this move. I didn't interfere though because I saw him keep his orchestra thriving and organized. I sensed he could and wanted to be his own boss.
>
> It wasn't until much, much later we recognized that the purchase of the store on Broadway was the base that our family business was ultimately built on. Roy and Walter Pouliot (his piano player in the orchestra) became partners, opening a small fruit, candy, and soda shop at 353 Broadway just five minutes from Cross Street where we were living.

Two new ventures: The birth of the first daughter, Catherine Marie, "Kay," two months before the birth of what would become the Dunfey family business. Fast forward to 1958, six years after my father's sudden death. Kay, now 38, wrote a letter to my mother on Father's Day, recalling the young LeRoy in 1920 when he purchased that first store at 353 Broadway, The Acre, Lowell, Massachusetts:

> It's not too challenging for us to visualize the appearance and personality of the young man, LeRoy W. Dunfey, on that memorable day when it became "his" store: He must have been about Walter's present age (26), with Jerry's handsome features, Roy's initiative, Paul's vision, Jack's executive ability, Bud's understanding of human nature, Bob's business acumen, and Dick's

eloquence. It's no wonder that you, Mother, lost your heart to that irresistible composite, animated by the great unique soul of our dad!"

—Kay Dunfey, Give Me Wings, 1958

Although things were not easy, they went fairly well until Thanksgiving week, when Walter Pouliot's pregnant wife was in a car accident. His concern was so great that he wanted out—so Roy bought Pouliot's share.

My mother not only observed her husband's motivation and hard work, she managed to find a young woman who would come to the Cross Street apartment to babysit now and then so that she could walk the two blocks to the store to help out:

> Here it was—all ours—a family of three and 353 Broadway where all the kids would go through boot camp, so to say, under the guidance of Dad. Over that counter, he taught them how to treat all people—at that time mostly Irish, French, Greek, Italian, and Lebanese, such a life lesson for my children to have. Little did we realize what their dad's example would lead to in the years ahead.

With a brand-new baby and a brand-new enterprise, Roy Dunfey had to make his store a success, and he wasted no time doing so. Space was at a premium, so he set up a fruit pyramid in the left window. A newspaper rack hung on one side of the entrance. He sold bread and milk. Coffee was a nickel, if you had one. If you didn't, you could also get a "food coupon" from St. Patrick's rectory or simply wait a minute and Roy Dunfey would serve you one. The warmth and odor of the kerosene oil burner were free.

Kay memorialized the first dollar our dad earned there:

> This is the dollar that Dad never spent. With it he purchased the homespun fabric of happiness to clothe us warmly...the spacious shelter of a love that was proof against stress...an inner security, the unmeasured fare of a living faith: unquenchable faith in God; generous faith in all of God's children; and a humble faith in self. This is the dollar he never spent, and with which he procured the imponderables that money cannot buy. We are rich, indeed!

1920: Lowell's Acre: Location—location—location

The City Barns was the center of the Acre not only for equipment storage but also for laborers who emerged from their hovels and gathered at 6:00 each morning. The lucky ones had "coins" issued by "friends in high places" or another source, giving them a permit to work. When there was a storm, each would be assigned a city intersection to maintain. Four barrooms, over one of which my mother had lived, lay within a stone's throw of the store. They offered other kinds of "spirits" to warm customers' systems temporarily and empty their pockets permanently. Lacking education and weighed down by burdens, men often tried to ease desperation by drinking away their meager wages. The women's "escape" was more often hidden in bottles under their threadbare sweaters and the cover of night.

There was no food or warmth in sight on Broadway. So my father went out and bought an apartment-sized kitchen counter and enough turkeys to fill it.

> "In between nursing and caring for three young children," my mother muses, "I started roasting extra turkeys at home as my contribution to the sandwich making. I did a lot of cooking and baking anyway, just to feed the family. I'd bake a dozen pies at a time—two of each of the family favorites: apple, cherry, blueberry, pineapple, lemon meringue. But I never had to make pies for the store. Mrs. Talty, who lived around the corner from the store, baked wonderful pies and cakes to sell."

In the Acre there also was a Greek coffee shop. In winter, you could look in and see a couple of old Greek guys drinking coffee but a long line of tattered overcoats on hooks along the wall. Those belonged to men who were downstairs drinking and playing Baboot, a Greek gambling game. Every once in a while, the shop was raided. The cops were Acre people, though, so they often left their clientele alone. The teasing, the pinball games, and even the "one-armed bandit" provided brief escapes but did not diminish the reality of the hardships.

The perfect family: two boys and two girls

My parents' fourth child, another daughter, whom they named Mary, arrived in 1922. According to my grandmother Eleanor Smythe Dunfey, Catherine and Roy now had "the perfect family, and she made her opinion known!" My mother adds, "so then I went on and had eight more!" Sixteen years and another eight name-decisions later, my parents would baptize me, their twelfth child, "Eleanor," as much for Eleanor Roosevelt as for my grandmother. In the early 1920s, my parents also marked the growth of their fledgling business with a new name: Dunfey's Luncheonette replaced Dunfey's Variety Store. When he decided to sell food, my father called a friend and carpenter, Mr. Burns, to build a sandwich board for which there was no room, so it was set in the window. In this Wild West of the East Acre called Broadway, Roy Dunfey planted his feet, his drums, and his hopes.

My parents had no experience in the hospitality business when they started the luncheonette at 353 Broadway. No matter. In Lowell, the Bay State's second largest city, hospitality began in the kitchens of the mill workers themselves. So, while it is true they started from scratch at the luncheonette, they were not exactly novices. In our home, with ten to fourteen hungry mouths around the table, every meal resembled restaurant service. In Dunfey's Luncheonette, which we called "the store," Dad installed seven counter stools (and later two booths) to serve his hungry customers, expanding the menu beyond turkey sandwiches to hotdogs, hamburgers, and tuna and egg salads, while still stocking a variety store inventory of newspapers, a fruit pyramid displayed in one window, penny candy in a small glass case, milk in the ice box, bread on a rack, and cigars and cigarettes secured on shelves behind the counter and sold singly.

It wasn't long before "Dad Roy" was singing lullabies to a new baby boy and a whole new refrain on 353 Broadway. The fifth child, Jack, was the first whose birth exceeded my grandmother's idea of "the perfect family." Throughout his currently ninety-five-years of life, Jack has exceeded expectations in many significant ways, shaping the trajectory of our Dunfey family and business.

Father, businessman, citizen

On the doorstep of the Great Depression, our dad's rituals focused on making a livelihood. In the darkness before dawn of many days, he pulled open the store's squawking hinged screen door, leaning back on it while rotating the hefty key in the lock. The heavy wooden door reluctantly gave way. Lights. Heater. Coffee. Cash drawer. Dunfey's Luncheonette was ready for another day of business. Business involved more than selling food and basic household necessities. The business of politics also awakened in Roy Dunfey during those early years as a storeowner. Where better to listen to and identify people's needs than at the central artery of the Acre, 353 Broadway? Believing he could make a difference in the lives of his Acre neighbors, he volunteered as an unpaid health/welfare commissioner in a city of 105,000 people after the former commissioner went to jail for graft.

Regular customers generated the store's modest success. Among them was my paternal grandfather, Nicholas "Nick" Dunfey, who lived above Marie's Seafood Place on Moody Street. Nick added personality if not profit. He was a familiar, amiable fixture, seated at the small round table reading his newspaper just a few feet beyond the counter's soda fountain. The other "regulars" assumed that with only a third-grade education, he was not actually reading: "Hey, Nick," one of the Broadway characters would tease, "You're reading that newspaper upside down!" With a mere lift of an eyebrow and without moving the pipe set firmly in the corner of his mouth under his bushy white mustache, he'd answer, "Sure I am. *Anyone* can read it the other way!"

And so it would go each day, the banter, the "razzing," and calling out French, Irish, Greek, and Lebanese nicknames, a common practice among working-class folk. It was a pre-TV version of *Cheers*, a place where everybody knew your name—or, in this case, your nickname. Nobody had a real first name. It was Soup Campbell. Spotsy McNamara. Banty Shanahan. Chowda Qualey. Tights Carney. Squash Conlan. Star Flanagan. Suitcoat Rowley. Biscuits Leahy. Here, you entered a colorful, politically incorrect atmosphere. Over that counter we met men and women from cultures different from our Irish roots. What was the common bond? Hands down, the universal language of humor, hard work, a hot cup of coffee, and stories that built trust in that Acre enclave.

The commonalities among the clientele in no way eliminated accents, brogues, customs or heritage—or even deeply rooted prejudices. The razzing could have an edge. In that luncheonette, undertakers, policemen, serious political thinkers such as Charlie Connor of the *Lowell Optic*, and a slapstick, motley assortment of down-on-their-luck folks found seats at the counter and willing ears for their woes. When you sat down at the counter, you knew it meant you would not simply drink or eat. You expected to be interrupted: "Pass the pepper..." or the salt or a napkin. You knew if you had a newspaper even partially open, someone would be reading over your shoulder. You expected to be teased into conversation. Comments, quips, and conversations were part of the "daily specials." That was *Counter Culture*. That was the way customers also saw they could trust Roy Dunfey. He accepted them, acting on their behalf not only by inviting them in out of the cold but also by representing their needs in City Hall.

While learning how to cook a hamburger and make change, we young Dunfey kids observed firsthand the many personalities of an intergenerational, ethnic, and economic mix of people whose raw pain and often scary behavior played out on the street and in the store. It was on-the-job training, a kind of "counter intelligence" that informed our counter culture. One reporter later described *when* our lifelong training started: "For the Dunfey kids, it was shortly after they learned to walk!"

Four decades after those "not so affluent years," and seventeen years after our dad had died, my brother Jack received a letter from the long-ago *Lowell Optic* delivery boy. As a lad, Ernie Berry had assisted his boss and newspaper owner, Charlie Connor, in delivering the weekly political update. Berry expressed memories of that era at Dunfey's Luncheonette:

> *November 17, 1969 [the first anniversary of the Dunfey family's purchase of the Parker House in Boston]*

> *Friend John (Jack):*
> *Dad Roy's picture in yesterday's* Lowell Sun *brought cherished memories immediately to mind.*
>
> *Memories racing back to the not so affluent days of the 30's on lower Broadway, Lowell, when your genial dad presided over a combination variety store and luncheonette; a regular stop on Saturday trips with Charlie Connor when I would help him and his wheelchair up the three steps into the store to deliver copies of his weekly political gazette—the* Town Optic.
>
> *We always had to pause, chat-a-bit, and enjoy hot coffee and sandwiches. Roy's hospitality would have it no other way.*
>
> *Dad Roy was a good Christian, devoted family man, and source of encouragement and sound advice to all in the Acre.*
>
> *Were he in our midst today, your father would be extremely proud of the great progress made in all directions by the younger Dunfey generation.*
>
> *Best regards to your mother, brothers, sisters and their families. And success to Roy F. on his recent association with the Dunfey Hotel operation.*

> *Cordially, Ernie Berry*

Roy Dunfey, proud owner of
Dunfey's Variety Store (later Dunfey's
Luncheonette) 353 Broadway, in
Lowell, Massachusetts, Acre section.
Purchased in 1920, it was the first
of what would become the Dunfey
Family Corporation, then Omni Hotels
International. Twenty-two years later,
in a letter to his "first girl" who had,
by then, joined the convent, our dad
describes his store updates including
"our brand new swell stainless steel
backsplash and refrigerated sandwich
board unit."

My mother's original
scrapbook, a page of pride
in my father's entrepre-
neurship: orchestra gigs,
and two newly installed
booths. Pat Paterson, too,
always on hand when
cameras were around
(see front book cover).

CHAPTER 4

Surviving Birth and the Tumult of Living

At midnight in our home, Dr. Leahy performed a tracheotomy
on two-year-old Jack—right on the kitchen table.
                                        —*Catherine Dunfey*, Memoir

Beyond the fact that the twelve of us—and my mother—survived our birthing process, it also seems a miracle that we all survived the tumult of living.
More than once it was a close call. The firstborn arrived in 1917 on the verge
of an influenza epidemic which claimed an estimated fifty million people
(compared to sixteen million lives lost in World War I). Like most working
poor at the time, my mother delivered nine babies at home—the first five
in the Acre's Cross Street tenement. As she recalls in her memoir, "I was
put out of the picture, things were so difficult, and where the ether began,
my recollections end." She awoke to find herself the mother of a baby boy
whom they named Roy Francis after my dad, who was at her side for that
birth and the following eight home deliveries (the last three were hospital
babies and fathers weren't allowed to be present, something of an irony
because he probably had more experience than some of the obstetricians).

Our dad was not simply an onlooker. In fact, when my brother Paul was
ready to make his appearance on a Sunday morning when my grandmother
and aunt—the traditional midwives—were in church, it was my dad who
recognized the imminence of the delivery. My mother relates his order:

> "You'd better get into bed, Kate." Before doctor or midwives
> could arrive, "Whoops!" Here comes my Paul into the world—
> almost on the kitchen floor with only his mother and dad on the
> reception committee!

Kate was, perhaps, too young and too new at birthing to recognize the
courage that women have brought to bear in enduring the hardship and
uncertainty of home delivery. Early century statistics recorded in historian
Judith Walzer Leavitt's remarkable study, *Brought to Bed: Childbearing in
America 1750 to 1950*, states: "An almost permanent expectation of mothers was to lose children either at birth or in the first year of life." Beyond
birth, infectious diseases became the worry. My siblings Roy (1917), Paul
(1918), Kay (1920), Mary (1922), Jack (1924), Bud (1925), Bob (1928), Richard

(1929), and Eileen (1930) were born before the widespread use of inoculations against TB, polio, diphtheria, and scarlet fever.

At the age of two, Jack contracted diphtheria, a disease that had not been a serious threat since 1913. My mother writes:

> Jack was in such a bad way that the doctor advised an emergency operation to save him. At midnight, Dr. Leahy performed a tracheotomy—right in our home—on the kitchen table.

My mother stood over her toddler while the doctor cut a hole in his neck and inserted the breathing tube. Early the next morning the doctor returned, demonstrating to my mother how she would have to remove the tube, clean it with a pipe cleaner and then, of course, place it back in his neck. She would write later, "I don't know how I followed those orders. I guess I just knew I had to."

When my sister Mary contracted scarlet fever in 1928, before the contagion was controlled by disease-specific antibiotics, one of the rigors patients endured was isolation. Jack remembers a man hammering the *Quarantine* sign to our door. My siblings were sent down the street to stay with my paternal grandmother, Eleanor, leaving my mother and Mary alone in the house.

At age seven, my brother, Bud, also faced a life-threatening disease—at the brink of another birth of a sibling. In late January 1932, my mother arrived home from her first experience of delivering a baby in a hospital (Walter, #10):

> I was already six children beyond my mother-in-law's idea of "the perfect family." But I was happy. Walter was a healthy boy. That first night, though, I noticed Bud was snuggling and not wanting to leave me. I thought it was just that he had missed me. That may have been true, but he took ill that night, and when the doctor arrived in the morning, he announced that Bud had Scarlet Fever. My Buddy was scooped up and taken, by motorcycle, to the isolation hospital where I could not visit him because of the new baby. The quarantine sign, warning all to keep away, was once again hammered onto our front door.

Fortunately, the second half-dozen Dunfey babies—Bob, Dick, Eileen, Walter, Jerry, and Eleanor—were born healthy. There would be health challenges along the way, but we all got off to a good start.

First four children., left to right: Kay, Mary, Paul, Roy. "Now you have the perfect family," according to Kate's mother-in-law: "two boys and two girls." Kate went on to have eight more.

My paternal grandfather, circa 1890s,
a witty, winsome and goodhearted
"scamp" behind that mustache.

My paternal grandmother, Eleanor
Smythe Dunfey, circa 1890s.

The Birthplace *(with apologies to Robert Frost)*

By Kay Dunfey, Give Me Wings

This corner, wrested from the wood,
My Father bought to raise his brood.
Five were Acre-born, beside the store,
Here Mother bore him seven more.
When life spilled over everywhere,
Our neighbors came to be aware
That our snow lasted until spring,
And our yard fostered everything
(But grass!) Our wall kept no one in,
Just marked a world outside to win.
If spirits linger there today,
They laugh and quarrel, care and pray—
For angled on this corner slope,
Depression head-on met Mt. Hope.

CHAPTER 5

Upstairs, Downstairs

119-121 Fifth Avenue is at the corner of Mt. Hope Street in the Pawtucketville section of Lowell, Massachusetts, and there, as my sister, Kay, writes, "Depression head-on, met Mt. Hope."

For the first ten years and five children, the Dunfey family lived in the nine-tenement block at 138 Cross Street. To buy a home in those days was a big step. My mother's joy about the move to a home of their own, and the arrival of baby #6, is tangible in her writing:

> It became 'Mother's Day' the day we left Cross Street to live in our own home across the bridge in Pawtucketville with our very own yard for the children and more room for comfort—never realizing that there would be six more children added to the Dunfey family to fill up what seemed a spacious place in 1925. To say I was on cloud nine would be putting it mildly! I was as excited as any bride moving into her home. That happiness was passed on as a gift of singing, I think, to my unborn. Through the years, we always knew when Bud was coming—You could hear him singing morning, noon, night and the wee hours—even in the shower, belting out, "O Holy Night," in the middle of the summer! He had a song in his heart even while the neighbors tried to sleep!

I often wonder how our growing family fit, even in these "spacious" living quarters. The twelve-foot square kitchen was home to a black Garland stove with four removable plates to feed it coal and a front steel door that opened. We put buttered bread on a sliding tray to make delicious crisp toast, that we called oven bread.

An icebox kept food cold as long as we were on the ice man's regular route for deliveries. We graduated to a Westinghouse refrigerator by the mid-thirties, when my dad also eased the burden of my mother's mountain of ironing by purchasing a sit-down steam-ironing machine.

Our young cousin, Marie Hart, a "sweet angel" according to my mother, was part of the Westfield/Springfield O'Connor, Fenton branch of my mother's family. Marie was the only child of a cousin, Pat Hart, whose wife became seriously ill after the birth of their daughter. They returned for some years to Ventry, near Dingle, where Marie's mother was cared for. Pat Hart became a direct link for all of the family in the States when we were first reconnecting to our roots. He and Marie often visited the Dunfeys and Keefes in Lowell, and she recalls as young as five, being in awe of my mother. "She was always so kind and looked after me along with Aunt Josie Keefe…I remember her in the kitchen where there was a huge ironing machine. Each of the five doors off the kitchen had hangers with pressed shirts and blouses [uniforms] ready for school each day."

The expandable—always expanded—kitchen table found its place between a 6-by-8-foot bathroom on the left (called "Dick's bathroom" because he took so much time combing his hair in front of the medicine cabinet mirror) and the pantry, a bit larger than the bathroom. The pantry housed a wringer washing machine which was often the destination for unwashed cast iron pans—"hidden" by siblings on KP duty. They were anxious to get away from the stack of dishes in the over-sized, black-stone sink, and out to a "hoodsie hop" (teenage dance) at the CYO or movie at the downtown Strand Theatre.

Soon after the Dunfeys settled in at #121 on the first floor, my Aunt Josie married Tom Keefe. Along with my maternal grandmother, Nanna Manning, they became the "family upstairs" at 119 Fifth Avenue. The upstairs Keefes and the downstairs Dunfeys never lacked a sibling or cousin to "create incidents that would be omitted [my mother concedes] from a book on how to bring up children." For instance, at about age ten, Jack figured out how to start a steamroller that had been parked in the cow field overnight during roadwork. He was able to steer it onto Mt. Hope Street where the younger kids, including our five-year-old cousin Ed Keefe, got a front row seat along the curb to watch the spectacle. Jack had not managed to figure out, however, where the brakes and reverse gears were. He and the steamroller came hurtling down the hill and the machine went out of control.

To his horror, he rolled over Eddie Keefe's foot. Believing that he couldn't possibly face the consequences from our Aunt Josie, Jack decided to save himself by running away, heading a couple of miles up Princeton Boulevard. Younger brothers Bud and Bob and cousin Joe Keefe joined him. A drenching rain short-circuited their getaway. Starved, soaked, and scared in what he had figured would be the "shelter" of pine trees, Jack decided it might be less punishing to face Aunt Josie's verbal wrath after all. He never did mention a word about the wrath he faced from our parents, but he did note that his soggy partners in escape had made themselves scarce as soon as they arrived home.

Jack always had a trail of peers and younger kids following him around, more often than not more than willing to participate in the serious business of deciding the day's or night's agenda. The boys turned to other, less-punishable but similarly creative pranks, while Eddie could now proudly claim to be one of the "walking wounded" at an early age.

Our back yard was bordered by a good-sized plot which, after Cross Street, felt like a large farmyard. The "cow field" as we city kids called it (grazing land for at most one calf), provided a great place for sports and a spot to meet up with pals. Our neighbors were mainly of French and Irish origins. In fact, St. Joan of Arc, the French-speaking Catholic church, was almost at our back door and provided free movies in its hall every Sunday, a real bonus for the kids. The teenage Keefes and Dunfeys also thought it an added bonus to go to confession on a Saturday afternoon at the French church, because they figured the priest could not understand English. They knew, from experience, that Fr. McGuire and Fr. McGrath in St. Rita's parish understood the English language only too well.

New ages and stages

The move to the Pawtucketville section of the city meant our family also changed parishes, but all the kids continued to attend St. Patrick's School—now a two-mile walk over the Moody Street or Pawtucket bridge. Our good-natured neighbor, Mr. Bedard, allowed Keefes and Dunfeys to pile in the back of his truck for the trip across town. Connection with two parishes doubled our activities, both religious and social. The Catholic Youth Organization (CYO) was the center of our active teenage years. The Catholic Church was divided into dioceses with a bishop as the leader of each. During the Great Depression, Father Shiel, a prison chaplain working with youth in Chicago, saw the need to provide activities for teenagers. The 1930 program focused on athletic leagues for boys and grew from there. It became a core principle of CYO not to discriminate on the basis of race, religion, or gender, as was common in other youth organizations of the time. St. Rita's CYO not only bragged about its sports, but also its award-winning marching band and cadets, and its wide range of social events. Keefes and Dunfeys squeezed in as much as they could with school and work. Kay was leader of the drum majors; Mary, like our dad, was the drummer; Bud and cousin Joe Keefe were our basketball tournament stars; Dick excelled as a baseball pitcher.

The siblings and cousins still managed to find time for a host of pranks that the CYO, school, work, and family rules had been created to avoid, or at least minimize. Police officer Francis "Francie" O'Loughlin, a neighbor, made frequent house calls on the many days when the gang managed to weave in the antics. His cruiser would pull alongside the low brick wall that Kay later said in her poem "kept no one in"; she forgot, perhaps, that the wall kept no one out, either. When some Dunfey or Keefe kid would spot the cruiser, word traveled at the speed of light. Upstairs and downstairs suddenly went silent. One day, as the thankfully sympathetic policeman chatted with my mother at the back door, Jack was within earshot of the exchange and knew my mother would be pretty upset—with him. Once the officer left, she went directly to find Jack because, out of the corner of her eye, she had seen him run into the bedroom that housed two full-sized beds with hardly an inch or two left over:

> I called to him to come out, but he wouldn't, so I grabbed a broom, went to the bedroom doorway where I crouched down and started swatting the broom at the culprit in the far corner.

Years later, Jack would tell the rest of the story:

> Here I was as far into the corner as a 10-year-old could fold himself and Mom's telling me I'd better come out or else. I felt the "or else" was a better option than crawling out, so I secured my position even more as I saw the broom come swishing toward me. All of a sudden, there was Mom, on the floor, staring at me. I was really "in for it" until the most unimaginable "or else" happened. She burst out laughing! At that moment she recognized how funny the whole scene was, and her sense of humor saved me that day!

"Yes. Jack is right," my mother confessed with a smile. "There I was on the floor reaching under the bed with a broom, and Jack was cornered. It just struck my funny bone at how absurd we looked!" Jack says he never forgot that incident and our mother's ability to laugh, a practice she had learned well, living with our dad: "She knew intuitively when to 'lower the boom' or the broom, and when to 'let it go,' a skill I needed later on when trying to figure out how to handle a business deal heating up." My mother was not naïve, though. My brothers had a fairly good sense which pranks would push the envelope, and they did their best not to get "cornered at the other end of a broom under the bed" as Jack had done.

They also managed to keep mum for a couple of decades about a "paint job"—sharing it only in a "Remember when we..." session long after the family had moved out of state. The prank took place on Halloween back in Pawtucketville, not far from our home. The police stopped the Dunfey/

Keefe cousins and their friends to question what they were up to. Several of the more talkative chaps leaned over to respond to the policemen through the two front windows of the patrol car, assuring them that everything was under control. Satisfied with their exchange, the cops drove away, unaware that while they had been chatting with the group at the front of the cruiser, the rest of the gang had been painting the back of the cruiser bright yellow. The boys never did get blamed for that prank. The police "knew," for once, that the Irish kids were innocent because they had stopped and talked with them. That practical joke and many others remain unrecorded: "Thank goodness I never knew some of those shenanigans," my mother quipped. "You'd be in reform school if you attempted even half of those pranks today."

During the kid days, the teenage days, the courting days, the "wedding days," the Depression years, the war years over holidays, in joy and in sorrow, my mother marveled, "The Keefes and Dunfeys held fast to our bond. We are still speaking to each other, and that is a record for the books."

All the while, more Dunfey babies kept arriving by home delivery. For my mother, "heading upstairs to the Keefes" was the plan. There, she benefited from the experienced care of my aunt Josie Keefe, Nanna Manning, and my father. After each delivery, my mother signed off with what became her familiar words of gratitude: "Thanks for the use of the hall, Josie!"

At these times, the older siblings were farmed out for a brief stay down Fifth Avenue with our Dunfey grandparents. My dad's sister, Myrtle, was living at home. Family lore has it that Myrtle did not inherit her brother LeRoy's culinary talents. She would make what my brother Jack describes as the "stinkiest possible fish sandwiches." With sheer delight, Jack adds that "On the two-mile walk to St. Patrick's School in the Acre, we crossed either the Moody Street or Pawtucket bridges that stretched over Lowell's canals." Many a fish sandwich was fed back to its school of fish in the Lowell Canal before it ever made it to lunch at school and down the alimentary canal of a Dunfey or Keefe kid.

Whether or not my parents knew the tale of the stinky fish sandwiches at the time, no one knows. But in 1929, when my mother was about to deliver baby #8, she relates that my dad had an idea that eliminated the stinky fish scenario. Not only had he made room at the store for his usual food prep, he also decided he should have food for the mind and he managed to squeeze a two-shelf book case "lending library" into a corner for the extra time that the kids would be spending there. That nook became my sister Kay's favorite spot when she wasn't serving up an ice cream soda or staring down a (prankster) brother.

It seemed that the Dunfeys and Keefes were collecting as many "new additions" at home as there were books in the store's lending library. In fact, within four weeks that autumn, there were two new acquisitions on Fifth Avenue. Aunt Josie gave birth to the Keefe's third child and second son, James (Jim), and Dunfeys added #8, Richard (Dick), to their score:

> At 4 a.m. on an October morning in 1929, my eighth baby, Richard, was ready to be delivered. I felt it might be a slow labor and had visions of the other children getting up and off to school. Of course, at that time we had our babies at home; I did not want them to see their mother going through that stage of labor. How timely that Dad had started a lending library in the store. The kids considered this a big project, so as a favor, Dad woke, dressed and hurried them off for a special breakfast at the store where they could see the "new library." To me it was like sending them on what kids now call a "field trip" to a museum, and I could be at ease bringing my eighth child into the world!

Roy Dunfey was a natural "host," as comfortable behind the counter, holding a cup of coffee in his full-length, white bib apron as he was on stage holding his drumsticks. Eight children in, he was still the orchestra conductor, directing and learning, always seeking to make harmony out of life's dissonance, and humor from its disillusions.

Although my father, like many in those days, did not have any formal education beyond age twelve, he was resourceful in finding ways to learn and to share that learning. He advertised theatre productions by placing posters in the store window. In return, he was given coupons for dramas, and I remember the special treat of walking with him downtown to the Opera House to see plays.

And, out of that immigrant Acre, Roy Dunfey's was one of three businesses that would become regional, national, or international in reach: Dunfey's Luncheonette became Omni International Hotels; the Highland Cleaners, owned by the Antonopoulos family directly across from our store on Broadway, became Anton's Cleaners; and Demoula's Market (now known as Market Basket) at the end of Broadway has become well-known in the past decade.

The realist and the rogue

Even with his creative and daring spirit, my father was the realist in his family, while his younger brother, Richie, earned his reputation as the rogue. My uncle Richie was a brilliant pianist (although he could not read music), artist, and tradesman, for which he had no formal education. He joined the army and found his way across country. During the WWII years that my brother Bud was on leave in Los Angeles, he and a group of his brother Marines received an invitation to a party at actress Irene Dunne's *(I Remember Mama)* home in Beverly Hills, California. Bud recalls arriving to the refrains of very familiar music wafting through the beautiful mansion. He made his way to the source and found Uncle Richie seated at the piano playing any and every request hummed briefly while he picked up the tune and went on from there. Richie was the affable uncle who continued his wandering ways, telling my grandfather on one occasion: "I'm going out for bread, Nick. Don't eat 'til I come back." He returned two years later. Neither did Uncle Richie return to his wife and two daughters in Maine except for periodic visits through the years.

We kids were unaware of any of Richie's more serious omissions. We just loved his arriving "out of the blue"; it was like having an entire party package delivered. Richie played the piano almost non-stop. When I was six, he painted a portrait of me. Unfortunately, his choice of canvas—a large brown supermarket bag—must have suffered the fate of most paper bags and with it was lost the grinning kid and the long blond curls my mother created with her deft way of rolling my hair in rags. The loss of the painting did not make as much of an impression on me over the years as did the dawning of the fact that my mother actually made time to roll those rag curls every night.

Uncle Richie would disappear as unexpectedly as he had arrived, but he always left his thank you message—in chalk—stunning seasonal murals on the two front windows of the store on Broadway. My favorite was Currier and Ives-type winter scene one Christmas. I was crushed when it wore off.

In summers, while we were growing our business on Hampton Beach, we would have a piano near the front of our restaurant at the corner of C St. during August festival month. The place was hopping with Richie at the piano and all the wait staff dressed in costume theme, e.g., Gay Nineties or Roaring Twenties. One summer there was no mural as a sign of Uncle Richie's leave-taking, just a passing comment to Jack that he hoped his "gift" would help. Then Richie was gone again along with the memory of his "passing comment" until late September when no electricity bill arrived. It seems that, before leaving, Richie had re-wired the building to bypass the meter.

In the end, though, Uncle Richie, the gifted artist, musician, and warmhearted veteran-turned alcoholic died from injuries suffered when he was struck by a taxi in Boston in September 1957. Of his three siblings, it would be only my dad's younger sister, Leila, who brought her gift of simplicity and calm to their family for many years.

On the backsteps of 119–121 Fifth Avenue. Left to right: Back row: Mary O'Connor Manning (Nanna Manning), Paul, almost eight; my mother, Kate, holding her youngest, #6 Bud, the first to be born in the "new" home; two visitors. Front row: Kay, age five; visitor holding Joe Keefe, age three; Rose Langlois, who lived with us for a year, holding Mary, age three. Lowell, MA. 1926

My grandfather, Nicholas "Nick" Dunfey; inset: my uncle, Richie, my father's younger brother. The former was considered an amiable scamp; the latter, a creative rogue. My father, LeRoy was the dependable realist among the men in his family.

Left to right: Mary, Jack, Bud, Bob in front of wall that "kept no one in, just marked a world outside to win."

Model T car, yes. Model kids, questionable. Left to right: Kay, Bud, Roy, Mary, Joe Keefe, Jack.

The "perfect family" plus one, make their parents proud. *Lowell Sun*

Chapter 6

Rituals, Rituals, and Rules

We all have vivid memories of our dad, in particular, finding ways to spike our rituals with humor. Our collective family memory places him at the hub of any antics associated with religion. We were always connected to church, but current stereotypes of the word "church" may not adequately translate what that word meant to us. Somehow, all the involvement, obligations, and commitments morphed into a whirlwind world of weekly services, music, marching bands, sports, and dances curbed only slightly by our work and school schedules.

Perhaps it was my father's penchant for fun and teasing that made it hard to think of him as "religious." He could turn what was supposed to be "serious" prayer into sidesplitting laughter. (Why was everything more hilarious when it happened in church or while saying the rosary?) We did not recognize our dad's kind of spirituality, which I see now as expressed through his brand of hospitality. Make people feel included through fun, music, and caring. The Irish put it simply, "Look after one another."

It was more natural to assign rituals associated with religion/church/ spirituality to the women. It was my mother who saw to it, for instance, that we were scrubbed and dressed properly for church every Sunday morning. She was the one, for instance, who on a Christmas morning, sent Jimmy Keefe and Dickie Dunfey home before Mass when she discovered one arm of each of the two "bandits" locked together—with the key lost under the Christmas tree somewhere in the discarded wrapping paper. Richard "Dickie," the future Justice of the New Hampshire Superior Court had an early introduction to handcuffs on the other side of the Bench.

It was she and Aunt Josie and their women friends who held countless bake sales to support the Maryknoll missionaries (an impressive religious group of priest and sister missionaries which I almost joined). It was my mother who rounded us up to pray the rosary, a Catholic ritual of repetitive prayers remembering important moments in the life of Christ. My mother tried (with emphasis on "tried") to honor that ritual each October and May (the months dedicated to the Virgin Mary in Catholic tradition) every evening after supper.

Whoever happened to be in our house after dinnertime—girlfriends, pals, or a stray kid from down the block, Protestant or Catholic—knelt down with the rest of us for that ritual. We "regulars" knew enough to grab a pillow or choose a spot around a bed, even if one of us happened to be in that bed, sick, as Eileen was a few times. She remembers Jack tickling her toes and making her giggle when she was trying to look more distraught to gain sympathy. My brother Dick was known for burying his head in his pillow to muffle his voice when his turn came to lead the prayer and he couldn't remember what he was supposed to say.

If the phone rang, we'd all scramble to answer it, to take a break from the twenty-minute ritual lengthened by what were called the "trimmings," prayers added on just when you thought you were finally finished. At that point, my father would be sure he was directly across from my mother; he would catch her eye and stare straight at her while exaggerating each syllable of the final prayer. Determined to make her laugh, he "got" her every time. And as soon as we saw the smile break through her attempt to stay serious, we'd all laugh, signaling the "Amen" to another night's ritual.

It was a Catholic tradition, at the time, to honor the Sacred Heart, symbol of love and protector of the family. Much against my father's will, my mother placed the large framed picture of the Sacred Heart on the wall above their bed. Dad was sure it would fall on him and, sure enough, one night as he stretched his arm up over his head in his sleep, it hit the frame. The picture fell unceremoniously hitting my father on the forehead. It was Walter who cracked, "See, Dad, what you get for all that fooling during the rosary? That's a sure sign you better change!" The cut on his forehead mended, but Dad, fortunately, never did mend his ways.

We became adept at interpreting "traditions" in creative ways. Even on Good Friday, when we were supposed to keep silent from noon to 3 p.m. in honor of the passion and death of Jesus, we managed to develop a sign language at the store and among our friends, allowing us to communicate without saying a word. (I would hone that skill of "schemes in silence," and it would get me in big trouble when I was training to become a nun.) My sister Eileen remembers working the Good Friday three-hour shift without saying a word to the customers she was serving.

We learned Dad's lesson well. Push the limits a bit, get a laugh, and don't be afraid to rattle the norm. When my father fell and broke several ribs, for instance, Jack, Bud, and Bob conspired to smuggle their nine-year-old kid sister—me—to visit him in the hospital although rules stipulated: "No children allowed." While one brother distracted the woman at the information desk in the lobby, the other two hid me between them in the trench coats they were wearing. I played "statue" while they scooted me up the open circular stairway of St. Joseph Hospital, holding me up by my elbows. My feet never touched a stair. I was scared stiff, too, but so happy to see my father until a knock at the door jolted us back to reality. My brothers shoved me under the bed as the nurse came in. Lucky for all of us, the night nurse assured us that a visit from a father's nine-year-old would help him heal more quickly as along as we didn't make him laugh too hard with those sore ribs! There I was—another Dunfey kid under the bed. Thank goodness for that nurse who could laugh, who knew when and when not to lower the boom—or the broom, an echo of my mother's common sense. I was the happiest girl in the world that night.

Always a reason—and season—to party

Given our horde of siblings, cousins, and other family members, there were very few days in the month that we did not sing "Happy Birthday" with homemade cake, candles, party favors, ice cream, and rollicking games of musical chairs. Nanna Manning's birthday was the most anticipated. She claimed she did not know her age (not uncommon for first generation Americans whose birth certificates had been left behind in the old country's parish records). She very wisely chose St. Patrick's Day as her birthday. Before breakfast, my Aunt Josie would help dress her up fancy, often with a big green bow for her hair. No darning socks that day, nor would Nanna Manning be sewing her small scraps of cloth around the hundreds of milk bottle stoppers we collected for her to hand-sew her one-of-a-kind quilts. This was a day of ongoing congratulations as friends, neighbors, and Father Maguire from St. Rita's Parish showered her with blessings, gifts, and singing. The presents we bought Nanna Manning were original and within our limited means. My brother Paul earned the "most creative" gift one year—a gentleman's handkerchief embroidered with a capital "P." That certainly ensured that Nanna Manning would remember, with every sneeze, that Paul had given his gift to her.

One year, near party's end, neither Jack nor Bud had appeared with their gifts. If you imagined that our grandmother let this go unnoticed, you'd be wrong. Her feelings were roundly expressed in a string of Irish words that we, who knew no Irish, strangely enough still understood. In the silence that followed, "what to everyone's wondering eyes did appear" but Jack and Bud, lugging a case of beer up the back stairs to present to Nanna. Presto! Jack and Bud were, for sure, "the best lads in the land," words Nanna uttered in her best English (with an Irish brogue, of course).

Thanksgiving was a typical feast of turkey and trimmings, with a not-so-typical fourteen or fifteen homemade pies which my mother prepared starting the Monday before the holiday: apple, squash, mince, and the family favorite, lemon meringue. She had to hide them in unexpected places, like the chilly front hall closet—a place we kids would never check. Her pies rarely lasted through second helpings. When I was ten and already an experienced waitress at home and in the restaurants, I had an unforgivable accident involving the "last" lemon meringue pie, which my mother announced was still hidden in the front hall closet. Sent to retrieve it, I tripped on the rug. I don't recall any concern that I might be hurt. The shouts were all about the ruined pie. By age thirteen, I could make the most delicious lemon meringue pie imaginable, but even after I entered the convent, when my brothers visited, they invariably arrived armed with a lemon meringue pie whose topping had always "happened" to get squished on the trip.

Belonging: The roots

Our two-story tenement (upstairs and downstairs apartments) on the corner of Fifth Avenue and Mt. Hope Street was an all-embracing, spilling-over home base of rituals for the sixteen Keefes and Dunfeys who lived there at any one time. Our rituals forged a bedrock of values that stuck and would play out in lifelong relationships far beyond that primary family circle. Rituals and rules rooted us physically, socially, and spiritually. Those practices helped bind, comfort, discipline, annoy, and guide us. The stories I share here may sound familiar to others. No one tribe has the corner on youthful pranks and parties. Sebastian Junger agrees: "We have a strong instinct," he says, "to belong to small groups defined by clear purpose and understanding."

Such groups create a culture of security: our religious, ethnic, racial, or geographic customs. Rituals show us, often in hindsight, the need to gather around the table, chew on the issues as well as the food; talk, listen, argue, welcome others, and know we belong. Rituals change—as they should and did—in our family's life. Some of those changes left a sense of loss, which later stories in this book reveal. But, thanks to an inherent gift of recognizing the transient face of rituals and rules, Kate and Roy Dunfey never got caught making rituals and rules "ends" rather than "means."

It may be easier to remain in a cocoon of the familiar than to risk charting new courses. My parents somehow managed to avoid the extremes of complacency and intractability. Of all their traits, I think their ability to adapt to new, diverse situations and people has most affected my life. How did they manage that? They stayed rooted in the core spiritual values which are at the heart of genuine hospitality: looking after one another and the universal Golden Rule, "Do to the other...." My mother expressed it as "treat each person like a guest in your own home." My dad complemented those words with an ease and enjoyment in inviting those "guests."

On Christmas Day, 1951, I was with him, for instance, when he was closing the store about noon. Riding home to Pawtucketville from the Acre, we passed the downtown bus station, my dad noticed a boy, fourteen or fifteen years old, sitting alone on a bench. In typical fashion, Roy Dunfey pulled over, rolled down his window and called out: "What are you doing there?"

"Waiting for the bus to Dover," came the reply.

"It's Christmas. There aren't any buses going to Dover—or anywhere. Get in the car." As a thirteen-year-old girl, I was pretty embarrassed by my father's invitation (or order!), but the teen didn't seem to mind. He hopped into the back seat. A tiny picture from that Christmas shows all of us eating dinner. Sitting to the right of my mother and looking very happy with his plate of turkey and mashed potatoes and gravy, is a slight young man with much darker complexion and black hair.

That turned out to be our dad's last Christmas. He died suddenly six months later. I stored up all the songs and stories that reminded me of him, especially from that winter of my thirteenth year. My mother lived for another thirty years, but that Christmas story still reminds me of both my parents. When our mother died, our family asked Ambassador Andrew Young to share a reflection about "Mother Dunfey." He and his mother, Daisy, had become dear family friends over the years. Andy spoke of my mother as a "light—a Lady Liberty welcoming a world of diverse people." He had asked me before the service for a brief example he might share as an example of his metaphor. I immediately thought of our unexpected guest that Christmas Day three decades earlier. Andy loved the example and told the story as part of his reflection.

As we all exited the church, my brother Paul took me aside and asked me where Andy "got" that story.

"*I* told him," I said, surprised at his query. Paul shook his head and chuckled, "Do you know where they sent that kid for supper? To our house!" Of course, Mom and Dad would send the teen off to Rita, Paul, and their four little children, who lived in a tiny apartment in the Veterans' housing project! Paul (Dunfey #2) had never heard the first part of that story, and I (Dunfey #12) had never heard the rest of the story. It was refreshing to laugh at that moment in gratitude for the parents who had left us such stories to discover and pass on, examples of their lived spirituality— genuine hospitality. It also offered yet another lesson about adapting. (World War II had already taught my brother Paul and his wife Rita a much more critical lesson about being adaptable. That story has its own special place later in this book.)

Roots...then wings

By the 1930s, the family numbered eleven. My oldest sister, Kay, a budding thespian, had plenty of siblings and cousins in the wings to populate her backyard theatrical productions. Younger brother Jack was within her purview and, therefore, automatically in her troupe whether he liked it or not. He did not! He recalls pleading with her, "Please, please, Kay! Don't make me be in it!" To no avail. At first staged in the backyard, her productions were often about priests and nuns and processions, probably because of familiarity of topic and the availability of white dish towels and black pants. The productions later migrated next door to Bouchers' barn loft. That setting proved to be a distraction because the reluctant actors (including our sister Mary) much preferred jumping from the large side opening of the barn loft into the hay that had "magically" fallen into just the right spot for the kids to land.

Acknowledgment of Kay's thespian talent stepped up a notch when, at her high school awards ceremony, she received a full scholarship to the Mary Frances Rooney School in Boston. Kay however, had even loftier aspirations. After a semester at Mary Frances Rooney in Boston, she chose the Sisters of Notre Dame in Waltham.

Meanwhile, our two older brothers were playing real-life roles in those Depression years. They found themselves in a different sort of drama in their new setting. Roy and Paul had graduated from Keith Academy, a former jail in Lowell, and with no script to follow, had gone "West" (which we considered to be any place beyond Springfield, Massachusetts). With eight children still at home, the store's daily earnings were hardly enough to keep us fed. Roy and Paul took jobs working on the factory floor of a safe company in Hamilton, Ohio, where our aunt's husband, George Bickford, held a white-collar position. Roy and Paul lived in their home. Aunt Myrtle—an intelligent but quirky young woman—provided meager meals for the two teenagers and steamed open letters from their girlfriends in Lowell. Her intrusion into their long distance relationships had no effect except, perhaps, the irritated brothers' letting off some steam of their own. Regarding the meals, given Jack's description of Myrtle's lunches as "the stinkiest possible fish sandwiches," Roy and Paul may have fared better with "meager" meals.

The neighbor's barn in Pawtucketville section of Lowell,
Massachusetts, scene of my oldest sister Kay's drama productions.
Upstairs side opening provided escape route from rehearsals,
delivering reluctant thespians into previously prepared hay piles
below.

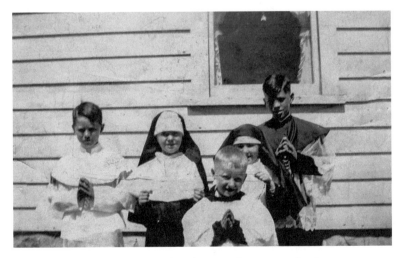

Some of my oldest sister Kay's reluctant thespians after being
snatched from the hay and transformed for pious productions often
about priests and nuns, probably because "costumes" were easy to
come by with black pants and white dish towels. 1935

Sh-Sh—You'll Wake the Baby

Catherine M. (Kay) Dunfey, Give Me Wings

Sh-Sh—You'll surely wake the baby
Was it Roy or Paul or Kay
Who disturbed the sleeping Mary
On some far-off Cross Street day?
Soon they joined "suburban" dwellers
And poor Bobby lay at rest
In the room where Jack and Buddy
Held their nightly muscle-test.

"Sh-Sh—You'll wake the baby
With your wrestling and your roar
Glory be! It's good the landlord
Lives with us on this first floor!"
Drums and marching, dancing,
*   laughing,*
Sunday song-fests, noisy cheer-
More to march, and sing, and frolic,
With a brand new boy each year.

Six to two—the score was standing,
So the noise was largely male
When the time-worn admonition
Hushed Eileen's protesting wail.
Walter's slumbers knew strange
*   rackets*
Drumsticks, trumpets, rush and go,
Stage-struck ravings, campaign
*   speeches,*
Blaring horns and teenage beaux.

"Sh-Sh—You'll wake the baby,
*   Guys and gals and Keefies all,*
*   With your Bingo games and penny sales*
*   Your Irish nights and Maryknoll."*
And the tempo kept increasing
Noise pressed down and flowing o'er
So that Jerry slept the day shift
Joining the nocturnal roar.

"Sh-Sh—You'll wake the baby!"
Nor did Dad escape the cry,
As he tip-toed in with ice cream
For our Mom and all still standing by.
The ageless song was not abated
Tho' two had gone beyond the nest
For ten were left to hail her coming,
And to shatter Eleanor's rest.
Wedding plans and happy furloughs
Parties that were rich and rare
Comings, goings, and sad partings,
Were your infant baby fare.
Soon you woke to understanding
In this Dunfey family
That real joy is all in giving,
And that love means unity…

CHAPTER 7

1938–1941

The First Phase of Dunfey Convent Years

Our family was intertwined with the social mission of the Catholic Church in New England. The women in our family were drawn in particular to the Sisters of Notre Dame de Namur (not to be confused with the School Sisters of Notre Dame). Its founder, Julie Billiart (1751–1816), had been paralyzed for twenty-two years from an early childhood trauma. Her father was shot in view of young Julie at the family's small Cuvilly shop when thieves robbed him of materials and fabrics. Her physical condition deteriorated to the degree that she was almost completely dependent on others. Physical constraints did not prevent Julie's spiritual strength from soaring, and her spirit inspired many at a time of upheaval across Europe, notably in Belgium and the Catholic Church. While still paralyzed, she met Françoise Blin de Bourdon, a woman dedicated to service. With Françoise's resources and Julie's spiritual gifts, the two founded a religious order.

They were astute, independent women dedicated to educating children in dire poverty. To pay for those schools, they simultaneously opened day-schools for middle-class and the wealthy, and those supported the free schools. They continued to act on behalf of the poor, and other women were inspired to join such a community of outward action (in this case, education) based on spiritual conviction. Women taking such initiatives were bound to rattle church authorities. In this case, on seeing such positive outcomes, authorities would stretch out the arm of paternalism:

> The bishop of Amiens, France thought the Sisters of Notre Dame de Namur belonged in only one diocese—his in Amiens! Sr. Julie knew that God was calling her far beyond those boundaries. The bishop finally expelled her from Amiens. It was a very painful time for Julie, Françoise, and the Sisters. Julie left each Sister free to choose whether to remain in Amiens—and separate herself from the original Congregation—or to go with her. Most Sisters did choose to go with Julie, and they found a home in the diocese of Namur, Belgium (where the Motherhouse still resides).
>
> —*From "Who We Are,"*
> *www.snddenca.org/who-we-are/history/earlyhistory/*

Julie and her sisters did not get stuck in the expectations society, the church and politics had of them: "In spite of her vulnerable position, she had to speak the truth: the priests who had sworn an oath to the French revolutionists were wrong, and it was wrong to accept their ministry. At one point, in order to save her life, Julie's friends hid her in a hay cart and carried her to safety at Compiègne, France" ("Who We Are," as above.)

These women who wore the ordinary garb of their day and culture—a dress that would over the centuries become stylized and called a "habit"— were anything but the ordinary. They became women leaders, college presidents, educators, missionaries, and advocates (other religious orders produced hospital administrators, founders of homes for children and elders). Boarding the Eliza Thornton from Antwerp in 1839, eight women pioneer Sisters of Notre Dame set sail for Cincinnati. They arrived on October 31, 1840. Within a year, they had opened the first Notre Dame School, located on Sixth Street in Cincinnati, using a model similar to their European initiative: launching a day school and a free school enabling impoverished children to gain an otherwise inaccessible education.

Within a decade, the Sisters had expanded in numbers enough to respond to calls for Sisters to go west to Oregon and California—and east to Lowell, Massachusetts. One hundred and sixty-five years later, the SNDs are still serving immigrants, refugees, and others in need at St. Patrick's School and Educational Center in the heart of the city's Acre. It was here that all sixteen Dunfeys and Keefes attended elementary school. I think the SNDs' experience with our clans was a test of their endurance. The arrival of the Xaverian brothers to teach the older boys may have helped.

Coming to America
Around this time, young women from all over the European continent were also leaving a war of famine and hardship to find hope in America. Many became housemaids or took factory jobs. On the East Coast, where many immigrant girls landed and settled, they were joined by even younger girls coming down from Canada to find work in the mills along the Merrimack River, the engine of the American Industrial Revolution.

The great migrations of young people, often from Catholic backgrounds, into industrial cities this side of the Mississippi, provided religious orders with a significant pool of candidates. Some accepted girls as young as thirteen. To its credit, the Sisters of Notre Dame did not.

My great-aunt Ellie was one of the thousands of Irish youth who made their way to America, lived with relatives from the "old country," working long, hard hours, and then entered convents to be trained as teachers or nurses or cooks or dress (in this case, "habit") makers. Compared to working in the mills, such training must have been regarded as a more meaningful way to live.

From my earliest years, I recall visiting our great-aunt Ellie, known in the community as Sr. Marguerite Joseph. She lived at St. Augustine convent in Andover, Massachusetts. Rosy cheeks were her natural make up and a sweet smile always brightened the small space between her bonnet blinders. I heard much later that she and my other aunts were very strict in any dealings with my older sisters when they entered the convent, never wanting to show favoritism to relatives. Auntie Ellie appeared to me to be otherworldly and unassailable, and situated squarely in a convent parlor chair, hands folded in her lap, shoes not quite touching the highly polished floor. Hovering around her was an aroma of freshly baked cookies, a hint of her job in the convent bakery. When she spoke, though, the Irish brogue that marked her questions about our comings and goings reminded me that she hadn't always been a nun.

Fast forward to 1956. My mother and I took our first trip to Ireland, to a tiny hamlet situated off map in the wilds of County Kerry, reachable only by a narrow, well-traveled dirt path on the southwest tip of the Dingle Peninsula. My cousins were expecting us. The night was anvil black, lit by windows reflecting turf fires in the bungalows along the way. I don't remember that first, late night visit as well as I recall the next morning. I woke to a sun-filled room and was invited for a walk up the path by my mother's cheery, ruddy-faced first cousin, who surely had experienced many a dark night and sunny morn on that wild coast.

"And how's my Ellie?" Dinny-Ban asked, in a brogue that brought her to mind. I easily conjured up my image of the dear old Irish nun in Andover and assured him that she was just fine. "Ah," he said wistfully, "Sure, I can see her now, walking up this path with young Jack taking him back to America. You know, Ellie wasn't even your age. I never saw her again." I froze. My "little old nun" had been a teen when my grandfather, James Manning, died aboard ship. Fifteen-year-old Ellen O'Connor was selected to "take Jack back to America," and that is how she ended up in Lowell working in the mills before entering the Sisters of Notre Dame.

In that moment on the remote path in Ireland, I realized how ignorant I was about my Aunt Ellie's life and sacrifice. I recognized, then, that her story was more than the journey of one girl. It was inextricably tied to the stories of thousands of young women who had walked up similar paths on journeys into the unknown—never to see their homelands or loved ones again. I was embarrassed and awed. I felt a certain envy of the courage of those teenagers who had left family, friends, and cultures behind and dared to risk the unknown "beyond."

A Catholic girl's place was often—"in" the convent

During the 1940s, when my great-aunt Ellie's generation of immigrant girls was nearing their seventies, the Dunfey sisters would add to the ranks of the Sisters of Notre Dame, which had grown to several thousand women worldwide. A large number of those women set out to educate new generations as missionaries in Africa, Asia, Latin America, and in cities and rural areas across the United States, totaling seventeen countries on five continents. Even in today's global village made even more accessible through social media, those figures are impressive.

Worth noting here, the terms "nun" and "sister" are often used interchangeably, but within Roman Catholicism, there is a difference between the two. A Catholic *nun* is a woman who lives a contemplative life in a monastery, which is usually cloistered (or enclosed) or semi-cloistered, e.g., the Carmelite Order. A Catholic *sister* is a woman who lives, ministers, and prays within the world. A sister's life is often called "active" or "apostolic" because she is engaged in the works of mercy and other ministries that take the Gospel to others where they are. (There are differences in the extent of the vows each takes, as well.)

Although my own sisters did not leave for distant missions immediately after entering the convent, their new life and culture were drastically different from the only world they had known. The twenty-two-miles between Lowell and Waltham must have felt like a thousand. It had to be extremely difficult for them to "shift their life gears" away from home, boys, work, social life, and war worries. In fact, during Kay's first few months, she was so unhappy, she ran away from the convent—an echo of Monica Baldwin's 1949 book, *I Leaped Over the Wall* (although Baldwin had been in a cloistered community.)

Kay found her way to our cousins' home in Brookline, Massachusetts, not too far from the Waltham Novitiate. Many years later, Kay and my mother would tell the story of Kay's arrival home in Lowell, thanks to the Brookline Dunfeys. My mother had only one concern, and it was for Kay: "I have no problem with your coming out of the convent, Kay. We all want what you want, but I do think you should go back and come out the same door you entered. I wouldn't want you to be ashamed or regret this decision for the rest of your life." Kay never shared what happened when she returned, but she did not leave the convent for another forty years, after traveling the world from Boston to Tokyo, to Rome and back, influencing thousands of students across the continents. Even within the confines and restrictions of convent life, my sisters would not be defined in any final way.

My second oldest sister, Mary—born with our dad's drummer gene—was a majorette in St. Rita's Cadets. Perhaps being the fourth child and second girl led her to develop that drumming talent to make herself heard lest she get lost in the maze of the growing clan. Mary would not need drums to be noticed, however. She would use logic and persuasion. She became an award-winning debater in high school. When Mary was given teaching assignments as a nun, she was more than qualified thanks to her debating skills, her life experience living with eight brothers, and her time spent behind the store counter.

Years later, Mary told me that her greatest heartache when she entered the convent was leaving me, her baby sister. "Eleanor. You were only eighteen months old, and I was so attached to you. I thought I would not be able to leave home." But Mary did, also remaining in the convent almost forty years, an exuberant presence in classrooms of boys from South Boston to Honolulu, San Francisco to Baltimore. To me, she was the embodiment of my drummer dad's gregariousness and my mother's generosity.

During the 1940s, many young men and women answered a call of another kind, to serve around the world. Thousands of them would never return to their loved ones. Keefes and Dunfeys were represented in that corps, as well, enlisting in World War II after the attack on Pearl Harbor. Despite still having six children to care for at home, my mother made it a priority to write letters every day to my three brothers who served in the armed forces, in addition to sending frequent letters to my sisters in the convent. At holidays, relatives at home would be rounded up to take a turn writing what was called a "Round Robin." This sample demonstrates its format:

Mother also made sure that my father joined her writing circle, and he did with positive updates that reflected his pride, to my oldest sister:

> Hello Kay—just thawed out after being quite frozen, and busy, these last four or five nights after midnight until the early hours of the next day when it was then time to start all over. We have made a lovely place out of 353 Broadway with tile walls, new mirror, new place for the telephone, a fine new 11-foot counter, etc.
>
> The booths are all painted with blue tops and cream colored body. The old top of the back bar has been replaced with new cream and blue tile squares with the latest lighting system on either side of a new round mirror giving a beautiful appearance as you enter the door.
>
> In front of the new counter, we have 2 new cabinets with 8 swell drawers and down where the ice box was, I have a new lunch board with a system of refrigeration for all the food you need in making up sandwiches quickly.
>
> This is my contribution to the "Round Robin" as Walter is on my neck waiting for his turn.
>
> With a lot of love, Pa [the name we called our father until the 1949 TV show featured "Ma and Pa Kettle." Then we shifted to "Mom and Dad."]

Left to right: Bud holding Jerry, Eileen, Walter, Jack. Dad, Paul. Bob, Dick.
Missing: Roy working in Ohio, Kay and Mary in the Sisters of Notre Dame
de Namur 1940.

If Nanna Mary O'Connor Manning's birthday wishes included wearing party hats,
most Dunfey/Keefe kids donned them. Left to right, back row: Kay Dunfey, Mary
Keefe, Buddy Dunfey, Joe Keefe, Jackie and Bobby Dunfey, Jimmy Keefe. Front
row: Eileen Dunfey, Eddie Keefe, Nanna Manning, Walter and Dick Dunfey.

My sister, Mary's, entrance day to the convent. I was eighteen months old and,
according to Mary, "I didn't think I could leave you."

Six Dunfeys gone to the west, the war, or the convent. Roy Dunfey turns to the second half dozen to run the Broadway store. Left to right: Front row: Walter, Jerry; Second row: Bob, Eileen; Roy Dunfey in rear. I would "join them" a few years later, when I turned seven. Here, Walter on duty at the luncheonette. 1943

Chapter 8

1940s: World War II

A Changing Acre—A New Half-dozen Dunfeys

Our dad, now almost as much a pro in the birthing thing as my mother, started the 1940s with a new half dozen kids to train at the store: Bob, Dick, Eileen, Walter, Jerry, and later, me.

My brother Jerry, the youngest of eight boys, was six years old by the time his older six siblings—Roy, Paul, Kay, Mary, Jack, and Bud—had left home for work, war, or the convent. I never saw Jerry as the "youngest" of anything. I was the youngest. In fact, on November 6, 1938, exactly nine months to the day that Kay had entered the convent (a source of much teasing by those "in the know" about "the birds and bees") my mother delivered her twelfth child, me, the youngest of the dozen. Kay remembers that "coincidence" in a poem, a few lines of which read:

Proxy

The Dunfeys have a baby!
Her daddy has a joy...

Perhaps I have a namesake,
This holds no prodigy,
And Mother has a daughter
To substitute for me.

I was only my parents' third child to be born in a hospital. My mother was admitted to St. Joseph's Hospital thinking her twelfth child was ready to meet the world, but as our Nanna Manning often said: "Time come. Child come," and I was taking my time, so much so, that the doctor suggested my mother go home to wait. The experienced birth-giver replied: "I came here to be delivered, and I'm not going home until I am!" She confided much later to me, "I knew if I went home, I might not make it back in time with nine children all around me. Being in the hospital was like a vacation!" Although women might be nudged to "go home" if delivery did not appear imminent, there was no rush to discharge a mother after she gave birth. At the time, it was common to have mother and baby remain in the hospital as long as ten days.

Jerry was my older brother, so it never occurred to me that he had the burden as well as the benefit of ten older siblings, seven of them brothers. Between my birth and our two doting sisters, Kay and Mary, entering the convent, Jerry lost a lot of attention in the clan. Once again, Kay penned her emotions:

> *From the oldest girl to the youngest boy*
> *The measure of years is long*
> *But a sister's joy in a baby boy*
> *Forged a bond both tender and strong...*

When he was barely six, Jerry had to have missed his loving Kay's attention. All he remembers is being scooped up into the daily charge of Bob, Dick, Eileen, and Walter, all of whom were in St. Patrick's School as well as working what most would consider fulltime. According to Jerry's memory, his siblings being "in charge" of him meant that they assigned him the jobs they didn't want to do: sweeping the floor, sorting tonic (soda) bottles, working the penny candy counter, folding boxes for the new popcorn machine (we had started selling popcorn at local churches and at city parks), putting the ten sections of the Sunday paper together, and most despicable of all—cleaning the cellar!

Eight-year-old Walter had the responsibility of bringing his kid brother to school for his first day of first grade. He took Jerry by the hand from the store down the few short blocks to St. Pat's for registration where the two joined Walter's best friend, Bucky O'Connor, who had his little brother, also a Gerry, in tow. Well almost in tow. Within what seemed just seconds and for reasons not even Jerry can recall, two punches flew. The exchange must have been a rite of first day passage because Jerry recalls only that he and Gerry O'Connor became great friends.

Jerry does have vivid recall, though, about remarks made back at the store—comments that had to have stung more than a kid's punch in the schoolyard. Even at his young age, he knew some of the so-called banter of the store's regulars seemed different:

> There were very few people of color in the Acre or Pawtucketville where we worked and lived. I only remember one Black family living in a tenement a few blocks up from the store.
>
> It was a different laughter from that directed at George, a Greek painter and regular who would shout his order, BUTTA-TOAS-NO-BREA. You'd ask him to repeat and he'd just repeat the same thing over and over, louder and louder. When you did

start to put the buttered toast on a plate in front of him, he'd slap your hand and yell "DOUNTOUCHAWITHYAHANS…"

It was different from the way everyone treated the elderly, bedraggled "Gimmee-cup-a-tea" homeless woman yelling, "Bag broke—gimmee nutha bag!" She got many a bag; that's for sure.

We bordered on nasty, for sure; we kidded and joked as Irish with the French, Greeks, and Italians. But I just felt—even as a young kid—that there was something more hurtful in the comments people made when they watched this Black family walking by.

Jerry frequently saw Dad go to the pay phone to call Arthur DeLorme, an ambulance company owner, when one or another down-and-out alcoholic would fall into the gutter across the street. He'd be picked up and taken to a hospital or rehab. Jerry also remembers "Chubber" with that mysterious disease called "TB" (tuberculosis), being brought for treatment to a hospital, the cruel but accepted term for which was "insane asylum."

Whenever ten-year-old Jerry was briefly left in charge of the store, he would take out the Billy club that Lieutenant Marty Laughlin had given to our dad. The club hung on a hook on the shelf within easy reach under the register: "I remember swinging it, now and then, but I never saw any one actually use it." However, young as he was, he knew he could grab that Billy club if he had to.

One day, he thought he would have to. Eccles was the huskiest, toughest, most violent drunk in the Acre. If you had any smarts at all, you would not pick a fight with Eccles. He had left a trail of broken bones and blood from Donahue's to Drooney's, to Brooksy's barrooms and beyond. Eccles arrived at the store one day, his glazed eyes squinting through blurred evidence of his latest row. Jerry was in charge. The few customers froze when the burly, scarred-faced Eccles started his shenanigans. Jerry remembers quaking in his shoes but walking directly to the pay phone. He shouted to Eccles, "I'm calling my dad!" Talk about immediate sobering up. As soon as Jerry removed the phone from the hook and began to dial, Eccles took a long dive, tumbling out the door.

"Wow," Jerry marveled. "Did that ever work!"

Our dad had instructed Jerry to do exactly that if he ever sensed any trouble starting. "For some reason Eccles was 'scared shitless' of Dad," Jerry quipped decades later.

Although we all wore scars, physical and emotional, from various skir-mishes, nightly wrestling matches and accidents, they came mostly from hot water, hot syrup, and later hot fryolater grease—the tattoo-branding requisite for food service employees, perhaps. Burns came from making coffee in the tall steel tanks as we'd try to pour boiling water over the huge strainer of ground coffee beans. We also cringed when it was our turn to pick up Mrs. Talty's delicious but scalding homemade apple pies and carry at least two of them from her home just around the corner back to the store at lunchtime. It was an impossible feat to accomplish without spilling some of the hot syrup on your hands and arms. We carried the pies daily; we car-ried the scars on our hands and arms for years. No wonder we didn't mind thrusting our arms into a freezer to scoop out pints and quarts of ice cream or making an ice cream soda, cone or "frappe," which was New England's name for a milk shake with ice cream.

It was during those years that Marty Sepè worked for Savoy Soda, which provided all the soft drinks a variety store such as ours would sell. When the teenage Marty made a delivery, it was a one-person, tough slog of an operation. He would back the truck into the empty lot next to store, lining it up alongside the bulkhead door to unload the heavy wooden cases of soda. He would then have to off-load the large gas tank and carry it down into the cellar to hook it up to the soda fountain (pipe), allowing the carbonated water to flow for making those ice cream sodas. During this ordeal, he would also have to put up with the Broadway kids who loved to take stale donuts (there were always stale donuts in the store drawer) and pelt Marty and his truck. He would not be outdone. The following week, he'd return and, timing the donut assault perfectly, would open the spigot on the gas and begin spraying soda water! Marty's quick wit, daring-do, and good-hearted Italian spirit endeared him to our dad from the outset. The feeling was not only mutual, it also spread to all of us kids and espe-cially my mother. Soon, Marty and his brother Matt, were working with the family expanding our "staff" as we expanded the business to the beach as well as building a restaurant in that empty lot where Marty had parked his truck as a delivery boy. Marty was a good-hearted fit, right at home, too, as a hard worker and practical joker.

Paul McGaunn, was an Acre-born-and-raised kid and, as much as any-one still alive, is the best witness to where and how the Dunfeys began the journey from clams to corporations. Paul, like Marty Sepè, got to know the Dunfeys even before the family sold clams. He describes the Broadway store and neighborhood of the forties:

The Acre was St. Patrick's Parish. Most everybody was a laborer working in the textile industry. Two steps up past the newspaper rack, and you were in. There was an ice cream cooler to the right of the front door and a candy display case on the left. A couple of tables, three booths, a pinball machine known as the fitness machine for Dunfey brother, Dick, who was teased for having built his upper body strength playing it. Not much space between the intentionally half-hidden 'one-arm bandit' and the counter with six or seven stools. Behind the counter was the all-important, sturdy brown cabinet that held the heavy metal, single drawer register and a salad unit.

The register

From our earliest days at the store on Broadway, we discovered that the cash register was of paramount importance in the business. First of all, its weight was significant, a sturdy metal with a hefty brown painted cabinet.

We learned our math, measured our height and our responsibility against the protruding keys, each with its own number that spread across the front of the curved metal chest in two rows. If pressed properly and with pressure, the selected key would ring and the number would appear across its top window while the wide drawer across the bottom front would spring open for the transaction. We saw the cash register migrate from its lowly place near the backroom, to the middle of the counter in our Broadway luncheonette, to its prominent perch right at the entrance (and exit!) of all our restaurants afterwards, a lesson experience taught us, no doubt. And to this day, Dunfeys are conditioned to sit facing the register and front entrance even when we are the customers in a restaurant, a challenge for sure when there are several of us in the party.

The register was also a surface for notes—handwritten reminders—for instance, to let one of us know when an order of soda would be delivered. Concern about leaving money in the register drawer overnight was such that whoever was on at closing was supposed to hide the cash. My brother Dick—probably age ten at the time and attempting to secure the profits (such as they were!)—wrapped the few paper dollars with a larger number of coins and safely tucked them in the small new freezer unit that stored ice cream—no one would look for the cash there! The only drawback was the note he scribbled and stuck on the register drawer: "The money's in the freezer!"

"If the note did not give the hiding place away," brother Jack quips, "the first ten–twenty customers would know because whatever coins they got as change were ice cold!"

Learning responsibility went beyond hiding the cash. In Jerry's six-year-old mind, it meant generosity. At age seven, he was a second grader at St. Patrick's School where each class competed to be #1 in generosity to the missions (donating to the work of the Sisters of Notre Dame around the world). Each day the children would excitedly watch as a "Black Sambo" bank nodded his head in a gesture of thanks for each coin donated. The source of Jerry's donations was the cash register at the Broadway store. For a while, all seemed grand. Happy teachers and Jerry's class were right up there at the top of the competition. Until…one day, Jerry's hand got caught in the proverbial till when Dad was within sight. Eileen, all of eleven, was horrified to watch the scene play out; she could not believe that Jerry was taking money out of the drawer! Sensing Jerry's motivation but knowing Jerry needed to learn a lesson, Dad, as Jerry put it, "made his point."

A lens on the Acre: 1940s
Paul McGaunn's lens on the Acre is pure local color:

> The Dunfey gang worked under their dad's watchful eye before and after school, as well as during lunchtime when we all walked to the store to eat. Many Acre children were latchkey kids before it was a buzz word, before there was a hint of social concern about underage kids running around loose. Younger kids followed their older brothers and cousins. That was the case, at least for working class folk.
>
> The North Common, the green area, was also a common home. My brothers played pick up football in a city league of kids who played for their own ethnic groups. The Greeks were the Blackhawks. The Irish were the Shamrocks' team, naturally. No one had a whole uniform. Monk Casey was the Shamrocks' organizer. One year he attended a city council meeting to see if he could get a football for the team. They got one but Monk had to make a strong case for it. Every year the Shamrocks played the "game of the year" against the Blackhawks. Every year after the game there was an enormous fight.
>
> When they weren't playing pickup football or baseball, they swam in the public pool nicknamed Lake Huron (a pronunciation more or less like "urine"). Of course, that was before

filtration. The teens swam the canal all day in summer, ignoring the raw factory sewage. A couple of mouthfuls of that and you had immunity for life!

Roy Dunfey's strong arm

Many of our arguments—we always called them "fights"—at home were about work, especially when the schedule was competing with teenagers' social wish lists. You'd find large, handwritten notes taped to the bottles of milk: *Dick—Your turn to close tomorrow. Walter—Remember you're opening.* We fought over working weekend nights. The younger you were—translate "Jerry"—the more likely you'd end up behind the counter and not at the movies come the weekend.

We didn't see our dad argue over small matters, although he loved a strong debate about politics. He was mostly a negotiator. He could, however, teach us in more forceful ways (as several brothers experienced) if he felt he should. Because St. Patrick's was a private school, tuition was charged, and with five-to-eight Dunfey kids in the school at a time, that bill (along with Jerry's generous donations from the register, to the missions) shrunk the scarce resources cobbled together from store sales, orchestra gigs, and my two brothers' very generous $18 sent home weekly from their Ohio jobs.

Jack has vivid recall of an occasion when our dad did choose a more forceful way to address a situation. The Dunfey kids' tuition payment was late, and Brother F. had decided to make that fact known by publicly calling out my brother regarding the missing payment. Of course, Jack told my father at the store. Without a word, Dad took off his white apron and headed from the store on Broadway straight down the two blocks to Adams Street and St. Patrick's school where said Brother was overseeing a yard full of rambunctious kids at recess. Jack and several other Dunfey kids followed closely so as not to miss what we'd now call a dialogue.

What they saw and heard was more of an in-your-face monologue. LeRoy Dunfey grabbed the Brother by the cassock (an ankle-length, close-fitting, often black garment worn by the Brothers, their "habit" of sorts) and pinned him against the side of the building with muscled arms made strong by his arm-wrestling record at the store (he won against burly truck drivers, shovel diggers and his bowling league competitors): "Don't you EVER talk tuition payments with ANY of my children," he said. "Do you hear me? If you have anything to say, you come and say it directly to me." Not surprisingly, Brother F. had nothing to say. My father released

the brother and his cassock and stormed out of the yard leaving his kids—
and most likely Brother F.—stunned and silent in his wake.

Dunfey difference

During the 1940s, my father's personality, pride, and progeny showed the
beginnings of what might be termed the Dunfey difference. His large family and entrepreneurial eye urged him toward an added business possibility:
a basic luncheon buffet service packed to travel. Each of us would help fill
the orders, usually for Campion Hall, a Jesuit Center in Andover, MA,
where Dad joined his brother Knights of Columbus or Elks men's group for
retreats. On the menu were ham and cheese, tuna, egg, and chicken salad
sandwiches, each wrapped in cellophane paper and packed in a large black
suitcase with long straps securing the broken lock. Even years later, each
of my brother's cars had a trailer hitch in case someone called in a catering
order. All orders were accompanied by a ten-gallon thermo-tank of coffee.
While providing plenty of food for all to enjoy at these retreats, the gregarious Roy welcomed the time to reflect, pray, and enjoy a serene atmosphere.
He could, of course, count on his Knights of Columbus friends to liven up
any retreat.

The confidence my father gained managing the luncheonette gave him
the impetus to purchase the empty lot next to it. In 1946, he tore down a
billboard and built a catering and take-out restaurant, one of the first of
its kind. It became popular, and Eileen was the staff star. She and a bevy
of other "hoodsies," as teenage girls were dubbed, attached trays to car
windows, took orders and delivered countless vanilla and chocolate frappes,
root bear floats, hamburgers, cheeseburgers, and French fries. Carhops had
first made their appearance during the Gilded Age, which makes sense
given the mass production of cars at the time. Even then, Americans
wanted fast food and they wanted it brought to them in their "four-wheeled
living rooms." But it wasn't until World War II that women replaced males
as open-air walking and skating waitresses. As in so many realms, World
War II opened the eyes of the public to the wide range of work women
could effectively do in a marketplace hitherto principally cornered by men.

Music as message—stories in song

With the ever-present challenges of the store, a wartime economy, and the
reality of supporting a large family, Dad instinctively turned to singing.
It was his, our mother's, and our release. Singing was as natural to us as
arguing over whose turn it was to open the store or do the dinner dishes.
Dad created medleys so that you didn't stop between songs (lest you catch

your breath or start fighting). The medleys continued as long as the drive or the chore and were probably his way of minimizing inevitable arguments. Harmonizing did make it harder to fight. All twelve of us had good voices, loved to sing, and unconsciously knew that singing diverted attention from the drudgery of boring rides, household chores, or a current gripe with a sibling. We knew, from experience, that singing long into the night at a party was, hands down, the best way to snap out of the utter fatigue of working long hours. We were all pros at that.

At least weekly, Dad would set up his drums and my mother would take her sheet music out of the piano bench. They'd harmonized to all the old songs, many of which they must have danced to during their courtship days! Dad's repertoire included the lighthearted tunes like, "There's a Red Light on the Track for Boozer Brown" or "That Little Old Red Shawl." Some songs were tearjerker ballads like "Please, Mr. Conductor, Don't put me off the train, 'cause my mother is dying in pain, and I want to see her again." That song referenced those who were quarantined in TB hospitals. I remember sitting on his lap night after night crying my heart out for that poor boy—always hoping in my four-year-old heart—that he would not be put off the train.

A favorite of our dad's rousing songs describes post WWI poverty and Depression-era woes:

> Rufus, Rastus, Johnson Brown: Whatcha gonna do when the rent comes 'round? Whatcha gonna say—Whatcha gonna pay? You know you haven't got a cent 'til Judgment Day...Landlord'll throw us out in the snow...

We all sang in full voice to the "whatchas" matched by Dad's knee-slapping rhythm. Often the lyrics didn't matter as long as the tune lent itself to harmonizing. We sang songs so often that we could belt them out by heart thirty years later at family reunions or on car rides with our own kids; Kay had contributed an easy tune that concluded all those medleys:

> As we going marching, and the band begins to play, Hear the people shouting, "The Dunfey gang is out again today."

My oldest brother Roy's favorite ditty, still heard down the generations, was "Tiddly winky winky winky—Tiddly winky woo—I love you!" How shocked I was to meet some children from Canada in those early years and hear them sing a version of those same lyrics. Hadn't that song been the sole possession of our family?

Family songs were so palpable to me as a five- and six-year-old that I associated each of my brothers with one of their favorites, so if anyone started singing "Oh, How I Miss You Tonight" or the "Whiffenpoof Song" after Jack had joined the Army Air Force, or "My Buddy" after Bud joined the Marines, I would run into the bedroom, bury my head in a pillow and sob. Perhaps that's why seven years later when I was thirteen and my father died suddenly, I could no longer sing a family favorite, "Last Night Was the End of the World." The ballad had come painfully to life.

Singing was—and remained for decades—the heartbeat of our lives. Given our well-earned reputation as a ragtag clan, we did not fit the image of *Cheaper by the Dozen* or the von Trapp family in the *Sound of Music*. For one thing, we never "fell in line" to the sound of a whistle. Period. The only way we fell in line was if some sibling "accidentally" pushed us. Neither did we suffer as a family the way the von Trapp family did on their journey to freedom. Years and what must have seemed "worlds" later, their mother Maria, and youngest son, Johann, became business colleagues and personal friends of my brother Jerry when both families owned inns in Vermont.

Jack, second from left, demonstrating his leadership skills early in the 40's with left to right, Jim Keefe, Walter Dunfey, Tim Considine, Jack and Tom O'Connor in spirited Christmas singing, possibly enhanced by other spirits.

Always ready to serenade my grandmother, Mary Manning, this photo features our favorite Italian tenor, Marty Sepé.

Tom and Jim Keefe (left front) join our dad and a mix of Dunfeys to serenade my mother, a Christmas tradition.

It's convenient that the beach was just across the Boulevard from the Clam Stand. Bob, Dick, Bud, and Jack would have to get back to work before that hole they dug for Jerry and me got any deeper.

Six brothers in search of a restaurant business. Left to right: Roy, Jack, Bud, Bob, Dick, Jerry, late 30s on Hampton Beach.

Father of the twelve of us wasn't fooling when he called this group "The tribe." According to a local reporter, "The Dunfey tribe can handle most any situation from a football contest to 32,000 customers. The chief, Roy Dunfey, says his summer business at Hampton Beach broke all records when that number were served..." Left to right are Paul, Walter, Jack, Dick, Bob, LeRoy, Eileen, Jerry. The other six members of the tribe, not included here, were also on duty, adding to the numbers served.

A brief furlough for Paul Dunfey to marry Rita Frechette, Lowell, MA. 1942

Photograph taken in school yard of St. Mary's Convent, Lawrence, MA. where our sister, Mary, was teaching. Nuns did not come home in those days, so the family went to them.

Campion Hall
North Andover, Mass.

Mar. 1, 1947

Dear Kay,
Well here I am again, at this fine retreat house with a nice gathering of K. of C. members. We have a new head of the retreat a Fr. Riley and he is a dandy. There isn't much time to write or get away as he has a list that keeps us quite busy.

In this note to my sister, Kay, our dad lets her know he's thinking of her. Usually, he and a couple of orchestra buddies would play for the school productions Kay directed for thirteen years at St. Bernard's in West Newton, MA, 1940s. I was so proud of my sister and excited to have a seat reserved for me in the front row at those shows, all through elementary school.

I received the song sheet from Witmark but the one Water-melon time is quite slow in coming. Hope your show goes off with a bang and that I'll be able to see it Mar. 9 next Sunday.
With all my love
Pa.

CHAPTER 9

1941: A War Over There Comes Home

"Extra! Extra! Read all about it—Japs bomb Pearl Harbor."

Jerry remembers Pearl Harbor Day through his six-year-old lens. He helped cousin, nine-year old Eddie Keefe on his paper route, tagging along and shouting the headlines to sell papers.

The war changed everything. The same young lads whose world up to that time had been focused on teen sweethearts, a job, cars, and hanging out, were suddenly off to places beyond their wildest imaginations, and action beyond their worst nightmares. Many of the same young carhop "hoodsies" took on new roles as Rosie the Riveters in mill cities along the Merrimack River. Three of our brothers and cousin Joe Keefe joined the Armed Services: Paul and Bud signed up with the Marines, Jack with the Army Air Force. Joe enlisted in the Navy. While on a brief leave as a Marine in 1942, my brother Paul married his hometown sweetheart, Rita Frechette. My child's-eye recollection of the wedding was pure fairy tale, infused later with pictures and stories worthy of best-selling fiction. In the wee hours of the morning before the wedding, Paul's Marine buddies found their way to the Pawtucketville section of Lowell where we lived, but they got lost on our street. My mother describes the scene:

> At 2 a.m. they started a chorus of DUNFEY—DUNFEY! There was no doubt that the Marines had landed! They had found Fifth Avenue but didn't know the actual house. Of course, it was the one with every light on, even though shades were supposed to be down during wartime. One Marine brought his girlfriend and we put up all of them for the night—no motor inns then—just a place where they could get a couple of hours of sleep. Picture our house in the morning as we all tried to make it to the church on time. What a gal that Marine brought with him. She played angel to me, put every bit of the house in order before we left for the church, and then, her boyfriend sang a solo in the choir at the ceremony—beautiful voice!

In the framed picture, Paul and Rita stand in the schoolyard of St. Mary's convent in Lawrence, Massachusetts, where my sister Mary was then living and teaching. Paul, in full Marine dress uniform beside his bride, fit a "happily ever after" photo, a storybook start that the war would soon alter. Rita gave birth to their son, Paul Jr., on April 30, 1944. My brother's frequent letters home, like this one penned to my parents from Guam in August 1944, describe his dire situation in lighthearted terms:

> Here's your jungle jogging marine trying to scratch off a hurried line to his loved ones after a busy day of patrolling of snooping and pooping as we call it. Yes, our real fighting is over…Believe me when I say I'm tip-top physically, mentally and spiritually. Good night, give my regards and thanks to my sister nuns and all and I'll be seein' ya. I'll try to write again soon. Your Paul

My brother would maintain that tone even into October 1944, in a thank you for the wedding anniversary greetings my mother had sent to him on the battlefront:

> I received your very nice anniversary card today and was very pleased…Rita tells me that our Paul has his third tooth. Hell, he's got nearly more than I have now.

Drs. Callahan and Virgoropoulus had pulled many a tooth from all twelve Dunfey mouths. But our brother Paul would spend little time thinking about the teeth he had lost thanks to the popularity of extraction in dentistry. His focus was on surviving and then writing letters minimizing the danger and horror. Only decades later did Paul share, in a *Lowell Sun* interview, the reality of war: "Our Sixth Marine Division is somewhat distinguished by the fact that we were formed overseas, fought and won overseas, but never made it back to the United States as a unit because we were disbanded after our hard-fought battle on Okinawa." Having been promoted to first lieutenant in the Marines, Paul had led a reconnaissance mission on May 9, 1945, and had seen, firsthand, the numbers and efficiency of the enemy:

> Every ridge was honeycombed with defensive positions allowing the Japanese to always hold the high ground and employ relatively small numbers of infantryman, machine gunners, and mortar men against a numerically far-superior adversary who had to move through ravines, across rivers, and up hills resulting in a dramatic advantage for the Japanese.

When Paul attempted to express his concerns to the commander, he was met with a curt "Dismissed" response, although a second officer did call Paul back and allow him to state his hesitations. So much for Lieutenant Dunfey's misgivings:

> At three o'clock the following morning, Dunfey's weakened platoon (from the earlier reconnaissance mission) was the second to cross a rope bridge strung across the Asakawa River by engineers earlier that night. The men had orders to hold their fire, light no cigarettes, move soundlessly.
> —Marine Corps Gazette, *"Okinawa Final Great Battle of*
> *World War II: an American triumph through bloodshed"*

A few at a time, he led his men in twenty-to-thirty-yard sprints before "hitting the dirt." Just as he led the last group forward, machine gunfire hit his stomach. It was May 10, 1945. Paul lay in the rice paddy for seven hours before he could be rescued. A medic gave him morphine, but Paul never lost consciousness. He said it was a "helpless feeling. All I could do was yell for the other men to "get down, get down!"

At a reunion years later, one of Paul's men confided, "I saw you when you were lying there in Okinawa with your guts all over the ground. I can't believe you are alive." In fact, word was that Paul had died of his wounds. He was grateful to report, like Mark Twain, that rumors of his death had been "greatly exaggerated." Well, maybe not "greatly":

> Paul Dunfey, the first lieutenant who scouted south of the Asakawa...could not be evacuated for many hours because Japanese fire was too fierce. A bullet had severed his bowel and a probable second drove fragments of his belt buckle into his intestines. He was saved when doctors on a hospital ship used a new technique, later described in a collection called Miracles of Surgery, to fuse his bowel.

The author explains at the bottom of the page:

> But its long-term effect wasn't known at the time. After Dunfey spent ten months in hospitals, a doctor told his wife to take him home and have a good time because he had about five years to live. He was vigorously alive forty years later.
> —*George Feifer, Tennozan: The Battle of Okinawa*
> *and the Atomic Bomb*

My mother's memoir shows her admiration for the way Rita, now a mother of a one-year-old son, Paul Jr., coped when word came that Paul had been severely wounded and was not expected to live:

> Rita, like so many others, was the "Valiant Woman" persevering with no news through anxious days and nights when Paul was on secret missions, and then dealing with the news—the extent of his injuries.

I was six-and-a-half-years old when Paul, my second-oldest brother, was wounded. In the next eleven years, I do not recall him ever uttering a word about the war, much less about his leadership and heroism in the war's bloodiest battle. Even then it would be brief. Immediately following my high school graduation, on a sunny June afternoon in 1956, Paul and I walked together down a tree-lined roadway. We talked about "life" andall that was ahead for me—and all that he wished for me. I'm embarrassed to say that, up to that time, all my conversations with Paul had also been about "me." In that exchange on my graduation day, though, Paul made me feel I had grown up during four high school years. Our conversation seemed more a sharing between a wise elder and a young adult, rather than an older brother and kid sister. That was the real gift I received from him that day. I'm not sure what led up to his comments, but I have never forgotten how fittingly they concluded our serious conversation about the need to live in peace: "Eleanor, I have seen enough killing to last lifetimes." That was it. And that was all I needed to hear. The stark effect of war was the lesson he taught me more poignantly than all the words in any history course leading to the diploma I had been handed a few hours earlier.

Paul was true to those words, too. In 1987, the *Lowell Sun* interviewed him about the purpose of his decision to return to Okinawa:

> The friends I lost on Guam and Okinawa can never be replaced. I have long since learned to live with the fact that many good friends died so that I could live, and I have also learned to love the enemy I have fought.

Paul's grandson, Michael Downes, visited Guam, just one of the battle-fields where his grandfather had fought. Michael wrote:

> I just got home last evening. I had the opportunity to go the National Park War in the Pacific Museum and learned in more detail about the Battle of Guam. Paul was in that battle. I went to Agat Beach where he and the USMC waded into the beach

(because their transport vehicles got stuck up on the reef) under heavy fire. The heat and humidity was brutal while I was there. It's hard to comprehend trudging through that heat with your military fatigues and gear, let alone the hostile circumstances. The Battle of Guam commenced on July 21, Paul's 26th birthday—kind of a crappy birthday gift. July 21 is also Liberation Day in Guam and they still celebrate it fervently. To have stepped foot where my grandfather served and sacrificed for his country and the world was especially moving for me. I'm very blessed to have had such a grandfather, and I'm privileged to have had such an experience.

A star in the window, a telegram at the door

War's most tragic reality struck our cousin Joe's household—one flight up in the Keefe family home. Families had been given a star to place in their window for each son or daughter engaged in military service. We had three stars in the window of our first floor flat. The Keefes had one star in theirs. Their oldest son, Joe, a star basketball and baseball player, had joined the Navy in 1942.

At the beginning of March 1944, Joe wrote a letter to my sister Kay, his favorite cousin and best pal, whose birthday month he shared:

> We're sure getting old fast aren't we, Kay? The 15th of this month I'll be 21! It seems like only yesterday that we were 12 or 13 and having all those good times—walking to St. Pat's every morning, taking trips with the Cadets, going to parties at LEAST once a week, dances, outings, lawn parties…The other day I received a Christmas package from Fr. Maguire (still spending all his money on the guys in the services) and it contained one of the bulletins which the C.Y.O. sends every once in a while. There was a list of engagements and what a list. There was Mary Stapleton and some O'Brien fellow, Kitty Powers and Davie Gerow, Helen McDermott and Joe Quinn, ANNE COYLE and Bob Hannifin (she must be all of 17) and oh, a host of others. From the look of things, I must be slow. Oh well, lots of time for that after the war…

March 27, 1944, twelve days after Joe's twenty-first birthday, I heard the screams from upstairs when the Naval officers arrived with the telegram. Even as a five-year-old, I knew something horrible had happened. Through the blur, someone told me that the arrival of a car and military people silently making their way to the door of a home meant a "soldier had been killed or was missing in action."

Joe was "missing in action." I had no idea what that meant except that it was awful. I ached with guilt because I had been pretty upset with my handsome teenage cousin when he had come home on Christmas leave the year before. It must have been a mild day. Joe and my brothers were all gathered outside the house just off the porch. It was a short walkway and my doll carriage, adorned with the white silk coverlet my mother had made for Christmas was parked, I should say squeezed, into the corner by the steps. I had gone into the house for a few minutes. Without realizing it, Joe had flicked his cigarette behind him. The ashes burned a hole in my irreplaceable coverlet.

It was only much later, maybe when further word came that Joe had been killed by "friendly fire," that I began to realize what "irreplaceable" really meant: my cousin wouldn't be coming back—ever. The cigarette burn on my doll's coverlet was nothing compared to the fact that I would not see Joe again. My sister Kay would remember Joe, cousin and friend, in her heartfelt poem:

Salute

My heart, defying distances
A rendezvous is keeping
Where cradled 'neath a slender cross
Our Joe finds quiet sleeping.
It pauses at the lonely grave
With foreign grasses growing
And suddenly is fiercely glad
You turned and waved in going.

For Joe, 1944

Post-war sorrow and strength

There would be a plaque installed on a corner light post, dedicating the area at the end of our street in front of St. Rita's Church as Joseph P. Keefe Square. It was a gesture of a brokenhearted community holding on to young heroes who had made the greatest sacrifice of all. In those years, sadly, there were too many such plaques, too many such dedications.

The emotional drain on all families was palpable, but it failed to unravel our parents' underlying optimism. The government decided how many rations a family would receive, but our parents never rationed their resilience. If the government dictated they must lower shades on all our windows, drive with headlights covered like half-moons during the darkest hours of the night, they obeyed in order to be safe. But government could not dictate how to hold fast to hope while grieving and supporting those whose families had been altered forever. Behind the scenes, my mother was there for the Keefes. She helped our dad keep the store going and kept the six younger Dunfeys, plus a host of drop-ins, fed.

My sister Eileen recalls, in summer months, that my mother would have a full-course meal ready for her and my brothers Bob, Dick, Walter, and Jerry—sometimes at 2 or 3 a.m. when they would arrive at the tiny Hampton Beach "Camp Comfort" after closing up the store in Lowell. They would have used some rations to add enough gas (hopefully) to the car to get them to their destination. They'd hope to make at least one trip with the Pontiac's old rubber tires staying inflated. That rarely happened. Bob was always fixing flat tires. They'd check to be sure there was still black tape on the top half of the headlight and then set out during the darkest part of the night after double-checking, as well, that all the shades were drawn at home in Lowell. Eileen also spent some summer nights all alone in our Lowell home. "How creepy it was especially with all those shades down."

During the War, my brother Bob "came into his own" on Broadway. My mother describes that time in his life:

> I register Bob as Dad's right-hand man because, during the War
> when his three older brothers were in the Service and his two
> older sisters had entered the convent, Bob kept the business
> going and doing this in wartime was a very difficult task, indeed.
> During rationing of gas, long lines waiting for butter, sugar and
> other items, Bob put in extra hours so Dad could have a little
> time away from his grinding schedule of 5:30 a.m. to 1:30 a.m.
> Bob was one of many who kept peace on the home front and
> were the mainstays of keeping families together. Those serving
> Uncle Sam were given medals, and I believe the guys helping to
> hold things together at home should at least be given honorable
> mention.

Bob also had his own beyond-the-call-of-duty experience on the home front, right there in the Acre, saving the life of an older, alcoholic tenant, during a fire in her tenement, two flights over our store. The slim, fifteen-year-old Bob carried Mamie D—very much against her will, and probably his—down a ladder to the safety of the street. There were cheers and kudos on Broadway that day.

Homecoming

Kind was the grave that they dug
    for you
And we bless the hands of your
    comrades true,
The care and the reverence that
    you knew
In that resting place afar.

But love has longed to have you
    near
In the land whose liberty you held
    dear,
And we greet you with remembering
    tears
Our hero - home from the war.

Now does the Master's design unroll,
And now is Faith's harmony made
    whole,
For we echo the welcome accorded
    the soul
Of our hero - Home from the war.

For Joe   June 27, 1948

My cousin, Joe Keefe, killed in action by "friendly fire," on March 22, 1944, ten days after his twenty-first birthday.

Kay Dunfey *Give Me Wings*

CHAPTER 10

1945

Flying Home

My brothers Jack and Bud returned safely from World War II. For all his aversion to his older sister's stage dramas, Jack was front and center in his own dramatic flight back to Fort Devens where he had enlisted. It was Christmas Eve, 1945. A PT-19 open cockpit. White-out weather conditions. Unplowed runway at Great Barrington Airport in Massachusetts. Low fuel. Nightfall. It may sound more like a Santa Claus journey gone terribly wrong. It was, however, my almost twenty-two-year-old brother Jack's account of his flight from Denver, Colorado, following his discharge from the Air Force.

"Not exactly what I had in mind for my re-entry to civilian life that blustery night," according to Jack. He could have used the skis from St. Nick's sleigh. These were not included with the excess planes stored in the Arizona desert. Jack and a fellow captain had bought twelve of the PT-19s, each for $350. They had to retrofit them for civilian use, adding fire extinguishers, for example. At the end of the licensing process, each plane was numbered: The plane Jack kept for himself was licensed and identified with the painted number 50,000 (recording the total sold to that date). The two enterprising pilots rounded up colleagues to fly the planes from Arizona to Denver where they sold eleven of the twelve for handsome sum of $1200 each. The new veterans were flying high with the profit.

This particular wintry evening, however, Jack was flying as low as he could, trying to stay under the clouds: "All our local flyers have skis on their planes," the crackling voice reported from the control tower at Great Barrington Airport. "The landing strip has at least four inches of snow and won't be plowed." Jack was obviously not your "local flyer."

"Low fuel. Permission requested to land," Jack replied in a strained but cool tone (I should say "cold," given the PT's open cockpit).

"Given," said the control tower voice with yet another caution about conditions. During the night, an additional four inches of the white stuff accumulated on the runway. The following morning, the controller was reluctant to allow Jack to take off. Jack was concerned, too, especially as he assessed his chances of clearing a four-foot woven wire fence at the end of the runway. Could he get up enough speed in the deep snow? Despite his own anxiety, Jack persuaded the controller to give him "permission to make some tracks and crunch down the snow."

After two runway round-trips scoring those tracks, Jack put on the brakes, then revved the motor and taxied along the narrow wheel paths. Picking up speed, he cleared the fence and was on his way. But which way? At 3,000 feet, he and his PT-19 were embedded in low cloud cover. He knew he was in the Berkshire Mountain range; his compass said he was flying east. "Trying to confirm that from the terrain below, I dipped down under the clouds—carefully—so as not to hit a mountain peak. After two or three tries, I spotted a few small streams flowing eastward. I knew, then, I was headed out of the Berkshires in the right direction."

Using navigation-by-ground-observation, Jack identified the Springfield, Massachusetts, airfield and got permission to land without skis, gas up, and take off again for the last leg of the flight to Fort Devens. Four years earlier, my dad had waved goodbye to his eighteen-year-old son at the Lowell Depot. The twenty-one-mile train ride had taken Jack to the same Fort Devens, to enlist in the Army Air Force after the bombing of Pearl Harbor. Regulations required discharge documents be verified at the location where the individual had enlisted. Jack was back, the Air Force pilot now a civilian.

CAMERA NEWS

OF GREATER LOWELL

By TONY ALVES
Telegram Staff Photographer

EX-PILOT STILL FLYING—Jack and Walter Dunfey about to take off at Richardson Field, Dracut, where Jack, ex-Army pilot, keeps his two-seater army trainer which you see flying over the city most any day.

Post WWII, Air Force pilot, Jack, ready to soar with fifteen-year old brother, Walter. Jack used his PT-19 to train Bud and Bob for their pilots' licenses; to delight Walter and Jerry with stunt-filled rides; to fly Eileen to work along with a sack of potatoes to peel for French fries at Hampton Beach. My ride as a seven-year-old, with Bob's arms around me as my seatbelt, left me with lifelong fear of heights!

CHAPTER II

1946

Hampton Beach: Turkey Sandwiches to Clams

Despite or maybe because of World War II, people flocked to Hampton Beach, New Hampshire, in the summer. It was the happening place. It had drawn throngs of fun seekers since the turn of the century, when new bridges, trolleys, and streetcars began to connect other regions in all directions to the beach. The new transportation lines made it easy and affordable for travelers who didn't have the kind of cash it took to stay in the White Mountains' luxurious grand resorts. Peter E. Randall's history, *Hampton: A Century of Town and Beach, 1888–1988*, describes the scene:

> Streetcars ran from the Merrimack Valley via the Seabrook line and the Mile Bridge. That route also was used by cars from Salisbury Beach. From the north, the Portsmouth Electric Railway…was extended to the Hampton-North Hampton town line in June 1900, and it brought tourists from Portsmouth and southern Maine…The 25.6 miles between Haverhill and Hampton Beach took 1 hour 45 minutes. Cars left the Casino at 15 and 45 minutes before the hour for Haverhill and Portsmouth and left on the hour and half hour for Hampton Village and Exeter.

During the war, we became human GPS experts, finding back roads from Lowell to Hampton Beach and back to Lowell in our Packard. I could have done without the shortcut through a cemetery in Groveland. But all routes got us to "Happy Hampton," and to Bill Elliot, the "Singing Cop's" favorite opening tune at the weekly band concert across from the casino. "Let's go down to Happy Hampton, Hampton by the sea." We did.

At age nine, I had my few minutes of kid fame on that stage during the weekly Talent Show. Elocution lessons were common at the time, and my teacher wrote a piece expressly for me, titled "Boys." I dedicated it to my eight brothers. The first line was "Boys! Do you like boys? Well, I don't!" My brother Jerry had good reason not to want to be seen with me.

By 1946, my father had been walking Hampton beach with summer neighbors for years. On one particular day when he stopped into Mr. Hayward's fried clam stand, he was thinking about new plans for post-World War II. Three of his sons—Paul, Jack, and Bud—were returning soldiers. How was he going to put them all to work? Fred Hayward, a taciturn fellow, owned the take-out stand situated between the Ashworth Hotel and DeLancy Rooming House. Hayward's was a popular spot and soon after my father put in his order, another customer arrived, taking up most of the available space inside. He was interested in talking to Fred, who was preparing my dad's order. In a few moments, not only were the clams ready, but my father had overheard the news that Fred was anxious to sell the stand because of a family illness.

Why not buy Mr. Hayward's clam stand? Dad digested the idea with the clams. Assisted in his negotiations by my brother, Jack, he bought Hayward's Fried Clam Stand for $26,000.

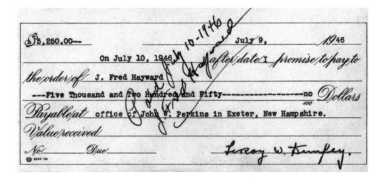

Our dad depended on Jack, and saw him as a natural leader. The B-24 heavy bomber pilot trainer was prepared to dive into the fray. He worked closely with and knew my father well. To hear Jack tell it, our dad inspired the hard, long work hours because he was always up first and down last. "There was no favoritism or shirking expectations when it came to us, either. Dad taught us the business by "feel" and by applying what he had learned every day." He switched his large family crew around from first to second to third shifts. One would have to wake up at 5 a.m. and go to work with him until school started; the next week, one would be required to get to the store immediately after school. "Sometimes, we worked shifts before and after school."

Dunfey's Clam Stand would test the success of Dad's training. A year earlier, he had bought a small cottage on Nudd Terrace. The cottages we first rented, then owned, had euphemistic monikers: The Restful, the Keefe rental, UNeedaRest, and Camp Comfort. "Camp" was a more accurate description than "Comfort." We did not merely live in these tiny spaces. We enveloped them until, bursting at the seams, we spilled out to porch cots and, on many a night, gave up on sleep altogether and just set chairs outside in what would soon morph into block parties full of joking and singing.

Willing or not (often not), renters around us were denied sleep as well. I recall seeing them out listening and laughing at our antics and songs; then when they decided they had had enough, they'd go in and call the police to come shut us down for disturbing the peace. We were guilty as charged!

My mother's turkey sandwiches may have been the first menu item the Dunfeys served, but clams would feed the realization that there might be a future in this business. We were about to create the secret recipe that would make selling fried clams profitable enough to feed growing kids and finance college educations. Taking over from Haywood after the 1946 Fourth of July weekend, the family had a successful season, selling ten to twelve gallons of clams daily and making a profit that equaled the purchase price. We had no idea the business could be so lucrative, as my brother Bud recalled forty years later:

> On hot nights and on Labor Day weekend, we stayed open 24 hours, selling clams and hot dogs until 3 a.m. We'd close for an hour to clean—and change the front window menu from hot dogs to donuts, serving beachcombers and adventurers who slept on the beach—back in the days when it was still allowed.

The Dunfeys needed more staff. Paul McGaunn, the Acre kid who lived across from the luncheonette on Broadway, happened to be sitting on his tenement stoop in Lowell one Saturday morning with his older brother, Harry. Now a seasoned Dunfey "alumnus," Paul, on that day, was about to begin his Dunfey career—unintentionally. My brother Bob, asked Harry to go to work at Hampton Beach for the weekend. Harry said, "No. I won't. But he will," pointing to his unsuspecting kid brother, and generously volunteering the services of the twelve-year-old sitting on the door stoop.

So, Paul filled a paper bag with some clothes and climbed into the borrowed O'Donnell Funeral Home hearse filled with Dunfey brothers and potatoes. That ride, balancing himself on an orange crate, not only led to Paul's first job peeling the potatoes for French fries on the back stoop of our first clam stand at Hampton Beach. According to Paul, his tenure with Dunfey led him around the world (traveling in more comfortable conditions than on a box in the back of a borrowed hearse) over "forty-five tumultuous, challenging, gratifying years." Paul retired as vice president of operations at the international executive offices of Omni-Dunfey Hotels in Hampton—just five miles uptown from that original clam stand where he peeled potatoes on Hampton Beach. But that summer of 1946, his only trip was from the hot tenement stoop in the Acre, to the even hotter back alley stoop of Dunfey's at the beach.

Still flying...and frying

"Our clams were a far cry from the fried strips you got at Howard Johnson's, two blocks down the boulevard," Jerry proudly states. "Ho-Jo's" had become an iconic rest stop, easily accessible along the new turnpikes, but it sold seafood that was previously frozen. "We only sold baby clams that had stomachs, and they were always fresh," reports Jerry, and he should know. At age eleven, he knew clams well, working fulltime at the take-out stand.

Our French fries were fresh, too, made with potatoes delivered in that borrowed hearse or flown from Lowell in Jack's PT-19. He would dip the plane's wings over the ocean in front of the clam stand as a message that a brother with a license should meet him at the Hampton Air Field, which was then a dusty, infrequently traveled strip of land five miles west of the beach.

One early June morning in 1947, Jack didn't use his plane for transporting potatoes. He and Bob took the open-roofed Ford. It was not a convertible; it just had no roof. It did have a windshield and rumble seat that popped up from the trunk area. The two drove sixty miles to a surplus equipment sale at Fort Devens and purchased what would be most welcome—a top-quality potato peeling machine. One slight problem, according to Jack, was that it "weighed a ton" and required the two brothers to enlist the services of several able-bodied men who had the misfortune of being within shouting distance. The machine had to be lifted, pushed, and then partly shoved and partly dropped into the rumble seat of the Model A Ford. At its destination, Dunfey's Fried Clam Stand, there was no shortage of muscled kids peeling potatoes on the back stoop or hanging around the front window. In the back alley, they hoisted and dropped the steel monster on the ground just inside Mrs. Lamprey's adjacent rooming house cellar, with her begrudging agreement, based on Jack's "promise," to move it in a "couple of weeks."

An extension cord was dropped from the stoop above. The machine started, worked well and fulltime in Mrs. Lamprey's cellar (for years). Before this automation, we'd crawl out the clam stand's back window—there was no back door. Eileen, Walter, Jerry, Paul McGaunn, and fellow Acre pal, Jim Cote, would crouch on those wooden tonic (soda) crates and peel potatoes by hand. Everyone celebrated the purchase of the potato-peeling machine, which reduced hard labor to the far simpler task of digging out a few eyes from the potato. From a PT-19 bought at Air Force surplus in Arizona to a potato-peeling machine purchased at Fort Devens, Jack had extended the life span and function of at least two armed-service-owned machines.

Marty Sepè continued to work at the beach and in the Dunfey's restaurant our dad had built in the vacant lot beside the Lowell luncheonette. The new establishment featured seafood in the city. Marty was one of the first to learn the secret clam batter recipe that my brothers had created at the Hampton Beach clam stand. The prep cook had the unenviable job of working his hands through an egg wash after it was coated in a mix of crackers and cornmeal. Then he would have to drop each clam separately into the sizzling grease.

Fortunately (for prank's sake), Marty could mix fun with his work as naturally as he could dip and drop clams into a fryolator. One afternoon, Pete Eliopolis, another Acre buddy, showed up in the new restaurant in his best suit (most likely borrowed), announcing proudly that he had a big date for the Greek Formal, but Pete was really nervous about the date and wanted a bit of his friend's confidence. Marty had to fill a customer's order so he asked Pete to join him in the backroom. He reassured him, enveloping the nervous lad with his all-embracing Italian hug, patting him firmly on the back. He coaxed him to relax and enjoy the date; then sent him out of the backroom, feeling a bit of Marty's own confidence. Off Pete went to his formal event totally unaware he also had more than a bit of Marty's huge cornmeal handprints on the back of his best (only?) suit.

No secret: a missing ingredient—sleep

Jerry had begun learning the ropes of the business at age six, two full years before I did. Then I joined him. Come Saturday morning I got up early, put on my white uniform and apron, and headed to the clam stand from Lowell or from Camp Comfort, around the corner. Weather permitting, on winter weekends and every day during the summer, our "production line" cranked out hundreds of hand-made Italian "grinders" (now called subs) on a board that stretched from the side wall at the front of the shop to the all-important but sweltering fryolator. Each grinder was wrapped in glacine and was sealed closed on the hot dog grill. All seven hundred would be sold through our front window within twenty-four hours!

What was lacking was enough sleep. My brother Jack still enjoys describing Bob at the 6:30 a.m. Mass at St. Patrick's Church at Hampton Beach. We Dunfeys would line up in our uniforms across the back of the church, so we could sneak out early and open for the after-Mass crowd. Jack says there was one unspoken rule: Bob must always have someone on either side of him to keep him from falling asleep. But one early Sunday, just as the priest was ready to lead the procession from the back of the church, Bob had no one holding on to him. His knees buckled, and he slid right into the middle aisle—sound asleep. What astounded Jack was not that Bob had fallen asleep, but that the fall didn't wake him.

Missing wedding gear—almost missing the wedding

My favorite "sleep" story, though, is not about Bob but about Jack—on his wedding day. That morning in 1948, all the rented shoes, suspenders, pants, starched shirts, ties, and cummerbunds which had been laid out in our kitchen were swiftly scooped up by my brothers and cousins, another upstairs-downstairs celebration in progress. Finally, after all the grabbing, fitting and tightening, the best man and ushers were out and off to the Immaculate Conception Church across the city where brother Jack would marry Joan Lannan.

My mother sent me to the front hall closet which we rarely used (except to hide pies) for her coat. I opened the dining room door and headed to the front room. There, on the sofa sound asleep, lay the groom! It was just after 9:00 a.m. The ceremony was scheduled for 10 a.m. All I remember after squealing and getting my mother's coat, was Jack, up in a flash and standing in the kitchen having managed to get "half" dressed. The problem was, there were no shoes or suspenders left for the groom.

Enter "Husky" McCarthy, right on time to pick up the groom, the parents and me in the large black sedan borrowed from Jimmy O'Donnell's Funeral Home. He was also right on time to complete Jack's wardrobe. Husky would not be chauffeuring us that morning. At the kitchen door, he was relieved of his suspenders and shoes. The next scene was of Husky, standing in our kitchen, barefoot, holding up his pants. Jack was in the driver's seat, and we were off to get to the church almost, but not quite, on time.

Three home from war—three now in the convent

Also in 1948, my sister Eileen entered the Sisters of Notre Dame, joining my two older sisters, Kay and Mary, who were then teaching, respectively, in West Newton and South Boston. Bob had to say goodbye to his younger sister and most dependable work partner; Walter had to say "So long" to his older sister and his best chance to date her beautiful girlfriends.

Humor belied the sadness of parting on Eileen's entrance day in August. Four of her good friends from Lowell were entering with her, so the family contingents were large. I was eight years old. Much of the emotion went over my head; I was excited to be wearing the new yellow sundress my mother had bought me for the occasion. I remember people milling around waiting for the bell that would call the postulants (the name given to those in the first phase of religious training). When it sounded, a silence fell on the gathering. There were some muffled sobs, then lots of tears and good-byes. Finally, the parting: The new postulants filed in the front door in their "nun" shoes and simple black dresses trimmed with white collars. Suddenly, a voice echoed through the convent yard breaking the silence and quiet sobs with its thick Irish brogue: "If ye behaved yerselves as ye should have, ye wouldn't be in there!! That's what ja git." Mr. Finnegan, the father of one of Eileen's best friends, shouted the remark through his tears, sending ripples of laughter through the emotion-laden air. Irish humor would mark yet another parting and mask the reality of a painful good-bye.

Dunfey's first Fried Clam Stand, Hampton Beach, New Hampshire, on Ocean Boulevard tucked in under the awning between the Ashworth Hotel and DeLancey Rooming House. 1946

Enjoying one another again, home from the service are Jack, (left front) and Paul, (right front). This "Camp Comfort" crew includes (back row, left to right): Roy, Jerry, Dad, Bob. Walter is front center. circa 1946

As a teenager in the 1940s, Robert "Bob" Dunfey stands outside Dunfey's Clam Stand in Hampton Beach, NH. That was just the start. Courtesy photo *Lowell Sun*.

Our dad loved his daily saunters along Ocean Boulevard. Here he is after stopping by Dunfey's Fried Clam Stand *(rear, left)*.

My sister, Eileen, takes a ride down memory lane in 1979 to see what had been Dunfey's restaurant, between J and K Streets at Hampton Beach. The entire block was later destroyed in a 1999 fire. The Higgins family, owners of The Old Salt restaurant which burned to the ground, later purchased Lamie's Tavern in Hampton Center and have preserved many Dunfey family traditions.

Dunfey's at 375 Broadway started out as a drive-in with carhops—my sister Eileen's "hoodsie teen" friends. My father built it on an empty lot next door to our luncheonette, then he added a full restaurant offering "seafood in the city." 1951

CHAPTER 12

Destination Durham, and Division of Labor

The trip from Lowell, Massachusetts, to Durham, New Hampshire, by way of Hampton Beach is only sixty miles on a map, but the War's intervention made it a circuitous and life-altering journey with training camps, killing grounds, and "friendly fire" touching all on the home front: Fort Collins, the Marshall Islands, Okinawa, and South Asian Sea. The physical scars and heavy hearts, effects of the Great Depression, exacerbated by WWII, had seared the soul.

Now thoughts and plans must turn to the homefront. With Jack's involvement in 1949, Dad bought the Rexall Drug Store at the University of New Hampshire in Durham, from Bob True. With that property, we inherited a soda counter, a bus stop, and Dennis, the store cashier, a "fixture in town here longer than I have been" according to Bob True. "All the Townies love him!"

Our dad admired Dennis from the start. At home in Lowell, my parents thought, "what a relief to have a 'father figure' up there in Durham" with the "boys" going to school and working. Dennis knew everyone. He was suave, sophisticated, and always ready to accommodate this Dunfey clan from Massachusetts as they learned "the ropes." Walter was now manager, putting in countless hours with Bob, often after opening and closing the restaurants at the beach. They depended on thirteen-year-old Jerry to assume significant responsibility, and even I, age ten, was added to the schedule at the beach clam stand.

It was during Christmas vacation in 1949 that the family transformed the pharmacy into a full restaurant, keeping the counter and adding booths and a kitchen; they used the hitches on their cars and rented trailers to bring equipment from the beach restaurants to Durham (which meant a reverse move of said equipment back to the beach in the spring). Later, the family purchased the property next door, Hamm's Market. Demolishing that building led to a new enterprise. We opened Town and Campus, one of the earliest student supply stores. Soon to follow was the "Speedy Laundromat," one of the first such services in a college town; located in the building's basement and entered from an outside stairway. Walter and his wife, Barbara Clark, managed the business. No longer living at home, my brothers, it appears, were assessing all the necessities of college students—including themselves—and then opening businesses to meet those needs.

Food—check. Class supplies—check. Clean laundry—check.

Trust—but verify

One basic item, however, was not checking out. Jack had crunched all the numbers with our dad when they decided to purchase the Rexall pharmacy. At the time, he had wondered why the previous owner, a hard-working, upright man, had not been making a profit. Even though Jack did not let on at the time, he recalls feeling suspicious about the "beloved" Dennis. Sure enough, my brothers began to notice small amounts of money missing.

Meanwhile, everyone's schedule was full. There were classes and work. Bob and Walter were renting a house on Edgewood Road. Jack and his wife, Joan, had a baby daughter, Susan, and were living on Mill Road. The businesses appeared to be thriving. Our parents even celebrated their thirty-fifth wedding anniversary in the Durham restaurant during the holidays. But there was a pall over the budding enterprise. Now the brothers began to notice that larger sums of money were missing. They were convinced that Dennis was stealing, but who could even imagine that—the stalwart town citizen, the real gentleman, the Dunfeys' trusted, mature employee.

If, indeed, there was a problem, surely the townies who admired Dennis would take his side over those young upstarts from Massachusetts. My brothers would have to cook up a plan to find evidence—if there was any—that they had the real culprit. Al Stadig, a local carpenter, was hired to "re-design" the front window at the restaurant's entrance. He built a two-and-a-half-foot cabinet with two "peep holes," through which one could see all the activity going on at the register inside the restaurant's front door. Next step: figure out who would be selected as the watchman. Unfortunately for Walter, he "fit" into the cabinet. "Oh, was he ever miserable!" Jack quips.

Each year, Jack, Bud, Bob, Walter, and Jerry attended the Restaurant Show in Boston, a three-hour drive from Durham in those days. Instead of joining Jack, Bud, Bob, and Jerry that year, Walter was assigned to hide out for three days in that stuffy, vertical coffin, looking through the peep holes and noting each transaction that the heretofore trusted Dennis made. Misery paid off. On the very first day, Walter saw Dennis pocket a $10 bill—a significant amount in those days. Dennis would also short-change each sale, ringing up only $2.00 on a $2.50 sale and pocketing the difference. The repetition added up and Walter was recording it all, feeling that his three-day sentence in a cabinet was painfully worthwhile.

Having hard evidence would not be enough. Given Dennis' untarnished reputation in town, there was every chance that he would be seen, not as perpetrator, but as victim. The brothers, especially Walter who had been closeted collecting the evidence, were infuriated. Wisely, they decided to go to a friend and advisor: the Dover sheriff, whom they invited to a meeting at Bob's home on Edgewood Road. Under the guise of holding a planning session, they also invited Dennis. Jack and Walter contained their anger as they watched an extremely defensive Dennis vehemently deny the theft, even in the face of the evidence. As anticipated, they got nowhere with him. So, they asked the Sheriff to come into the room. He sat down in front of Dennis and told him in no uncertain terms that he needed to "pay or face the alternative," the alternative being a public arrest. Dennis reluctantly admitted guilt and accepted the terms of the deal. It was not until the spring of 1953, a year after my father died, that the matter was settled.

My mother and I had moved from our tenement in Lowell, Massachusetts, to the town of Hampton, New Hampshire, where we could be closer to our family's burgeoning business in the Seacoast area. All I remember of the Dennis saga was that my mother and I suddenly had a house full of very lovely furniture and a "swell" stereo, which found a welcome home in what we called the downstairs rumpus room. It was perfect timing, as the room became the hub for many employee parties, as well as the sleepovers and dances I had as a teenager. I far preferred the furniture and stereo to the man who betrayed my parents' and brothers' trust.

My brothers had learned an important lesson: "Trust but verify." They were "seeing red" in their outrage over this ordeal, but they recognized its complexity. Rather than have the short-term satisfaction of humiliating this employee, they chose to deal with the matter in a way that required him to acknowledge his wrongdoing and pay—even if only with his furniture and stereo. There were ever-increasing responsibilities of running the businesses without our dad's leadership. My brothers might see "red" in their fury, but they had to choose their battles. They were coming of age. This experience was a major reality check. They would get back to school and business and growing families.

At that very moment, our country was experiencing another, more serious "kind of red."

National "Red" tremors
WWII may have ended, but it left in its wake a red tide, personified in the extremist agenda of Senator Joseph McCarthy. The "communist threat"

was sweeping the country and even reached into the outposts of the small state of New Hampshire.

In 1948, in the *Union Leader*, Bill Loeb editorialized that Jack Dunfey, then a young married father, UNH student on the GI Bill, and owner (with his family) of Dunfey's Restaurant in town, was holding Communist cell meetings at his home at 48 Mill Road. Loeb's "reasoning" for the claim was the fact that Jack and his wife were "harboring" a negro. What was accurate about the claim is that UNH freshman Albert "Buck" Johnston Jr., from Keene, NH, was rooming at Jack and Joan's home. After Loeb's column, Jack recalls, "Almost every night throughout the winter, cars with their headlights off would drive back and forth in front of our home on Mill Road, an unsettling experience for us, especially with our new baby."

Just as they were learning management in business courses on Main Street, my brothers were alerted to the heightened importance of citizen involvement, lessons my father had taught us when he got involved in politics. His example was affirmed by humanities professor Gwynne Daggart, whose courses Bud took and then directed his other brothers to take.

The family had been aware from the start that some people used politics for their own benefit. After all, my father's welfare commissioner's role began in Lowell because the sitting commissioner was in jail for graft. But it was the constructive role of politics in our democracy that peppered conversations when we were growing up. Politics was a good word, a vehicle for citizens to build healthy communities. Bud was a student, learning first from our father's example, affirmed by Professor Daggart's rigorous curriculum, deepened by Catholic social teaching as lived by Dorothy Day, and experienced in WWII and its red-tide aftermath. With this combination of personal, academic, moral, and spiritual underpinnings, Bud took on the challenge at hand: researching and writing the history of the Democratic Party in New Hampshire and establishing, with like-minded students, the first Young Democrats' club in the state's history.

Fledgling entrepreneurs on the move

When, in 1949, my dad and brothers purchased that small pharmacy in Durham, they had viewed their Durham and Hampton Beach businesses as ways to finance their college educations and support their young families. At the time, the family owned four businesses: two in Lowell and two at Hampton Beach. Just one year later, they were faced with a new set of decisions after a major fire on July 14, 1950, the peak summer season at Hampton Beach. The conflagration destroyed nineteen businesses in the center of the beach at C Street and the Boulevard. Three hotels went up in flames, as did two rooming houses, several summer cottages, and fifteen stores.

Bob, Dick, and several employees were at our restaurant on the south end of Hampton Beach. Because the blaze enveloped the area in between that south end restaurant and our clam stand at the north end, we had to carry armloads of supplies down on the beach when the tide went out far enough to allow us to walk at the water's edge. I remember feeling the heat and smoke as the blaze torched its path through the long night. We kept both of our small businesses open, serving the many vacationers who were left without lodging.

The fire was halted by a concrete wall situated between what was then the Exeter and Hampton Electric Company and Junkins candy store on Ocean Boulevard. The Ocean House next door was spared. Had it had not been, then the famous Hampton Beach Casino, according to Peter Randall's 1989 history, likely would have been destroyed as well. Randall writes:

> As with previous fires, businesspeople immediately began to rebuild. On the day after the fire, Henry Dupuis, whose business had burned, posted a sign, "Henry's Real Estate," against a fence with an arrow pointing to the Ocean House porch, some fifty feet away, where he had placed a desk. Just a week after the fire, the Hobbs family began a new building at the southerly corner of C Street and the boulevard, and others did the same, resulting in the present structures in the area.

Even though our restaurants did not sustain damage, the inferno challenged our family to make a whole new commitment to Hampton Beach. Real estate developer Paul Hobbs accepted our bid for a lease on his new building. This C Street location was prime real estate. If Bob had come into his own on Broadway during the war, and Walter had done so in Durham, to make it possible for Jack and Bud to go to UNH, then Jerry, recently turned seventeen, came into his own as manager of our largest restaurant, Dunfey's at C Street, a property that heightened my father's pride and energy. An impressive, multi-keyed register stood prominently at the entrance, a statement that Dunfey's Restaurant was, indeed, taking dining seriously.

Along the front window were cold drink dispensers, and a grill spread across the width of the building. Twenty-five booths lined the C St. side windows. Three counter bays filled the main section, framed by sparkling stainless steel backdrops, ice cream and soda fountain features, a new-fangled machine called the "cow" because of the tube which spewed forth fresh milk, and close to the door leading to the kitchen, too many fryolators for summer's already hot temperatures.

Left to right, back row:
Dad, Bud, Jerry, Jack,
Roy; front row: Dick,
Walter, Bob, Paul 1951,
the fledgling Dunfey
entrepreneurs.

G.I. Bill makes college within reach at the University
of New Hampshire. Time to open a Durham
restaurant; build a student supply store, Town and
Campus; and assure clean laundry in a "first":
The Speedy Launderette."

Anyone can advertise
the 25th Anniversary;
the Dunfeys advertise
our 26th.

CHAPTER 13

1951

C Street Hampton Beach: Dunfeys—for Good Eating

From the ashes of the fire that had destroyed the entire C Street block a new brick building had risen—with extra storefronts and a hefty mortgage—catapulting L. W. Dunfey and Sons into the real estate and insurance businesses, thanks to a growing entrepreneurial confidence and, probably, out of necessity. No one else would insure us.

Jerry's seriousness of purpose made it clear that this restaurant's standards would be as high as its new fire code. He did all the interviewing to complete a staff of seventy-five, and was in charge of all scheduling, as well as strict codes regarding personal appearance and impeccable work behavior. He circulated a full page of instructions about uniform and personal habits, including such points as "clean finger nails" and a rule "never to touch hands to face" when serving food, as well as a host of other specifics—all attached in the letter of welcome to a new hire.

Sixty years later, my niece, Ruthie, (daughter of my oldest brother, Roy) and her Ohio neighbor and best friend from childhood, Marlene, produced the famous "Requirements for Staff" list which each had received while working for Jerry in summers during college. Fortunately, there were no rules about staff dating one another. Summer romances abounded, some fleeting; others, like Marlene and Bob Doran's now in its sixtieth year. Marlene would fall in love and marry the handsome counter man, Bob, a veteran of the Korean War and six years older. Even though he was also older than Jerry, Bob admits that, except in his love life, he was always sure to obey his seventeen-year-old manager!

At thirteen, I was Jerry's partner, working full-time alongside him. I don't remember being taught to waitress. I just knew how. In fact, the only major blemish in my career up to that time had been dropping the lemon meringue pie after Thanksgiving dinner when I was nine.

My brothers were concerned that as a thirteen-year-old, I didn't look old enough for my waitress role. I needed to look fifteen. I remember listening through the paper-thin wall of Restful Cottage while Walter asked my mother if I could wear lipstick. "Even though she's five-foot-eight, she still doesn't look old enough, especially in comparison to the girls she's

Available at Jordan Marsh in Peabody, starting May 25, Thursday.
New uniforms must be worn starting May 27, Saturday.

— Some light reading for your post-op enjoyment!

DUNFEY'S RESTAURANT

WAITRESS UNIFORMS AND GROOMING HABITS

1) Clean, neat, freshly pressed uniform daily.

   a) Kilt and blouse uniform. (2 kilts and 2 blouses)

   b) Green knee sox. (2 pairs)

   c) Tan, well-cleaned "buck-type" shoes.

   d) Clean, well-pressed apron. (2 aprons will be issued)

   e) Apron strings tied in a perky bow.

   f) Top button of uniform should remain buttoned at all times.

   g) Tam O'Shanter hat worn at proper angle.
     (1 will be issued)

   h) Carter's Green Pants. (2 pairs)

2) Hair kept short, neat and compact, or worn in a net.

3) Fresh lipstick at all times. *{ I wondered how I got hooked on it when I hate all other make-up ☺*

4) Only white or light colored sweaters may be worn over uniforms *It's Jerry's fault. Geez*
when restaurant is cool.

5) Clean hands and finger nails, colorless nail polish or natural gloss.

6) Keep voice low and pleasant.

7) Keep good posture and smile at all times.

8) Never bring hands to face or head while in dining room.

9) Blouse should be kept well tucked in at all times.

10) Apron should be treated as part of skirt and not as a hand cloth.

Kilts -- in Marsha Jordan Shop on Mail Level (5.98 ea)
Blouses - in Misses Sportswear on Mall Level -- Lady Manhattan - rounded collar(4.97)
Knee sox -- in Budget Hosiery Bar (next to Marsha Jordan) (1.50 ea)
Shoes -- in Teen Age Department on Lower Level (8.98)
Carter's Green Pants -- in Lingerie (opposite Marsha Jordan) ? (1.00)

List that my niece, Ruthie Dunfey, Hamilton, OH, and all other staff
received from her manager and uncle, Jerry, when hired to work at a
Dunfey's restaurant. 1958

training," he explained, convincingly enough to get my mother's approval.
Jerry hired a number of attractive high school seniors and UNH freshmen,
all of whom looked "so much older"; and most of whom had crushes on
their handsome, shy, all-business-boss. No wonder he did not include any
restrictions on dating among staff.

Until the summer of 1951, Jerry and I had tried to be in each other's
presence as little as possible. Were we to find ourselves on the same Moody
Street bus in Lowell, he would get off at Fourth Avenue and I at Fifth

Avenue, so we did not have to walk the two short blocks home together. Come summer, one would walk the boardwalk to work if the other happened to be walking on the store side of the beach. By 1952, however, you could not find a team that worked better, running our C Street restaurant at Hampton Beach.

No one, including Jerry, was aware that he had juvenile diabetes, despite his excessive juice and milk consumption—frappe cans filled one after another (made easier given the newly acquired "cow" milk dispenser) hardly raised concern. We were all milk drinkers. At home, several empty glass quart bottles would be stacked under the table after every meal and washed to be picked up and replaced with new quarts delivered to our back door in Lowell, sometimes by our brother, Paul, who worked for Brox's Dairies.

Fortunately, Bud had a close friend who had the then little-known disease, and recognized Jerry's insatiable thirst and weight loss (forty pounds that summer) as two of its signs. Jerry was diagnosed and soon on a journey that required testing his blood and injecting insulin several times a day. He's made history at Boston's Joslin Clinic, currently one of its very few clients to live a healthy life for more than seventy years with Type I Diabetes. Anyone who worked for Jerry would never have guessed—nor did I—that he was dealing with anything more than his full-to-overtime manager's job and a long list of admiring female employees. To this day, Jerry keeps healthy, still bicycling and advising the family (not-for-profit) founded in the 1970s.

1952 "Hey…Dunfey!"

Whether the issue was the health of a brother or the demands of a business, anything a Dunfey undertook, for better or for worse—and some times it was the latter—was a family affair, a big family affair. How it all worked was often random. From 1950 to 1952, when my dad took such great pride in our restaurants, he also had to make an extra effort to keep up with all of us. Half the Dunfeys were no longer behind the counter at the beach: Roy was in Ohio; Paul, in Lowell; and Kay, Mary, and Eileen were in the convent. That left Jack, Bud, Bob, Dick, Walter, Jerry, and me at Hampton Beach, still too many for our dad to keep straight when he needed us. As the restaurants grew and the pace intensified, if our dad couldn't remember the name of the kid he wanted, he would just call out from his familiar place behind the register at the entrance to the restaurant: "Hey…Dunfey!" We'd all turn around, and he'd point to the one he wanted. It was natural for the orchestra leader, pointing at various sections to raise its "voice," weaving rhythm and sound into a whole.

He had been doing just that in the family often in subtle but effective ways, especially after Paul, Jack, and Bud returned from World War II. It was at this juncture our dad saw the need for division of labor. Even with only a seventh-grade education, my father's astute, outgoing, optimistic manner along with his experiences as husband and father, orchestra and civic leader, mill worker and small business owner, had shown that he recognized each of our particular talents and savored new ideas.

He would point to Jack to assume a more formal leadership role in 1946, involving the twenty-two-year-old in the purchase of Fred Haywood's business, making it the family's first business beyond Lowell, Massachusetts. It was now Dunfey's Fried Clam Stand. He had encouraged the building of a catering and "car hop" take-out in the empty lot next to our Lowell Luncheonette in the same year, as well as launching its transformation into a full "seafood in the city" restaurant in 1951.

Both of our parents supported the major leap to Durham and the University of New Hampshire. Dad observed Bud's excelling in his UNH courses. He could translate its class theory into strategies necessary to grow a business by focusing on people, not just property acquisition. Bud was not only grounded in our dad's principles but had a uniquely warm personality that could make each person he dealt with feel respected.

By the end of World War II, my father had had plenty of time to observe Bob's growing years. The two of them had worked hand in glove as fifteen-year-old Bob assumed significant responsibilities. My father identified Bob's tenacity and single-minded sense of purpose and in 1949, called on Bob to "convince" Ben Butler he should rent us his south-end restaurant at Hampton Beach. It was a narrow hallway of space with a ribbon of counter squeezed in down the left side and nine booths on the right. The aisle seemed no wider than a yardstick, especially when as a waitress, I had to carry three fried clam plates in two hands to the middle booth. Mr. Butler still lived in the building above the market next door. Many a Dunfey employee slept in the building, catching quick naps on a cot in the restaurant's back room.

My father recognized that our Marine brother, Paul, had daunting challenges related to his war injuries, which would require frequent surgeries and procedures. Paul took over the two Dunfey establishments in Lowell and remained in the city, raising his five children with his wife, Rita. After he sold the restaurants, he would go on to a distinguished career for the General Services Administration in the Northeast.

Before an annual family reunion in the late 80s, their sons and daughters challenged their executive-level fathers. "We bet you never really 'pushed clams.'" Challenge accepted. Jerry described, and his master carpenter son, Sean, built the prep table. With their aprons on and secret ingredients ready, the #1 item on the day's menu was Dunfey's "original" fried clams. Challenge met.

Jerry, Dick, and Walter show their expertise "pushing clams" with their sons and daughters as "judges."

at the center of the beach!

Dunfey's FOR GOOD EATING

Sandwiches: *Larger & Better Tasting!*

Served with Krinkle-Kut Chips and Sweet Piklstix

Grilled Hamburg Steak	.45	Baked Sugar-Cured Ham	.45
Grilled Cheeseburg Steak	.55	Sliced White Meat Turkey	.95
Pepper Steak on Toasted Roll	.60	Bacon, Lettuce and Tomato	.60
Fresh Lobster Salad Roll	1.10	Ham, Tomato and Lettuce	.60
Hamburg Steak Deluxe	.55	Sliced Tomato and Lettuce	.35
Cheeseburg Steak Deluxe	.65	Baked Ham and Cheese	.55
Fried Clam Roll	.65	Grilled American Cheese	.35
Tuna Salad Roll	.55	Grilled Cheese and Tomatoes	.45
Ham and Egg Sandwich	.60	Bacon and Egg Sandwich	.60
Western	.60	Cream Cheese and Olives	.40

Side Orders of Fried Foods

French Fried Potatoes	.35 & .70	Fried Fancy Ocean Fresh	
Fried Onion Rings	.35 & .70	Scallops	.65 & 1.20
Dunfey's Famous Fr. Clams	.65 & 1.20	Butterfly Shrimp	.70 & 1.35

The "Parosol Delight"

A Feature Sandwich of Fresh Ground Beef topped with American Cheese, Sliced Tomatoes, Spanish Onions and Crisp Lettuce. Served on a three-decker roll in a basket with a helping of French Fried Potatoes

.99

Dunfey's Famous "Charcoburgers"

Quarter Pound of Choice Beef
Giant Sesame Roll
Shredded Lettuce & Sweet Pickles
Special Dunfey Sauce
.65
with French Fries .95

Triple Decker Club Sandwiches

CHICKEN CLUB: White Meat Chicken, Grilled Bacon, Sliced Tomatoes, Crisp Lettuce, Mayonnaise, on three slices of toast with Krinkle-Kuts and Sweet Piklstix 1.75

HAMBURG STEAK: Grilled Hamburg Steak, Crisp Bacon, Sliced Tomatoes, Lettuce, Mayonnaise, on three slices of toast with Krinkle-Kuts and Sweet Piklstix 1.50

SALAD CLUB: Tunafish Salad and Egg Salad, Sliced Tomatoes, Crisp Lettuce, Mayonnaise, on three slices of toast with Krinkle-Kuts and Sweet Piklstix 1.25

BAKED HAM AND CHEESE CLUB: Baked Sugar-Cured Ham, American Cheese, Sliced Tomatoes, Crisp Lettuce, Mayonnaise, on three slices of toast with Krinkle-Kuts and Sweet Piklstix 1.35

Desserts ★

Fresh Cut Pie	.20	Cake and Ice Cream	.35
Pie A La Mode	.35	Ice Cream on Brownie	.30
Fresh Baked Cake	.20	Brownies	.15
	Ice Cream or Sherbet	.25	

Beverages ★

Ice Cold Milk	.15	Iced Tea	.25
Coffee	.15	Iced Coffee	.25
Hot Cocoa	.15	Sanka	.15
Pot of Tea	.15	Soft Drinks	.15

*See our Fountain Treats on Back Cover

August was Carnival Month at Hampton Beach, complete with a parade and floats created by employees in businesses along the Boulevard. Dunfey's beach restaurant theme in 1955, had an irony to it; we had bought Lamie's Tavern in Hampton Center and were attempting to gain a liquor license. The beach and Hampton were "dry." Left to right: "The Unidentified Enforcer" Temperance Society members: Eleanor, Ruth Hession and my school friend, Barb Willey. circa 1954

Eleanor's elementary school scrapbook featuring third grade photo alongside junior high delegate badge. In the Dunfey family, education in the political process started early!

My mother learned to drive, unusual for a housewife and mother in the late 40s. She drove in style—a Model A with rumble seat.

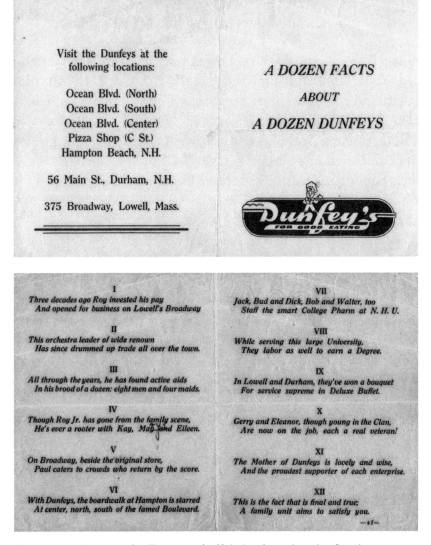

Visit the Dunfeys at the following locations:

Ocean Blvd. (North)
Ocean Blvd. (South)
Ocean Blvd. (Center)
Pizza Shop (C St.)
Hampton Beach, N.H.

56 Main St., Durham, N.H.

375 Broadway, Lowell, Mass.

A DOZEN FACTS

ABOUT

A DOZEN DUNFEYS

Dunfey's
FOR GOOD EATING

I
Three decades ago Roy invested his pay
And opened for business on Lowell's Broadway

II
This orchestra leader of wide renown
Has since drummed up trade all over the town.

III
All through the years, he has found active aids
In his brood of a dozen: eight men and four maids.

IV
Though Roy Jr. has gone from the family scene,
He's ever a rooter with Kay, May and Eileen.

V
On Broadway, beside the original store,
Paul caters to crowds who return by the score.

VI
With Dunfeys, the boardwalk at Hampton is starred
At center, north, south of the famed Boulevard.

VII
Jack, Bud and Dick, Bob and Walter, too
Staff the smart College Pharm at N. H. U.

VIII
While serving this large University,
They labor as well to earn a Degree.

IX
In Lowell and Durham, they've won a bouquet
For service supreme in Deluxe Buffet.

X
Gerry and Eleanor, though young in the Clan,
Are now on the job, each a real veteran!

XI
The Mother of Dunfeys is lovely and wise,
And the proudest supporter of each enterprise.

XII
This is the fact that is final and true;
A family unit aims to satisfy you.

—sf—

Our sister, Kay, now Sr. Franceca (-sf-) helped market the family restaurant although convent rules did not permit her to visit it.

CHAPTER 14

JUNE 14, 1952

The Twelve Together with Our Parents

> I am talking about the freedom that comes from choosing to
> remain open, as my mother did, to life itself, whatever it may
> bring you: joys, sorrows, triumphs, failures, suffering, comfort,
> and certainly, always change.
>
> —*Reeve Lindberg, describing her mother in the*
> *fiftieth-anniversary edition of* Gift from the Sea

That same June of 1952, back in Lowell's Acre, there was a celebration planned for the hundredth anniversary of the arrival of the Sisters of Notre de Namur and the opening of St. Patrick's School. It was a remarkable event for all parishioners, but for our family it was immeasurably significant. All three of my Notre Dame sisters would be there for the picnic-style festivities and, even more exciting, my oldest brother, Roy; his wife, Ruth; and their family would drive with three kids—no air-conditioned car and no disposable diapers—nearly nine hundred miles from Hamilton, Ohio, to make it a complete family reunion.

It may have appeared that the reunion was arranged just for the thirty-eight Dunfeys and Keefes in attendance. But while there were no limits on family numbers, other rules still reigned—or were supposed to—even at such a momentous gathering. Nuns were not supposed to have their pictures taken with family. On that day, however, rules went to the winds. Fortunately, my brothers, true to their penchant for rule breaking, arranged for a professional photographer-friend to take photos. His picture of the family would be the last we'd have of all twelve Dunfeys and our parents.

June 24, 1952—the night the music died

"You just go right on with your forty-five prayers, Kate," Dad teased, in response to my mom's third, fourth, maybe even fifth good-natured call for us to go to bed. My father took advantage of any opportunity to tease my mother about what he called her "forty-five prayers," a devotion Catholics (mostly women) in the era were drawn to, filling a prayer book with prayer cards and ending the day reflecting on different ones. For my mother, St. Anne, the patron saint of mothers, ranked first.

When my mother called for us to "go to bed," the "us" was my father, my close friend Maryjane Molloy, and me. Earlier that week she and I had burst out of eighth grade and into adolescence and were celebrating with a sleepover at the Restful Cottage. Three steps leading up and you were on a screened-in porch too small for the cot and two rocking chairs it held. The small first room inside had a fireplace, an overstuffed chair, and a rollaway bed that rarely rolled away because someone was usually sleeping on it. That night, it would be my mother who slept there, to give my dad a little space in the tiny bedroom off the kitchen.

Earlier that evening, Maryjane and I had walked the boulevard with our friends. Everyone walked the boulevard, unless you were on a date. Then you walked the boardwalk or the beach. You didn't just walk it once a night, either, unless you were Roy Dunfey. Dad sauntered from the Kentville Hotel at the top of Nudd Terrace to our closet-sized, take-out clam stand (now the lobby entrance of the Ashworth Hotel); the distance Maryjane and I covered in about three minutes took my parents at least fifteen minutes because Dad would stop and chat on every corner.

Sometime after 7 p.m., they would be standing on the corner of Highland Avenue outside Mrs. L's seedy excuse for a rooming house next to Dunfey's Fried Clam Stand. Lightly tapping the cigar in his hand, Dad would hold court with his cronies. About an hour later, you'd find them just outside our C Street establishment, the newest and largest of our seven restaurants. From there, my parents would make their way along the porch-lined sidewalks between the casino and our sliver of a restaurant between J and K streets.

That particular night, Maryjane and I had crisscrossed the boulevard several times. I knew where to find my parents when we needed more money for skee ball in the penny arcade. By 10:30 p.m., the four of us were back at the cottage, enjoying our nightly treat of coffee ice cream. Thinking we'd all soon follow her to bed, my mother said her goodnights. Dad started his goodnights as well, but as he leaned over to kiss me, he simultaneously gave his infamous squeeze-of-the-knee to Maryjane. Our giggles were all he needed to recognize he had an audience: two giddy adolescents looking for any reason not to go to bed.

"Did you ever hear," said he," about the answer the young woman gave to the suitor she did not wish to marry?" No need to reply. Dad was into his act, and it led him from one corny story to the next. Anyone who knew Roy Dunfey would guess that his next move was into song. The drummer and orchestra leader could burst into song any time, and he did just that, shortly before midnight. With me as his back up, harmonizing to my heart's content, he led in singing every song he ever taught me, pausing only to catch a breath or tease Maryjane before the next medley. My shy, fair-haired friend sat patiently, never imagining the gift she was giving my father and me by simply being our audience in those wee hours of June 24, 1952.

After once again teasing my mother to go right on with her forty-five prayers, Dad turned in, and so did we.

Jerry was the next to arrive after closing the C Street restaurant. He was bearing good news: After a number of Chamber of Commerce hearings aimed at blocking the sale of pizza—bias against Italians coming over the bridge to Hampton Beach, New Hampshire—Jack had finally secured the first permit to sell it in a storefront next to our C Street restaurant. My parents and family were close friends with the Zappala family from Lawrence, MA. The Zappalas had, and still have, an excellent reputation for homemade pizza at their Lawrence and Salisbury locations, both in Massachusetts. They "gave" us their most talented pizza makers, "Sam the Pizza Man." It was a positive step in building the business and, more importantly, cracking some stereotypes. On that night, though, it was simply great news for Jerry to be sharing with my father, even at 1:00 a.m.

Bud, the last to arrive at the cottage, opened the bedroom door to let some warmth from the kitchen heater on that chilly June night. He knew immediately that something was wrong when he heard what he thought was Dad's snoring became labored, and he could not wake him. An ambulance made its way down the graveled path of Nudd Terrace in the early hours of June 24.

Earlier that night, we had celebrated the ordinary rituals of our life. We had carried fried clams and French fries from #3 across to the beach. We had walked the boulevard, enjoyed our coffee ice cream, and even sung our favorite songs, punctuated with a bit of Dad's teasing our mom and my pal, Maryjane. Jerry had checked in with news. Bud had checked in, too.

But after that evening, nothing would ever be the same. Our dad suffered what was then called a cerebral hemorrhage. He died hours later at nearby Exeter Hospital. Ten days after our family's celebration at St. Patrick's in Lowell, a hearse, cortege, and hundreds of cars drove slowly by a window in that same Lowell St. Patrick's convent, a few hundred feet from where the photographer had snapped the family picture.

In the window stood my three sisters. At that time, nuns could not attend a parent's funeral; no exceptions. The scene from where I sat in the back seat of a funeral car in between my mother and Jerry is etched in my memory. Why weren't my sisters with my mom? I was no help at all. They should be with her. The rules, however, "fit" a culture and structure which, up to that point, had been obeyed blindly. My mother had not entered religious life herself, but her life was certainly affected, both positively and painfully, by its rules. Not long after the funeral, my sister Kay, wanting to capture our dad's spirit and give me some hope, wrote a poem about LeRoy whose life was worthy of his name— the king:

Semper Cantaris *(Always Singing)*
for Eleanor, August 1952

When God ordained his dear and distant birth,
Heeding the sighing atmosphere of earth
He sent him singing!

In tranquil hours, in times of stress and strife,
He faced the grim and gay of mortal life
Yet somehow, singing!

And when to one he gave his royal heart,
He found in hers a queenly counterpart
To share his singing!

God heard his prayer for rich paternity
And gave him gold in loving progeny,
To swell his singing!

And all their voices from the happy past
Were echoing that night, in mine, the last
He started singing!

Our songs were sweet, 'til mystic melodies
Ravished his soul with heavenly harmonies.
He set forth singing!

His faith is mine; his song, my heritage,
I shall walk worthy of my lineage
And seek him, singing.

"His song, our heritage…"—refrains for the future

> Many people die with their music still in them. Too often it is
> because they are always getting ready to live. Before they know
> it time runs out.
>   —*Oliver Wendell Holmes, Sr. (found in one of my sister Mary's*
>   *handwritten collections of reflections on living)*

If a real life is measured by finding the music within and sharing it, then our orchestra-leading, drumming, singing father had lived the fullest life possible in his brief fifty-nine years. But that summer I had no understanding of that. My sister Kay's touching sentiments were lost on me in the midst my self-absorbed, confused thirteen-year-old's emotions. It took me a long time even to appreciate what a tragedy my father's death was for others: my mother, for instance, and each of my other siblings. At that moment, it was my world that had crumbled. My close summer friend, Anne, confided long afterward, that she was so scared when my father died. "I had always watched your dad and you walking up Nudd Terrace, and he'd be holding your hand. I was envious. Now, I was heartbroken and frightened."

Weeks after the funeral, Walter and I were making our early evening trip to UNH from Hampton Beach to close the Durham restaurant. In addition to my day job waitressing, I had been assigned by my brother Bud to "ride with Walter and keep him awake." Two years earlier, Walter had fallen asleep at the wheel of our Pontiac on Route 108. The car had gone down through a field and onto the railroad tracks. It was the blare of the train's whistle—fortunately still in the distance—that woke him up in time to maneuver the car off the tracks. A good Samaritan on the same road stopped, so Walter fared better than the Pontiac which my brothers towed to our backyard in Lowell. It sat for a year, a sorry heap of bent fenders and broken glass, but still offered one benefit: Fifteen-year-old Jerry used it to practice shifting using a clutch. He didn't have to worry about having an accident since Walter had already taken care of that situation. I found the sight of the Pontiac a scary reminder of the reason I had been assigned a double work shift.

And on this particular night, it was probably to keep awake that Walter started singing, but I had no voice. Just weeks earlier on the night before he died, my father and I had sung, "'Til We Meet Again" and "Last Night Was the End of the World," two of our favorites to harmonize. Now, for the first time in those dizzying weeks since his death, I cried:

"Walter, I will never, ever sing those songs again."

"You will—in time," he said gently.

And I did. We all did.

Summer of change

In the meantime, if we were going to follow our father's example, we had to work. Summer was high season for our three Hampton Beach restaurants. The Durham restaurant remained open with abbreviated hours for summer-school students and townsfolk. Bud was in charge of the short-lived take-out clam stand just over the New Hampshire border in York Beach, Maine.

We also had to be politically engaged. I remember five or six of my brothers, along with some cousins and friends, huddled in our tiny Restful Cottage living room on July 26, that summer of 1952, trying to see the image of Governor Adlai Stevenson on our mouse-pad-sized Zenith television. The red scare of McCarthyism had ratcheted up attacks on the patriotism of politicians, celebrities, and other public servants, heightening fears and mistrust.

Between the number of people squeezed into our seven-by-ten-foot room, and the "snow" on the ten-inch screen, we could not see the candidate very clearly. What was clear, though, was President Harry Truman's introduction of the statesman-orator-turned-politician. Stevenson's speech was infused with a dignified moral tone. About his rivals in the primary, he noted their "vigor, character, and devotion." He added he was "heartened" by the conduct of the convention delegates: "You have argued and disagreed because you care, and without calling each other liars and thieves—without despoiling our rich traditions." Stevenson lost twice to another great American, Five-star General Dwight D. Eisenhower, but Adlai Stevenson, with his wit, deep intellect, and moral compass, would continue to be a force in the Democratic Party and was appointed ambassador to the United Nations after John F. Kennedy became president.

My mother, meanwhile, held her sorrow quietly in her heart and did not try to curb the activity, political and otherwise, that followed her sons everywhere they went. They were sensitive to her feelings, too. Jerry had an idea. Maybe our mom would consider working at our C Street restaurant for a few hours each day. Being surrounded by family at work might lighten her sadness.

In her memoir almost thirty years later, she wrote to Jerry:

> Do you remember when you were my boss, Jerry? When I filled
> in as cashier, stood at the grill in the front window making hot
> dogs and hamburgers and even, later, when I was hostess at the
> Anchorage and Lamie's? That was so good for me, Jerry, to be
> with you all after your dad had passed away. I was so lonely, and
> felt so lost that summer. To be near you all was my security. The
> rush and excitement of the beach, "pushing" hot dogs side by
> side with you, was the best therapy for me.

Regrettably, I lacked Jerry's sensitivity. I had no idea how to act or react.
The only "constant" was work, and that I could manage automatically.
Beyond that, the summer was a blur. I was so insensitive to my mother that
even my quiet, disciplined, Marine hero brother, who had his own family,
had to pull me aside more than once and give me a "talking to." I muddled
through the waves of unnamed, adolescent grief. So did Jerry in his own
way, but we never talked with each other or anyone else about it. You just
didn't.

That September of 1952, Jerry was a freshman at St. Anselm College
in Goffstown, New Hampshire. On weekends and vacations, he would
continue working in Lowell helping our brother Paul. I returned to Notre
Dame Academy in Tyngsboro, Massachusetts, as a freshman. We stayed
on that year in Lowell.

1952 family reunion at St. Patrick School's 150th Anniversary. It would be our last
complete family photograph. Our Dad, Roy, died suddenly ten days later on June 24.

CHAPTER 15

1953 Homestead: From Lowell to Hampton

> From looms to love; from a kitchen table to counters; from class-
> rooms and boardrooms to a circle of global citizens and—still
> around a table…

"Oh—but my mother was the homestead."

In 1983, I heard myself say that to a twenty-something acquaintance who told me she felt sorry that the Dunfeys had moved out of Lowell thirty years earlier, leaving us "without a homestead." I believe this person (new to the family) imagined that we had left behind some grand estate in Lowell's well-to-do Belvedere section. If only she had a window view into our two-tenement home, bursting at the seams with Dunfeys and Keefes in the working-class Pawtucketville section of the city!

I did not know what a grand homestead was, so I never felt deprived of one. That Pawtucketville tenement had been "our mansion," as my sister Kay expressed in a poem she wrote after our dad died:

> You built no marble mansion—on our Fifth Avenue
> But life was there; love everywhere, and laughter ringing true…
> You never took us all abroad to some quaint Swiss chalet,
> But Sunday nights were our delight, with homemade harmony…
> You leave no tawdry treasure now, to grieving family,
> But you live on in daughters, sons—a priceless legacy.

Ten months after my father died, my mother and I left Lowell and moved to Hampton Center, New Hampshire. There she would embrace the next phase of her life, even as she still grieved the loss of my dad. "We have to focus on the living," she said quietly, and she did just that. Our clan now included eight sons, five daughters-in-law; four daughters, three in the convent; and two-dozen grandchildren. My mother had no lack of family competing for her attention. No time to be self-absorbed, despite her grief.

We had grown decade-long summer roots at Hampton Beach in those rented cottages euphemistically named "Camp Comfort" and "The Restful." Now my mother and I would live two miles from the beach on Moulton Road in a lovely ranch home of "comfort" that was even at times, "restful."

My mother, now almost sixty, was still raising a teenager—her twelfth child—and a rebellious one at that. In the memoir she would write twenty-five years later, my mother took a literary pause after writing the stories of her first six children. She asked her grandchildren, the audience for whom she was writing, not "to tire," knowing there were six more births to come in the story. "I promise," she said, "that each will be different, but I'll admit that, by the time I get to Eleanor, I may be asking for a crayon and just draw her picture!" Fortunately for me, she managed to guide the last of her clan as though I were her first and only child.

Also assisting my mother in that "oversight"—especially of their youngest sister's social life—were Bud, Dick, and Jerry who were still living at home with us. Bud was the oldest of that trio. His oversight came mostly in conversations that were warm and sensitive. Dick's idea of oversight took a preventative approach. He regularly intercepted my phone calls by telling the caller: "Oh, she doesn't live here anymore!" Jerry took a more subtle approach to keeping me out of teen trouble: He scheduled me to work every afternoon after school and weekends, at our beach restaurant, which we kept open long after Labor Day weekend recorded the calendar close of the summer season.

Actually, I began to find my way and was happy in this setting. On the first day at Hampton Academy, I had made a friend—Sandy, also new to the area. It's obvious to me now that, in those years, even mere acquaintances of the Dunfey gang ended up washing dishes, peeling potatoes, frying clams, or waitressing at one of our restaurants. It was the risk an unsuspecting teen took by associating with one of us. Sandy was no exception. Jerry was quick to add her to our work force, and the pair of us biked to the beach to work each afternoon.

Living year-round in Hampton during 1953, I went home from school for lunch each day. Some of my happiest moments were spent in the kitchen, eating my mother's American chop suey. I was beginning to relate to her in a whole new way. She showed me that we "take our happiness with us" wherever we move. Bricks and mortar do not a homestead make. My mother *was* the homestead, not in an ostentatious, self-centered way; not even in her words, but simply in her presence and understanding. She was a good sport, too, going along with my continual party planning. Our rumpus room was the scene of frequent pajama parties, so much so that my mother starting inviting my new friend Sandy's mother—also a widow—to our house to help chaperone. In the middle of the night, they would often dress up in outrageous outfits and make their way through the rumpus room—a clever tactic, I now realize, to check up on us.

"Mother D," as she started to be called by Dunfey employees, welcomed folks to frequent parties in that rumpus room which had been "upgraded" with furniture and a stereo system courtesy of our former employee, Dennis, who had stolen money from our restaurant at UNH. His apartment furniture and "modern" stereo were all we saw of financial restitution, but that suited me fine. Besides employees and often their families, parties in those days included our friends and their siblings, and—always—Charlie Gallagher playing the piano. McGaunns, Keefes, Beaupres, Gilligans, Kelleys, and Zappalas (all Irish for the occasion) contributed to the often raucous and always mesmerizing strains of songs belted out in surprisingly fine harmony. Singing continued to sustain us.

Now we lived in a real New England town. I could walk or bike everywhere with a whole group of new neighborhood friends. I was fascinated by the fact that I was getting to know peers who were not Catholic or Irish. Out of fifty-four sophomores at Hampton Academy, four were Catholic. I loved hearing about the religious practices of my new friends and was thoroughly caught up in the whirlwind of their social lives. They were eager to include me in their church activities, but of course, a Catholic in the fifties was not even supposed to enter a place of worship unless it was a Catholic church. I never felt my new friends were trying to convert me. I felt at home immediately except once, when invited to a religious service in Exeter, where someone asked, "Are you a Catholic?"

"Yes."

"Oh—you're not to supposed to be here…"

I wasn't certain whose rules the person was going by: his or my church's. I didn't stop to figure that out. I slipped out the nearest exit and waited on the sidewalk for my pals to notice I was not at the service.

Most of the time, of course, we teens were immersed in the usual planning for football, field hockey, basketball, volleyball, and bowling when we were not going to dances at the Exeter Town Hall or skating on Taylor Pond in winter. On very special occasions, we'd go to Lamie's Tavern in Hampton Center. We'd pile into the hand-crafted, high-back booths and enjoy delicious, spill-over-the-top-of-the-dish hot-fudge sundaes. Little could I have imagined that a year later I'd be living one floor above those booths—and making those hot fudge sundaes.

Lamie's Tavern. circa 1940s

Come as you are... They did. circa 1950s

CHAPTER 16

1954

A Tavern in the Town—Lamie's

In 1954, the Dunfey family bought Lamie's Tavern in Hampton Center, New Hampshire. "I lived over a barroom when I married your dad," my mother said, "so it seems right I'd live over a tavern now!" Kate Dunfey had a way of framing her life in concise statements:

"Fate, Kate, a date, and oh how we did propagate!"

"I met your father on Labor Day and was in labor ever after!"

My mother had not only moved from her "known" Lowell world and culture, where she was mother, caregiver to neighbors in need, volunteer for missionary causes, and behind-the-scenes supporter of our dad and brothers' entrepreneurial aspirations and political pursuits. She now inhabited a whole new universe, in what was to be the family's first major venture into the innkeeping business. In a few short years, she would also be hostessing at Lamie's and greeting chartered busloads that carried tourists from around the country. Lamie's offered an experience of an "Old Yankee Tavern."

Before we bought Lamie's (pronounced Lamay's by townsfolk), six of my brothers—Jack, Bud, Bob, Dick, Walter, and Jerry—met regularly on Sunday nights at our home on Moulton Road or two blocks away at Jack and Joan's home. Bud admits: "We had no long-term plan":

> From Lowell and from the time that Jack, Bob, and I took over Hayward's; our first clam stand at Hampton Beach, it was a group project. There was no dividing line between fun and work. It was an adventure and home and family all rolled in one. You worked or you slept and that was it. I don't think any of us put in less than twelve-hour days, seven days a week. No one questioned it. No one added it up. And every penny that could be scraped together was used for expansion.

In the post-WWII culture, my brothers' priority in business acquisition was to earn enough money to marry and support a family. To me, it seemed like a combination of blind luck, good timing, and the dogged determination passed down that we should do something well and do it until we reach good-natured (and sometimes irritable) exhaustion. If you felt you

were flying by the seat of your pants, well, you probably were; that was part of the fun. Make it up as you go, failing, succeeding, resilient, with plenty of room for arguing and razzing. Humor housed our trust; harmonizing expressed it, creating an "easy hospitality." With a sizable assortment of brothers involved, you could usually count on one of them to inject a joke or idea or caution or all of the above at any given moment. When they bought the C Street business block at Hampton Beach, for instance, they still had one vacant store after they sublet the various spaces. So, according to Bud, "Rather than let it stand idle, we went into the real estate and insurance business." The story I heard from Walter was slightly different: We went into the business because "no one else would insure us!"

In 1953, we owned a clam stand, a small restaurant on "J Street," the Playland Arcade, and a pizza and grinder (AKA submarine sandwich) shop. We also tried promoting a "Charc-O-burger" in the front window service of our C Street location.

Who knows—had it caught on, we might have evolved into "O'Dunfeys" before McDonald's caught on. Or, if our more upscale Anchorage Steak and Lobster restaurant at Boar's Head on Hampton Beach had thrived, or the Durham Town and Campus student/office supply store at UNH had grown beyond expectations, our business journey might have taken a totally different trajectory. As it turned out, the 1954 purchase of Lamie's Tavern made us innkeepers "almost by accident," according to Bud. His comments appear in Peter Randall's Hampton history, *Hampton: A Century of Town and Beach, 1888–1988*:

> The purchase of Lamie's redefined conceptually what we were going to do. Prior to that purchase, we were short order cooks, selling clams, hot dogs, candy, and pizza at the beach, and selling hamburgers, pizza, and student supplies in Durham. Lamie's had a good reputation and we had to live up to it. We adopted the theme, set by the restaurant, of "good old" Yankee hospitality.

I was almost fifteen and happily overwhelmed with my newfound school and social demands. The only next steps I thought about were the ones that involved getting out of work in time to go dancing on weekend nights. My brothers were thinking next steps of a different kind, fully aware that 61 percent of Hampton's taxable property was labeled recreational. New Hampshire's economy was thriving. "Until the purchase of Lamie's," Jerry recalls, "we were all over the place in our businesses: seven restaurants; a student supply store; Playland, an arcade; real estate and insurance. Lamie's would provide a solid base for developing a New England innkeeping business. But we could not have imagined just how much more that acquisition would lead to." At that point, there were more challenges looming. My mother's amusing take on living first above a barroom and now over a tavern, omitted an important difference between her two experiences: Unlike Lowell, Hampton was a dry town back then, and only inns could serve liquor. Lamie's may have been called a "tavern," but it was not an inn. In New Hampshire, unless a lodging establishment totaled more than eight rooms, it was not considered an inn.

My brothers would soon discover that, despite their best intentions, they would be going "counter culture" to yet another "good old" Yankee tradition. What did the "Yankee spirit" look like? In her feature, "New Hampshire's Real Life Yankees," Lyra Tryba writes about some of those Yankee traits. She starts her essay with the nineteenth-century novelist Frances Trollope's description: "Yankee: In acuteness and perseverance, he resembles the Scotch. In frugal neatness, he resembles the Dutch. But in truth, a Yankee is nothing else on earth but himself." Tryba continues:

> And there's the ability to pinch a penny. "Though frugality and shrewdness in business dealings are traits characteristic of New Englanders as a whole, I think New Hampshirites are the most frugal of all," Judson Hale writes in his book *Inside New England*:
> But a Yankee preserves much more than material goods. The zeal for conservation also includes local culture, whether it's the mom-and-pop maple syrup operations, the traditional music of the state or how town government is run.
> —New Hampshire Magazine, *October 2013*.

According to Paul McGaunn, the first of our lifelong employees, my brothers had to "hurry up and build more rooms just to apply for the liquor license." Jack adds more color to the story. "There was a big uproar in town," he says. From his perspective, it was partly because the Dunfey brothers were considered brash, young, Irish and Democrats in an old

Yankee town. "Opponents organized opposition to our license, hired buses, and brought three hundred people to Concord to protest. The liquor commission actually had to get a bigger hall to hold our first public hearing." Jack says that on Dunfey's side, only two or three people spoke in favor of the license. "The liquor commission was impressed by the opposition," according to Jack, "but still they had to abide by the law. And we now met the law's requirements." We eventually got the license on the condition that no resident of Hampton could drink on the premises: "Can you imagine," Jack muses, "no booze at wedding receptions? The Kiwanis Club met there every month—of course they were going to have a drink."

What Jack and Bud devised was mimeographing hundreds of cards stating: "I certify I am above the age of 21 and not a legal resident of the town of Hampton." Every patron at the bar and dining room received one when ordering a drink and had to sign it before being served. After collecting a couple of thousand signatures, the staff noticed a lot more luminaries drinking at Lamie's: the likes of Abe Lincoln, General Grant, John Wayne and other notables regularly "signed" cards. Hampton was awash in prominent "residents." Finally, with "signatures" in hand, Jack showed the results to the liquor commissioners. Even they laughed. The law finally changed, and Hampton went wet.

Lamie's was popular for its counter service as well, and it proudly held on to its unique quirks, as John Milne describes:

> There used to be a white marble counter at Lamie's Tavern, the tiny mother church of the Dunfey hotel chain. It was paneled in wood and offered food and coffee to the Hampton residents who habitually ate there. One of the stools was broken; it rocked and it was hard to sit on. When a patron pointed this out, the polite reply was that it was the way one of the regulars liked it.
> —Business NH Magazine, *1984*

Besides the ten stools—including the broken one which we must have inherited in that condition because I remember it being there thirty years earlier—and the usual coffee urn and soda fountain behind the counter, there was a curious light switch attached to a support post under the counter. At the New Hampshire State Police headquarters' request, an electrician connected that switch to a blue light, secured and visible in the stately elm tree that stood just outside Lamie's at the corner of High Street and Lafayette Road, Route 1. In the fifties, when the State Police took over the task of patrolling the main travel route between Massachusetts and New Hampshire, fifty miles east of its headquarters, radio transmission to police cars was unreliable. Thus, the blue light was installed. The State Police dispatcher in Concord would call Lamie's when it needed to contact the only on-duty State trooper. The counter server would turn on the blue light, signaling that the passing patrol car officer should stop and call Concord from the area's only pay phone—inside Lamie's side door.

That stately tree would fall victim to elm tree disease; the flashing blue light would yield to more sophisticated radio transmissions; but Lamie's would continue to stand, a significant presence in the community and in our family business story, having evolved from LeRoy W. Dunfey and Sons, to Catherine Dunfey and Sons, and now to the Dunfey Family Corporation.

Managing a Tavern and Inn

At age twenty, Jerry became Lamie's manager. The landmark's survival, to say nothing of its flourishing, would continue to challenge the new innkeepers. In 1950, Interstate 95 had become a four-lane turnpike, bypassing the fifteen-mile New Hampshire Route 1 that ran through Hampton Center. A number of businesses along the Lafayette Road portion of Route 1 feared being victims of this "progress." There was no assurance of future business. Lamie's all-wooden construction also heightened Jerry's concern about its survival, fiscally and physically. One young busboy, on his first night tending the open hearth, almost burned the place down and actually did blacken the huge beam across the enormous fireplace. The busboy, Bob, was certain that his boss, five years older than he, would fire him on the spot, but Jerry gave him "a talking to" and additional lesson about the safe building of a fire. Some fifty years later, that teen is back at Lamie's as a night clerk and is considered the in-house historian, a welcome contribution and conclusion to his less-than-auspicious start at the tavern.

Jerry's managerial responsibilities included a most repulsive job: "I had the grimiest task of cleaning out what had been the tiny, permanent rooms of Richie and Nappie who had been living on the third floor, so it seemed, since the prior century, without ever the trace of maid service or evidence that they had ever thrown anything away."

Without a doubt, Jerry had inherited the "clean gene" from our dad, who was and had required us to be as sanitary as possible back in the days at our Broadway store. Dad would meticulously wipe the covers of canned goods before opening them. He was proud as punch to show off his "swell" new stainless-steel refrigerated units and backsplash that were "sparkling clean." We all remember how he tried to keep the cellar somewhat presentable for storage by having one of the Broadway locals whitewash its walls. Whether or not the wall's appearance improved is questionable, but in the process, the painter whitewashed a few four-legged critters, like the rat dubbed the "white monkey."

So, in keeping with his father's clean gene, Jerry dutifully cleared out that third-floor space, helping to upgrade the building's physical appearance. From the start of his management career at our C Street restaurant, he had earned the reputation of requiring that staff be impeccable in their appearance and sanitary behaviors. That requirement carried over to the cleanliness of the tavern, a much more demanding task as it turned out.

Lamie's would provide a good number of additional lessons for Jerry and the rest of us. In the early days, its waitress crew was not comprised of college-aged students new to restaurant work. Lamie's waitresses and hostesses were seasoned, no-nonsense, hard-workwomen who knew what they were doing and were quick to let you know it. They were a take-charge band whose style and loyalty played out in their daily service, from early morning coffee at the classic marble counter to the last dessert of the night in the Hearth Room. Mary, Edie, Doris, Kay, and Judy, among others, always had the situation "under control"; they were ready to stay a little later or arrive a bit earlier when they were needed. And no one doubted who was running the front—and maybe the back—of the house. In the "back of the house," head baker Kenny Lord worked for twenty-eight years perfecting his many specialties, especially his secret recipe for "crumb cake" and "three-inch deep pecan pie," along with other worth-coming-back-for homestyle baked goods.

The mothers of some of my close friends worked as hostesses with my mother. They were among Lamie's dependable staff. Kitty was always ready to assist in overtime, much to the chagrin of her sons—my friends—Loring and Ernie, who were her chauffeurs. They arrived late at many a party because they had to wait for their mother. Mary, a long time waitress, did not need her son, Fred, another of my school friends, to give her a ride to work. She lived less than a five-minute walk up Lafayette Road from the Tavern (as we always called it). Add up all the steps that Mary took walking to, from, and within Lamie's dining room, and she could have walked to West Point more than once; but it was Fred, who got there during my freshman year at Emmanuel College in Boston. I got there, too. Fred invited me to the annual West Point Weekend in March. It was so unusual for us to take a flight in those days, that all my dorm mates lined up on a large open deck on Marian Hall in the Fenway section of the city. As they later described it, everyone shouted and waved sheets and banners when they saw "my" plane fly from Logan Airport over the college.

Longtime manager Charlie Weinhold, who also lived only steps from Lamie's, served as the "heart and soul" of the enterprise, with his sons and a daughter-in-law joining the crew to pass on real Yankee spirit to his young Dunfey manager. The Dunfeys were the fledglings now, and we counted ourselves fortunate to inherit such loyal, talented, seasoned employees.

We no longer lived in largely immigrant enclaves or Democratic Party strongholds, but rather, in a state that had never elected a governor from the Democratic Party. We were in a place that looked askance at Irish Catholics, especially activist types like our tribe from Lowell. Front and center in Hampton, New Hampshire, was our traditional Yankee tavern and inn. We would have to work hard if we wanted local people to adopt this entrepreneurial Irish Catholic clan. The good news was that we shared the Yankee value of working hard.

Adding rooms—adding profit

In 1958, four years after my brothers bought Lamie's Tavern, we added a thirty-two-room motel, thematically designing the interior to invoke the Isles of Shoals, the historic nine islands located ten miles off the New Hampshire coast. My brothers quickly realized renting rooms was a lot more profitable than selling clams. They had an uncanny ability to know when to buy, when to sell, and how to resurrect a dying property. I think the "uncanny" part was the the combination of their individual talents gathered around the table for every single conversation, argument, discussion, vision, and plan. As one newspaper reporter described it: "They are five of the most competitive, easiest-going, hardest-working Irish Yankees in the Northeast." Irish—yes; we had always been Irish. Now, Lamie's was showing us how to be "Yankees."

A new upstairs, downstairs chapter—come as you are!

Meetings migrated from our homes to the second floor of Lamie's. It was a new upstairs, downstairs chapter, this time for business dealings. While the brothers were in the upstairs offices creating a new angle of Dunfey hospitality, they were aware that the entire downstairs operation was steeped in tradition. Preserving those traditions while nudging a more entrepreneurial, contemporary, casual style became a priority in shaping the Dunfey brand of easy hospitality. "Come as you are" was the message on our billboards. A Boston Globe reporter described it as "the Dunfey touch."

A lighthearted judgment of the success of the Dunfey touch came from an unlikely source, Judge Murphy from Lynn, Massachusetts. His son owned a home in New Hampshire, and he had suggested that his father stop by to meet the Dunfey brothers. Judge Murphy decided he would. Jack remembers him arriving at his office while the brothers were meeting. The judge didn't waste a minute. He let them know he had heard about the humble, hard-working, ragtag Dunfey clan from Lowell. He thought he might not even find where these modest fellows were doing business! Jerry adds some details he remembers even after all these years because they describe his and Bob's first marketing plan to draw travelers off the new I-95 to Lamie's. Along the fifteen miles from the Massachusetts/New Hampshire state line, billboards advertised Lamie's Tavern, with its "Come As You Are" welcome; others promoted Dunfey Real Estate and Insurance Company and four Dunfey restaurants at Hampton Beach—even a new Lobster Steak House! (Whatever happened to those fried clams?) There were bumper stickers on about ten cars outside the door downstairs. Jerry smiled, remembering that the judge concluded, "Yeah! You Dunfeys are just a humble ragtag gang from Lowell!"

Make a case for your pay

The judge's ribbing aside, my brothers were also recognizing they were on a fast track. Bud, in particular, saw that the quickly evolving business would require vision, strategy, and organization. Weekly meetings grew organically to serve this purpose, shirtsleeves conveying an informality with ambitious agendas covering a wide range of issues, as Jerry recites, "from the minutest detail to the most comprehensive of long-range projects." The atmosphere could simultaneously feel electric, argumentative, hilarious, and frustrating, especially when the topic was the brothers' annual pay. "That was the toughest meeting of all," notes Jerry. With six (Dick was working while pursuing his law degree) siblings, each believing he was the hardest worker, putting in the most hours and holding the greatest responsibilities, each brother prepared his own "case," hoping to convince the others that he deserved a certain pay level. The process unfolded as one brother at a time left the room while the others reviewed his case, and jointly decided his salary for the following year. The budding lawyer presented by far the best defense. According to Jerry, "Dick's was the most well-prepared with his judicious, thorough, methodical, lengthy testimony. When Dick's turn came, we all knew we were in for the night. You'd come back in the room to hear the outcome, sometimes being satisfied, sometimes asking for clarification, sometimes arguing, not liking the decision at all and letting that be known." But at the end of the process, they lived with the outcome because they knew each was pulling his weight, working what seemed like 24/7 each week, while always taking on new challenges.

How much the Dunfey organization could be simultaneously demanding and casual—and how much it depended on mutual respect—is indicated by the fact that my brothers' policy was to reach all major decisions unanimously. If a troublesome issue cropped up, as it could, it remained on the agenda until it was either disposed of or resolved. "It never even reaches a formal vote," Bud would say. "Either we agree or we drop it. But knowing you have five others to convince, makes you prepare thoroughly before you broach a new project." Perhaps that's why the "charco-burger" never made it to the big time.

President Dwight D. Eisenhower and his wife, Mamie, enjoyed a family Thanksgiving at Lamie's when grandson, David, was a student at nearby Phillips Exeter Academy. Jerry, not the Secret Service, escorts the President to his car after dinner.

Kate Dunfey loved to quip: "I was born over a bar, so I guess it's only natural I'd end up over a tavern!" Photo in Isles of Shoals lounge, Lamie's Tavern. Left to right: Bob, Walter, Jack, Bud, Jerry.

Near but far: Off to the Isles of Shoals, nine miles out of Hampton Harbor, for the first of many "isolation meetings" which provided time to consider business, political and social issues that needed time beyond regular meetings. Left to right: Dick, Bob. Second row: Jack and Walter, with Bud in the stern. Jerry is either taking the photo or hidden behind Bob. (circa 1955)

Kate Dunfey welcoming tours traveling from all New England States and stopping at Dunfey Hotels along the way; one of Jerry's many marketing projects.

In Lamie's kitchen, Mother Dunfey, as employees liked to call her, often chatted with Ray Morrissette who was chef at Lamie's for more than 30 years.

As upscale as a Dunfey family beach restaurant could get. The Anchorage at Boar's Head gave me a sense of a real classy restaurant—despite the fact we were still installing the booths two days before the 1955 Memorial Day opening. Chef McMullen was ready with steaks and boiled lobster. Even waitresses' uniforms seemed to look better in this restaurant.

Catherine A. Dunfey and Sons

The ANCHORAGE

**GREAT BOAR'S HEAD
HAMPTON BEACH, N. H.**

The peninsula GREAT BOAR'S HEAD has been a landmark for seafarers along the Atlantic seacoast for over 300 years. Legend has it that Leif Erickson, first white man to see the American continent, actually landed on this historic site. During the eighteenth century, Great Boar's Head served as an "anchorage" for widespread smuggling operations. Observed from the sea, this picturesque peninsula closely resembles the outline of an enormous boar's head. No longer a rendevous for smugglers, this rocky coast now provides an "anchorage" for some of New England's finest lobsters.

A La Carte

BOILED LIVE LOBSTER, Hot or Cold, Drawn Butter
1 lb. or over .... 2.25   2 lbs. or over 2.90
BROILED LIVE LOBSTER, Drawn Butter .

CHAPTER 17

Classrooms into Boardrooms: Integrating Life Learning

When Bud registered for classes at UNH, he signed up for Professor Fred Jervis's psychology course. Fred, a 1944 UNH alumnus, had lost his eyesight in WWII. His good fortune was finding a nurse, wife, and professional partner for the unimaginable journey to follow. With his gift of a seer's insight, intellectual depth, and teaching skill, Fred inspired Bud and others whom Bud directed to Fred's courses. Fred's psychology class served as a laboratory to shape a business philosophy that reflected the values and practices of our parents' lived lessons—spiritual roots, hard work, humor, and hospitality. Bud recognized his professor's personal insight and global vision. He (and later the whole family) never stopped being Fred's student. If the Dunfeys had been bitten hard by the entrepreneurial bug, they also saw the importance of Fred's expertise and guidance, which emphasized long-term planning and good relationships with employees.

So valued were Fred Jervis's insight, clarity, and advice that, early in his involvement, my brothers established the requirement that all key hires had to meet with Fred, their admired professor who had become the "family mentor." Stephan Lewy—child survivor of the holocaust and WWII veteran, applied for an accounting position with Dunfey. He loved sharing the story of his introduction to the family. Jack interviewed Stephan and saw him as a promising candidate, so he directed him to meet Professor Jervis, who by then had been mentoring my brothers for a decade.

"It was one of the old buildings at UNH and there were about eighty-five steps going up to the front door," said Stephan. "I went upstairs, I waited, and all of a sudden I hear this tap, tap, tapping. A gentleman arrives at the top of the staircase and says, 'Is Mr. Lewy here?' He looked me straight in the eyes and I saw he had a cane. And I thought to myself, 'Jack, you didn't tell me he was blind.' We went to his office, he took out his braille and said, 'From what I have seen of your background, I can tell you are qualified for the job.'"

The interview went well. Fred asked that Stephan tell him about his life. "Where should I start?" Stephan asked.

"At age five," was Fred's response.

"He looked straight at me the whole time, right into my eyes and listened intently. Finally, he asked, 'Do you have any questions?' 'Yes. I have one.

How does a Jewish boy get along with five Catholic brothers?' Fred leaned back in his chair, laughed out loud and responded: 'I can tell you, Stephan, that is one problem you will never have to worry about with any of the Dunfeys.' And I never did."

My brother Bud assisted Fred, his nurse-partner-spouse, Janice Williams, and May Sidore, CEO of Pandora Mills in Manchester, in the founding of the Center for Constructive Change in Durham. My brothers took it upon themselves to ensure that just about everyone they associated with would have the good fortune to participate in Fred's seminars. Those included Dunfey executives and managers, business employees, non-profit directors from organizations such as the NH Charitable Foundation, NH and Maine Community Funds, the Boston Foundation, the Odyssey House, and many hopefuls planning to assume responsible professional positions.

The Center for Constructive Change provided a framework for a mentoring relationship that would extend to several generations of Dunfeys and thousands of others for sixty-five years. A number of young adults who aspired to positions managing the political campaigns of candidates running for national office, received Dunfey scholarships for the center's seminars, which encouraged personal assessment of talents, values, and priorities, all built around one's big picture and long-term goals.

Additionally, one of Fred's specialties was the psychology of acquisitions. He could actively listen to you, sum up the parts of your statements and put them back together into a whole that he not only understood implicitly, but with which he could empathize. It was a powerful and disarming combination. At many a board of directors meeting, my brothers leaned on Fred's perspective regarding a situation before they made a decision. He knew the psychology of the deal, including the human elements.

Four fingers and a thumb

> "They were four fingers and a thumb that made a business-like fist."
> —*Jim Stamas, senior vice president and
> chief administrative officer of Dunfey Hotels, later Omni Hotels;
> a member of senior leadership team that transformed Omni into a
> major national hotel company and in 1995, founding dean
> of the School of Hospitality at Boston University.*

Fred Jervis had given my brothers a keen understanding of the importance of a philosophy, a strategy, and a brand. He recognized that each brother added dimension and breadth to the personalities of the others, characteristics grown from close interactions in the early years. He tapped and helped optimize that synergy. Collectively, they added different perspectives around what was, at that juncture, a fledgling boardroom table. Once a decision was reached, those fingers and that thumb came together as a fist, and not much could pull them apart. Every morning at seven-thirty, without fail, the five brothers were on a conference call.

Jack

No one ever beat Jack to the office. He was the thumb, no doubt about that; the first one there and the last to leave. He just grasped the entire business and loved it. In the 1950s, Jack was the oldest of the five brothers involved in the business. He had the natural gravitas to stay on top. Even early on at our beach restaurant properties before the glimmer of a thought about hotels, you knew he was in charge. Jack had the skill set to surround himself with talent that complemented the fist, and he didn't let his ego get in the way. Having trained fighter pilots in WWII, he knew the importance of being decisive, and especially of having to make split-second decisions. Pilots are intuitive and self-assured, and certainly not risk-averse. Jack displayed all those qualities, whether he was mastering business plans, traversing the highest ski slopes, or piloting even higher as a trainer.

Bud (Bill)

If Jack had innate logic and drive, Bud had vision. His contribution was organizational—he had a way of looking around corners to see where the business was going. He possessed the leadership, vision, and humility to bring in outside help who could instill an organizational framework. If Bud had his way, he would have modeled the company so that everyone, from the lowest position to the company president, shared in the employee meetings. He taught organizational skills in a style so unassuming that you didn't realize you were learning. He facilitated their regular retreats—isolation meetings—where they could hash out, more fully, ideas/causes that were too big to squeeze into the weekly ones.

Bob

When situations required tenacity, Jack was quick to say they'd put Bob on the mission. Bob's behind-the-scenes persistence "would reap results that the rest of us would probably not wait for." That trait not only marked Bob's business personality, but served him well in his longtime, dogged determination to help, behind the scenes, to bring all sides of Northern Ireland's factions together during that country's "Troubles." I also saw Bob as the first responder to our brother Walter's antics. The more outrageous Walter's humor got, the more Bob dissolved in laughter. You could count on Bob as your focused colleague and audience.

Walter

My mother had heard that the tenth child in a family should be pope or president. She noted such in her memoir. Few would doubt that the tenth Dunfey, Walter, had the temperament and inclination for the latter job, if not the former! Walter was a mentor for the long-time employees. Magnanimous. Gregarious. Charming. Sacrilegiously comical. Kind...

Nancy Hirshberg describes the close family friend, whom she'd known since her early teens: "Walter was Santa Claus, pope, and rainmaker rolled into one...No one was excluded from his circle, neither pauper nor prince." Walter had an expansive human touch and knew how to motivate people. He played a key role as "glue" for the brothers, with humor that could relieve tensions, clear the air, and find a way out of "dead ends." At such moments, Walter's resilience helped create the Dunfey culture before there were such things as company cultures, and he often helped us laugh our way to resolution. "Born with a sense of humor and the good sense to use it," the American Ireland Fund characterized him. He loved life and fun, and he charmed the socks off everyone.

Jerry

In the Dunfey family business, it was often Jerry from whom the most was demanded. As the youngest brother, he could not recall an age when he was not working, always trying to meet the expectations laid upon him. I realize on hindsight that when he was seventeen-years old, Jerry was probably the youngest manager of any business on Hampton Beach and then, at twenty, the youngest manager in the entire town of Hampton. Our older brothers knew how to give orders, and by the 1950s, they already had had a couple of decades of experience giving orders to their youngest brother. In the early years and without much if any budget, Jerry headed marketing/communications in newsletters highlighting employee accomplishments and activities like softball with each hotel property's team competing in tournaments; and through the long-running publication, the Private Line, sent out to all guests. He oversaw the successful marketing through what were called "rotogravure sections" (pictorial supplements) featured in the Boston's Globe and Herald, as well as the Portland Press Herald. Quiet by nature, Jerry, in turn, found his niche in the background, a slight comfort zone within the milieu of his four to six far more outspoken, sometimes overbearing, always well-intentioned and caring older siblings.

Much like my mother who always preferred one-to-one exchanges, Jerry is at his best communicating face-to-face. We joked when we'd see people give their business cards to Jerry. "They'll be sorry! Jerry will never lose that card!" It's true. To this day, Jerry not only has scores of those cards but has updated contact information written on them. What's more— he remembers the people and their affiliations, and still maximizes what folks now call "human capital." A South African legislator working on his country's new constitution in the 1990s, for instance, shared with Jerry his work framing a policy on gender issues. Jerry immediately connected him to good friend, Barney Frank, a United States Congressman, highly respected for his years of involvement in that issue. Jerry had the corner on networking long before the LinkedIn era.

Later, when he was introduced to Archbishop Desmond Tutu and South Africa, Jerry would hear the "Arch" (the title Tutu prefers) describe the term Ubuntu—translated as, "I am a person through other people... Your humanity is bundled up in my humanity..." Jerry and I would adopt that metaphor. As #11 and #12 in the family order, we each had eleven sets of shoulders to stand on, siblings who made indelible impressions in our lives, personally and professionally.

Not enough digits
Roy

While the "four fingers and a thumb" may fit as a metaphor for the five brothers who established the Dunfey Family Corporation in 1954, there aren't enough digits—even on two hands—for all twelve siblings who developed what was dubbed the "Dunfey difference." In addition to the influence of our parents and the brothers who were most actively engaged in the family business, our lives were formed and informed by brothers Roy, Paul, and Dick, each of whom possessed traits that played out in our lives and businesses throughout the years. Even as teenagers, our two eldest brothers, Roy and Paul, revealed their sense of responsibility and generosity when they helped keep food on the table for their siblings during Depression years, by sending home almost all of the meager weekly earnings from their jobs in Illinois and Ohio. With his boundless enthusiasm and initiative, Roy showed us from afar that he was capable of building a career and raising a family from the bootstraps up "way out there in the West" (Ohio!) After retiring from that career, Roy would join the brothers in the family business in 1968. His unique contributions are featured later in the book.

Paul

"Paul was our preeminent peace warrior," according to my brother Jack. When he returned home to Lowell, our brother Paul revealed sheer will to survive and thrive through the life-long effects of the near-fatal injuries he had sustained in WWII's Battle of Okinawa. Paul was disciplined. Self-pity was as foreign to his system as the scrap metal that more than a hundred surgeries would attempt to extract from his gut. His tenacity and courageous lifestyle adjustments made him unassumingly tough and resilient, a true exemplar of Semper Fidelis who, along with veteran leaders of the 6th Division, worked to get a monument erected on Okinawa. Many Japanese civilians were against the idea, so a retired Japanese meteorologist who had fought for his country in Okinawa suggested to the 6th Division that the Americans and Japanese do it together.

"This is the first time that any memorial has been put up in collaboration with the enemy," Paul wrote. "Erected by those who were once adversaries on the battlefield, it represents an epic moment in World War II history, standing proudly as a symbol of man's ability to effect a reconciliation from even the most adverse conditions." Paul walked the talk of a forgiveness that leads to reconciliation and peace—in an individual and in a community, local or global. Since my high school days, I had recognized the tough lessons he had lived through in the war, and the even tougher lessons of peacemaking. Asked about returning to the rivers, the rice paddies, and rocky ledges, Paul cracked to Lowell Sun reporter Kristopher Pisarik, "I want to see where I zigged when I should have zagged," then adding one clear benefit of the trip: "It'll be a hell of a lot better than the last time." When President Reagan appointed Jack to the inaugural board of the United States Peace Academy (which evolved to the United States Institute for Peace), Jack credited our brother Paul as his inspiration and assumed the position in honor of his older brother.

Richard (Dick)

As Richard (Dick) pursued his law degree at Boston University and beyond, he provided legal assistance to the family business. He was our expert in the exercise of considering every conceivable angle when facing dilemmas. Unlike our gregarious brother, Walter, whose humor oozed forth, Dick provided one-liners, a dry wit that would have you collapsing in laughter even as you tried to figure out whether or not he was serious. In 1988, for instance, our brother Bob (born in 1928) was honored by the Spurwink Foundation of Maine. The event organizer thought, understandably, that Bob's brother Dick (born in 1929), then chief justice of the New Hampshire

Superior Court, would be the perfect person to offer introductory remarks before Bob accepted the award. That event planner obviously did not know our brother Dick. The two bespectacled brothers could, at first glance, pass for twins and actually were what some call "Irish twins" (born in the same twelve-month period).

Dick began by telling the three hundred guests—most of whom did not know him: "I've never liked my brother, Bob." After that opening shocker, he proceeded to say that Bob always "took credit for all that I did, starting when we were six years old working at our family's store. He was always late and lazy." Audience discomfort no impediment, Dick catalogued several more stellar traits of Bob and "made sure" all present knew that it was he, not Bob, who really possessed those traits. Dick concluded: "I am the one—not Bob—who should be receiving the award, tonight." Silence.

Like the "wave" across the bleachers at a baseball game, a ripple of hesitant laughter and applause made its way across the banquet hall. Only Bob's pent up laughter and the hilarity that spilled over the Dunfey tables, finally replenished the air that had been sucked out of the room. Guests exhaled. It worked. Dick's, sober-faced and "serious charge" that the life-long mistaken identity between him (#9) and Bob (#8) had indeed led to Dick's being overlooked and under-appreciated. It was a tribute like no other.

That humor supported Dick as a lawyer, a judge, and a chief justice. His young daughter, Dianne, was very serious, though, when she called her father, "My Honor." Dick showed his "honor" walking the fine line between his professional and his paternal duties in a cause Dianne would espouse years later when she became a leader in protests with the Clamshell Alliance at the Seabrook Nuclear Power Plant. My brother Dick and his daughter had a secret signal of support that her dad could convey from a distance. She knew he had her back even when she and others were arrested and sentenced with her BU professor, Howard Zinn.

Still counting…the four sisters

Then, there are the sisters. As one of them, I cannot do justice describing the roles each of the four Dunfey women have had on our family's philosophy and trajectory. I am separated by almost a decade from my three older sisters, so I was influenced by them before joining them in the Sisters of Notre Dame. But the truth is that the whole family was entwined with and affected by an unusual reality: having all four daughters, or sisters, become nuns. Paul McGaunn's entire career from age eleven was with our family. He had a front row seat for over thirty years observing the "Dunfey convent phenomenon." He muses: "I really couldn't understand it—all four sisters entering the convent? The business was a bit easier to describe!"

One Sister of Notre Dame did find words. In her unpublished essay, "The Dunfey SND," Sr. Thomas Francis, Maryland province and friend of my sisters, Kay and Mary, penned her characterization:

> Dunfey SNDs come in assorted lengths, times, convents, and ages, but there is one thing they all have in common: each is an enthusiastic rooter for Dunfeys, Notre Dame, and life in general; and each lives a life full and rich in meaning. Pupils confide in her, older nuns admire her, young sisters tease her, relatives dote on her, brothers fly oceans to see her…She is poise with a bloody nose, fervor with a Boston accent, shrewdness with the US Government, simplicity with head of any department… grace in high speed…She can do anything: run a variety store, jerk sodas, melt ice cream for fifty, lead a band, tame a rose, be a spiritual director, charm a dignitary, patch a love life…
>
> The Dunfey SND may be headachy, weary, lonely, and missing all things North…she may be footsore and fatigued, but she will propel herself to the moon for you. She may be disappointed in you, but she will give you a middle-of-the-week grin…There's no fighting it. The Dunfey SND is a jim-dandy top-notcher, a 1960 Julie Billiart, and she's OK, OK! Here's to more Dunfey SNDs.

Choosing to follow such women role models certainly was a good decision for me. Maybe some of my sisters' verve would rub off on me.

True to her talent and prescience, my sister, Kay, (Sr. Francesca Dunfey), published a choral drama, *One with the Flame*, in 1961. The teenage Joan of Arc, considered a heroine of France for her role during the Hundred Years' War, was canonized as a Roman Catholic saint. Kay realized that "Most accounts of Joan, such as George Bernard Shaw's and Mark Twain's, are seen through the eyes of men. I wanted to reveal the Joan I studied in light of the women in her life." The drama, with twenty-eight women and four men, was produced at a number of women's colleges across the country.

CHAPTER 18

"Where have all the women gone?"

"Oh, we sent them all to the convent," my brothers, especially Walter, would quip. In the sixties, my sister Kay was a professor at Too-Dai, the Imperial University in Tokyo, the first Western nun to teach there. Mary was at Star of the Sea School in Honolulu, Hawaii, loving her diverse groups of eighth graders and teaching all their lessons in a foreign language—Bostonian English, an accent thick enough for local Honolulu administrators to conclude that her mimicking students might need speech therapy. Mary had earned her stripes and "perfected" her accent in Lowell's sister mill city, Lawrence, and in the heart of South Boston, where she had taught eighth grade boys for years.

Eileen was a reading specialist who unlocked the treasure of reading for hundreds of first graders, making it possible for them to master what might be their most important life skill. Evidence of her extraordinary success continues, a recent example coming from a sixtyish carpenter working in the home of one of my nieces. "Are you related to the Dunfey nun who taught first grade in Exeter, New Hampshire?" he inquired when he started the project. Once my niece figured out "which of her four Dunfey nun-aunts" he might be referring to, her affirmative reply brought this immediate reaction: "I would never have learned how to read had it not been for Sister Julie [my sister Eileen's religious name]." He was convinced that feat was impossible until his teacher made the "impossible" possible. Eileen served as convent superior and founder of the religious education program at St. Theresa Parish in Rye, New Hampshire. Adding to her impressive list of positions, Eileen was also principal of Presentation School, a remarkable treasure of a parish school in Brighton, Massachusetts, just outside Boston, where parish families like the McLaughlins credit Eileen's spiritual gifts for inspiring parents to be engaged in their children's moral as well as academic learning, and even in the exhaustive rounds of fundraisers to keep the school's ledgers in the black.

Perhaps my brothers were also thinking about keeping their ledgers in the black when I broke the news that I was entering the convent. "Oh—OK—but go in after Labor Day," Walter cracked, without a blink. It had been the brothers' go-to-line each time a sister had entered the convent, because the traditional entrance day was in August when our beach restaurants were still in high gear and required all hands-on-deck. Walter claimed credit when my entrance date announcement arrived: September 7, 1957, the day after Labor Day, the first post-Labor Day entrance date in memory.

My brothers need not have worried about staffing. Older nieces and nephews, several just a few years younger than I was, along with their friends, were ready to put on uniforms and put in time. Along with our Dunfey cousins from the Boston area, they comprised a new generation discovering the world over the counters, at booths, and in the dish sinks and kitchens of our early restaurants. Listening carefully, I hear my nephew, Michael, son of my brother Paul, tell so many stories that echo the "counter culture" that carried over from our dad's first store in Lowell, "where everybody knew your name" or rather, "your nickname." Michael's favorite is about "Benny," a C Street regular:

> Benny Lake was a fixture at the beach. I remember him shuffling into our C St. restaurant each morning for breakfast. To us he was this gentle, dare I say, old man, bald, with glasses and a great big smile, the longtime manager of Playland Hampton Beach's first "Arcade," which the Dunfeys then owned. Benny had his morning ritual. He always sat at the first counter bay, where my sweet and beautiful cousin, Ruthie, and her equally sweet and beautiful friend, Marlene, served. He ordered the same breakfast: two poached eggs on toast, and coffee. So before he even shadowed the doorway—like clockwork one of us would yell out: "Drop two for Benny!" Then, no matter how busy it was, each server would shout it. The "drop two for Benny" order echoed from the register, along the line of counter servers (and was even picked up by other "regulars") on its way to the back-order window and into the kitchen like a morning-has-broken wake-up call.

Although none of my parents' thirty-five grandchildren spent an entire career in the family business, almost all would cut their work-teeth very early as dishwashers, waiters/waitresses, pizza servers, bell boys, auditors, and front desk staff. Bob Dunfey Jr. might hold the record for having started work as a cashier in the change booth of our Hampton Beach "Playland Arcade" at age nine, and then filling other roles in the hotels until pursuing other ventures. Nieces, nephews, and cousins contributed significantly to the growing Dunfey operations. We Dunfey sisters could rest easily, leaving business operations to explore worlds beyond the counters, all the while remaining close through a communications network that had evolved from earliest years. Later, we would return to active involvement in what would be the family's most significant initiative. That part of the Dunfey family story must wait for another chapter in this book.

A different take on convent living

Counter to our culture's stereotypical view of nuns disappearing into some black holes, rarely to emerge again, my three sisters who joined the convent were the first people in our family—other than our cousin and sibling WWII veterans—to serve overseas. Far from disappearing into a vast black hole of the habit, and despite the myriad rules of convent culture, we remained a close-knit family thanks to a communications network of notes, "Round Robins," and letters to and from the battlefront and the convents. Writing kept us attuned to one another's lives—the ups, downs; the reasons for and concerns about all that was happening.

I think my brothers understood and respected the motivation behind their sisters' decisions, but don't ask them to admit it! When I was a college student, there was no Peace Corps or VISTA offering service opportunities at home and abroad. It was natural for me to consider the religious order of the Sisters of Notre Dame de Namur (SND). My mother understood this and was quick to alert and assure me: "Eleanor, people are going to tell you that you should 'stay home and take care of me.' I want you to know, I didn't decide the first one's life, or the sixth's, and I won't live yours."

In 1957, I entered the SNDs. The community's 150-year history of women in global service was compelling. Add to that my close-up view of three sisters and two aunts who were already demonstrating what dedicated service looked like, and my decision made sense, especially given my lofty desire "to save the world!" In *Erin's Daughters*, Hasia Diner makes reference to that motivation: "Nuns provided role models of women engaged in a variety of educational, charitable, and social welfare activities, often doing work deemed inappropriate for women.

It is a phenomenon that by the late 1950s—a half-century after a generation of immigrant girls, mostly from Canada, Ireland, and Europe, had entered religious orders—four thousand women educators had joined the Sisters of Notre Dame (SND). We had missionary sisters in Africa, Asia, and Latin America, and in cities and rural areas across the United States. In 1957, my entrance year, seventy-six young women formed the largest entrance class in SND history. Its philosophy was grounded in the idea that we were one in service. Wherever one was assigned in the world, she was connected to the service of each SND throughout the global community. I relished being "connected" to what a Boston Herald reporter described as "gutsy nuns, noble examples," writing about the Sisters of Notre Dame who "for years have lived in Boston's public housing projects and served in its soup kitchens and hospitals."

In the six-month introductory phase, we wore simple black dresses, short capes with white collars, and sturdy Oxford shoes. The half-year provided spiritual instruction, meditation, and other practices to help us figure whether we still thought this was our vocation after all. The religious superiors sometimes made that decision for us, in some cases with less than desired sensitivity, informing an aspiring candidate that she was not "suited" for convent living. Our cohort (we called it our "band") diminished by twenty-four young women in the first six months. The fifty-two prepared for the beautiful ceremony that would welcome us into a two-year novitiate. A white veil marked this new phase, the first year of which was dedicated to maintaining a strict schedule of meditation, work, discipline, and theological studies. In the second year, those spiritual "exercises" extended to service along with continued study. A profession followed. With permission from their religious superiors, novices chose to make temporary vows of poverty, chastity, and obedience. We submitted three choices of names, one of which would be assigned and symbolize a new identity and life. I was given one of my choices: Sister Catherine LeRoy—breaking the "Francesca" tradition of my sisters and aunts—to honor my parents. It also gave me a little anonymity when I needed it.

I was ready. I loved community life. It was a tectonic shift from my male-dominated existence, but our group was a creative cohort of young women with a generous spirit, and a love of and talent for singing. We even cut our own record. We shared a sense of commitment, humor and resourcefulness. I was at home in that kind of environment, male or female.

Not so quick for that white veil...

Our cohort's sense of humor played itself out many times over those two years, but especially on the night before we were to become novices. Although not a word was uttered that evening—none dared to break the discipline of the "Great Silence," which lasted from 9:00 p.m. to 6:00 a.m.—a bottle of Breck Shampoo, sitting innocently on the bathroom sink, caught someone's attention. The "for oily" or "for dry" hair words on its label had been crossed out. It now read "Breck's for No hair," and that one-word alteration was enough to get us laughing. Our silliness probably expressed an unspoken but real anxiety. The next day would mark a huge step in our training, and you can believe our well-meaning superiors had inculcated the seriousness of the solemn commitment we were about to make.

We really did take that serious lesson to heart, but on the eve of that occasion, we almost-twenty-somethings were more focused on the fact that before we received the white veil, we'd have our heads shaved. Yes. The next night, Breck's for "no" hair would be our choice for shampoo! The laughter illogically led to someone's (my?) idea, conveyed only in gestures, of course, to short-sheet about twenty beds along the hallway closest to the bathroom. Now that's a job, especially when you're not talking. Each bed looks perfectly made, but you can only stretch your legs halfway.

It must have been a pious postulant who felt obliged to report the raucous behavior to the postulant director. The following morning, all of us were ushered into the study hall, where on each desk, were a piece of paper and a pen. We were told to write down whether or not we had "broken" the Great Silence. Whew –Nope. I hadn't said a word (I was practiced in communicating without words from my early Good Friday noon to 3 p.m. silence rules!) Then we were to list exactly what we did do before going to bed. Curiously, my list was a tad longer than those of most postulants around me. I submitted my admission of guilt.

Our postulant director then informed us that a decision would be made later in the morning regarding the consequences of our actions. Oh no! What if I were sent home? I wasn't worried about losing my vocation; I was worried about facing my brothers' razzing. I could just hear them: "Eleanor, the Reject!" I also imagined the shock of my dear SND aunts, prominent elder figures in the community, in effect saying, "Eleanor, the Embarrassment!" I wasn't too worried about my sisters, who I figured would commiserate with me; nor about my mother, who was more than used to my behavior. She had survived my being "almost suspended" in the eighth grade for planning a hayride that included boys. Did anything *not* include boys? I could almost hear her say, when informed about this latest escapade: "This, too, will pass!"

The ceremony did go on that day as scheduled, but without the seven of us who, it had been determined, were responsible for causing the disturbance. Because the occasion was private, parents would not be visiting their "daughters, the new novices" for another week or two. All seven of us guilty souls had relatives in the order. No preferential treatment in this case! We would remain postulants while our permanent fate in the Order was decided. For days thereafter, we stood out among the sea of more than a hundred white and black veiled sisters. Much later, one of my sister novices admitted, "Oh, you were all lined up in the first row in chapel, and I was right behind you. I cried every day looking at you all." What empathy, I thought, but Cathy admitted the tears were for herself. She had the most gorgeous hair, the envy of any young woman. More accurately, Cathy had had beautiful hair until the day she became a novice. She was distraught about losing it. It was an era before girls easily expressed themselves in creative hair colors and styles or boasted that "Bald is Beautiful."

That week started with a mild sort of shaming—not shunning. No *Scarlet Letter*-like "A" on our capes, but it felt similar. Gradually, the situation morphed. We started receiving increasing support from many professed sisters who found a way to convey that they really thought the whole matter was actually funny—and not serious enough to warrant this delay. They would sneak treats to us, along with a wink of the eye or a thumbs up. We felt they really sympathized with us. Finally, "on the eighth day," unlike God who rested after his creation, we awoke to a surprise. We would not only be allowed to take the veil but would do so in an inspiring candlelight ceremony designed to welcome the prodigal daughters we were—a recognition, I guess, that we "seven foolish virgins" had finally wised up!

In the end, the reaction to our immature behavior made for hilarious re-telling, much as my brother Jack's re-telling of my mother's cracking up with laughter the time she tried to use a broom to get her prankster son out from his hiding place under the bed, following his latest misdeed. There were, indeed, times to lower the boom (broom) and times to see the humor of a situation. I wanted to hold on to the humor.

The sixties and sisters

As a new generation of SNDs, we were the young sisters in 1962 when Pope John XXIII opened the historic Second Vatican Council of the Catholic Church. I was a secondary school teacher at the new Bishop Fenwick Regional High School from 1960–1965 in Peabody. I taught in Lynn and Hingham, Massachusetts, and then was assigned as dean of women at Emmanuel College in Boston. I was only a few years older—and far less worldly—than the seniors I was working with. For me, it was total on-the-job training in an active campus community, influenced by the expertise of sociologist Sister Marie Augusta Neal and by faculty with advanced degrees in the arts and sciences. We were all coming to grips with navigating a growing tide of vocal expression and activism. The new Women's Liberation Movement held one of its first—if not the very first—meeting on our campus. The Fenway area, with all its colleges, provided fertile ground for Students for a Democratic Society (SDS). Our increasingly confident, articulate college student leaders protested traditional Class Day programs, holding their own activities on the tennis court and wearing Bermuda shorts under their academic robes, actions that shouted change louder than the chants or the messages they scribbled on pillow cases and hung from dormitory windows facing the Fenway. We had sit-ins and teach-ins and walk-outs protesting the Vietnam War, where so many of the boys I had taught at Bishop Fenwick High were now fighting our country's war there. Simultaneously, the Sisters of Notre Dame were addressing our religious order's directives to translate Vatican II's proceedings and spirit in a new world culture.

We faced cultural, economic, and seismic religious tremors with no script to follow. Our job was to find new ways to speak and serve, guided by rules, yes, but more essentially by dealing with the root causes of injustice. Long-simmering rage burst to the surface and broke the country's spirit after the assassination of three national leaders. Long-simmering injustices were finally being unearthed and addressed in the Civil Rights movement, the "Hippie" revolution, and Vietnam War protests. These harsh realities tested us to "walk our talk" and align with those who were re-defining themselves and our institutions, trying to reinvigorate us in light of all that was happening "in the world." By 1968, many sisters were starting to question the layers of the convent lifestyle. Some would remain and renew their communities; others would pack the lessons we had learned and lived, and move beyond formal religious structures and vows.

That same year, my mother was named "Catholic Mother of the Year in NH." Pope John Paul XXIII's Vatican II reforms had, as my mother described, opened the windows "to air out" the Vatican. Still, change was slow. Even a faithful woman with a seventh-grade education was aware of the inherent contradictions as her own understanding regarding what was truly spiritual and what were simply outdated rules and inadequate rituals. Many Catholics were now recognizing that the heretofore unquestioned "no exceptions" to rules and restrictions could unnecessarily spawn yet another paternalistic era.

Throughout the thirty years when my mother lived as a widow, she held fast to her spiritual base. But she moved beyond many rituals that had served a purpose in an earlier generation and now needed new forms and new meaning in the context of a new world. The "forty-five" nightly prayers my dad had teased her about had morphed into her own simple, home-grown prayer of gratitude—just "forty-five words." She began it after her sons returned safely from WWII and then added to it over the decades (often suggesting we add to it, as well):

Thanks be to God,
   For every hour of safekeeping; Every day of good health
   Every joy, every love, every sharing, every giving and
      forgiving
   Every understanding, every success, every companionship,
      every new life
   Every help and assistance sent to all of us throughout
      the years.

According to Meister Eckhart, Dominican teacher and scholar known for his spirituality and many quotable reflections, "If the only prayer we ever said in life were 'Thank You,' that would be enough." My mother seems to have shared the master's idea of genuine prayer although she never heard of the thirteenth-century theologian.

And the women will lead them

My mother had been silent for years, arranging our entire family schedule around the convent's hard and fast rules. She understood that, like it or not, Dunfeys went counter to accepted convent culture. We had so many relatives that we rarely "fit" stipulations of any kind (for example, only four visitors allowed for a monthly visit). Actually, I detested being an exception. I wanted to disappear into the sameness of the sisterhood. But our very numbers made us exceptions, denying me of my sought-after, non-worldly, virtuous compliance. "No exceptions" was the reason for the rejection my mother received in answer to the first and only request she ever made of the religious order.

In her mid-seventies, my mother asked that her four daughters be permitted to join our eight brothers and her for a first-ever family reunion with cousins in Ireland. Permission was granted at the regional level, but the request then had to go to the international Mother General. My mother wrote what she called a "plain down-to-earth plea," to request that all twelve of her children might visit the Irish hamlet outside of Dingle where both her parents had been born. It would be an "exception" to the rule, she realized:

> This is my first request to Notre Dame in the thirty-eight years of my daughters' service, and I would so appreciate your kind consideration of this matter...I feel certain the privilege I'm asking for now will be given freely in a year or two, but at the age of 74, I cannot count on being around for that...

At the time, many nuns traveled with students to various world destinations, but the practice did not apply to traveling with one's family. "They could have a holiday, but they would have to take it in America," the letter explained. On hindsight, we joked that we should have organized ourselves as a "class trip." We certainly had the numbers for that, and the four women in the family would have made impressive chaperones—finally lording it over the eight men! A Dublin, Ireland, reporter caught wind of the news, his source, no doubt, one of those male Dunfeys, and the consequent headline read: "Nuns banned from family reunion...."

My mother never blamed those in charge. There was an entire constellation of practices which, within the overall universe of convent life, "fit" the existing culture. The rationale within that universe made sense, and the Mother General tried to express it as kindly as possible. She could not allow an exception. Other sisters, after all, might like to go on trips with their families but did not have the means. And so it was. My mother simply continued as she always had, respecting all nuns—including her four SND daughters, two sisters, and aunts. She was very disappointed, indeed, but recognized there were far more urgent issues pressing for attention. She did, however, hope that something might change. Eventually, it did.

The times (and habits) they are a'changin'...

My world now included taking classes at Boston University. I was fortunate to study with Dr. Dugald Arbuckle, an esteemed professor of counselor education. He was always challenging, always inspiring, and always engaging his students. One Saturday morning, I gathered my books and my long black dress—the "habit," and settled at a corner table in the Boston University Library, hoping to finish a paper for the course. The library was a short walk from Emmanuel College, where I had recently been named dean of women. I needed all the help I could get, and Professor Arbuckle's course, with its thirty students from at least fifteen countries, was highly recommended. On this particular weekend, I was tackling one of his tougher assignments. Down the row of tables, I spotted a classmate. She looked my age, I thought—twenty-eight. My nod and smile met a similar, if more hesitant, response. Was it my imagination, or was she actually staring at me? Every time I looked up during the hour that followed, her eyes dropped to her book. When it was time for me to take a break, I walked by her table.

She managed a question: "Could we talk?"

"Of course!" Here was someone my age, and she'd like to chat—maybe about our challenging assignment. I collected my flowing yards of cloth and deposited myself in the wooden chair directly across from her.

"I've never spoken to a nun," she stammered. "In fact, I've never even seen one up this close except on TV." (Oh no! that "flying nun" image again, I thought, annoyed to feel grouped with the Hollywood "nun" stereotype. We couldn't take flight if we wanted to. Our habits would ground us!) I caught myself in the thought and said, rather lamely, "I'm glad we're getting the chance to meet."

"I'm Jewish," she remarked, as though from a memorized script she wanted to finish without interruption. "We've been in class for about three weeks now. I just see you and the way you're dressed. You're so different, but every time you open your mouth, you say exactly what I'm thinking, and it's driving me crazy!"

Did I hear her correctly? We think alike? Am I relieved, confused, dumbfounded? All of the above. Those emotions collided in that moment. Here I was, naively participating in a graduate class on counselor education, and the question absorbing my classmate was my outfit. Here I was, draped in yards of black serge, with only my hands, and my face, my dark eyebrows, and my chin visible. I was totally comfortable in the garb that had been a familiar presence in my Irish Catholic background. As a youngster, I had eagerly climbed on the laps of older sisters, aunts, and cousins who dressed this same way. I had played with the oversized rosary beads that hung from their waists, and I had scratched my face (now red with embarrassment) on their plastic capes. How was it that the way of life I had chosen, in order to reach out to all people, had become a barrier simply because of what I was wearing?

I'm separate, I suddenly thought. I'm shouting my difference through all these yards of laundry (my sister Mary's favorite name for the habit!) How many others have never approached me while I've remained oblivious to the barrier I raised?"

My classmate was honest. We shared some of the many ideas from the course and the assignment. We had a few laughs and off we went to finish our papers.

What was left unfinished for me was the question that arose that morning in 1967, about the artificial barriers between me and those who would come my way. Of course, I was already aware that any human encounter has its built-in barriers; cultures have their inclusive and exclusive tendencies. But did it make sense to add yet another barrier—such an unnecessary one at that? I had never paid much attention to the familiar remarks that "Sister has ears (or legs)" or "She's really human when you get to know her!" I was a stereotype, branded, and I was inviting such judgment by presenting myself in a costume that had been stylized over the centuries, originating in 1850 as the ordinary dress of those Belgian women who had founded the Sisters of Notre Dame. Each iteration, over the generations, made our bodies less visible. But for thousands and thousands of women and Catholics around the world, the "habit" had become habit.

That day's lesson in the Boston University Library did not come from the paper I was writing. The person who taught me a lesson had sat across the table from me, staring at the only part of my body she could see. A year later, I was given permission to be one of the first sisters in our region to try out some suits approved for those nuns who wanted to begin changing our form of dress. The rest of that story is too lengthy for this book. It was just another jolt to my system at the dawn of the Age of Aquarius, quite an era to engage in a conversation about clothes and culture.

Beyond, and far more important, than the change in the clothes we wore, was the path each of us Dunfey SNDs took in moving beyond formal membership in our religious order. In the following section, I share the decisions, along with some thoughts about my sisters' transitions.

Beyond the clothes we wore

During each of the summers of 1966–1970, I studied for my master's degree at the University of San Francisco. In 1969, I stayed on for a full year to complete my academic requirements. Thoughtful reading, discussions, retreats, and meaningful liturgies were opening my own thinking to a

...and changing even more! My University of San Francisco roommate, Nancy O'Brien, Sister of Notre Dame, California Province, and I, received permission to try out a modified "habit."

world beyond the convent. Over Christmas break that year, I planned to share three major considerations: that I did not want to go on at that point to study for my doctorate, that I was thinking of leaving the order, and that I had met a priest from Iowa who was in the process of leaving. I had not seen my mother in six months and figured I'd need the three full weeks to share the context of all these possibilities.

I might have been the one studying for a degree at the time, but I was simply "taking courses." My mother proved to be the real-life scholar. Case in point: On my first night home, she and I settled into our twin beds. "How are you, *really*, Eleanor," she queried. I thought, Well, that's a good opener; I can at least share that I've decided not to go on for my doctorate at this point. I did just that and she chuckled. "That's a good idea. I'm glad you're taking a break from the books. There's a lot of learning to do beyond the library." Well, that was easy enough!

I should have known my mother had thought long and hard about convent life. Much earlier in my training, I had excitedly shared news of the Vatican's permission to visit the graves of our parents if we happened to be passing through the city where they were buried. "Hmm," she had mentioned, cautiously: "Does it seem at all strange, Eleanor, that you can visit us after we die, but that when you drive the sisters to the chiropractor in Seabrook, NH, you can't come the six miles up the road to Hampton—while I'm alive—to visit me?" A mental light bulb must have blinked, but I had not seen it at the time. Now, sitting on the bed across from her, I realized that it wasn't simply a specific rule she had been respectfully challenging when she had asked whether her daughters might join the family excursion to Ireland. She had been trying to nudge those in charge to look at rules through a different lens in this new era. Now, she was gently questioning me: "Have you ever thought of leaving the convent?"

Did I hear what I think I heard? This mother of four, sister of two, and niece of two nuns was asking me this question. She really is way ahead of me.

"Well, actually I was planning to talk with you about that at some point—this month."

She had obviously anticipated such a moment happening, sooner or later. She propped herself up a bit against the pillows and said words, most of which I've never forgotten:

> Ever since Vatican II, Eleanor, I've been wondering when one
> of you…might think of leaving…The world really needs people
> out here with the values nuns live by. You can serve out here, too.
> So many people are struggling. Mark my word, in ten or twenty
> years, all this will seem normal.

I was still trying to fathom the depths of our conversation when she asked a logical follow-up question: "Do you think you'd ever get married?" She seemed as comfortable with the direction of our chat as she was in leaning back into the propped-up pillows.

"As a matter of fact, I was in class with someone…He's a priest and his name is Jim, and he's from Iowa." I couldn't believe I had strung that series of statements together and uttered them aloud to my mother, all within forty-five minutes of my first night home. I've no doubt what she said next had been percolating quietly in her heart and mind for years while she waited patiently for the Church, the religious order, and her daughters to catch up with her:

> You know, I've often wondered why the Church has made it feel that a vocation to marry is not quite as worthy as a calling to the priesthood or religious life. Believe me, month after month, year after year as I had four or six or eight kids trailing behind me going to visit peaceful and quiet convents with the nuns seeming so contemplative, I questioned if I had chosen the right vocation!

We both laughed at that, our lightheartedness dispelling any sign of what could have been a shattering conversation. She wasn't finished, either:

"Oh, my! Do you know who must be happy tonight?" Then answering her own question: "Nanna Manning!" Her mother and my maternal grandmother who had lived upstairs with the Keefes, who had assisted in the home delivery of many a Dunfey and Keefe baby.

"Nanna used to say," my mother continued: "'Oh, Catherine! You've got eight sons and divil [meaning not one] a priest!' Or she would scold: 'You've got eight sons and divil a Jim!'" (This referred to my grandfather James—Jim—who had died almost seventy years earlier.) With genuine delight, my mother quipped: "Well, Eleanor! Now Nanna Manning just might get both in one: a James and a priest, so I'll finally be off the hook!"

And there it was. I would remember just about every thing from that conversation especially my mother's prescient "Mark my word" remark. Most of what she had sensed was coming actually did come, but in fits and starts and setbacks. That night, I promised myself that I'd also try to remember her tone as well as her words. No rancor. No self-pitying sighs or "If onlys." Just wisdom. The straightforward reflections of a faithful woman whose universal spirituality was not constricted by rules or rituals but was, rather, undefined in any final way.

It seemed that centuries of other "absolutes" the Church espoused, many of which I practiced in my religious life, were also up for questioning. I had believed the Church held the answers to life's big questions. I trusted the truths as I trusted America's democratic form of government. "Ours not to reason why; ours but to do or die," was Alfred Lord Tennyson's statement, printed and framed on our convent refectory wall. I could not imagine being comfortable with uncertainty. But once again, the women in my life, along with my brothers, put things in perspective. My mother's response to my decision made it significantly easier for me to begin dealing with the guilt I felt about leaving a community I had wholeheartedly dedicated myself to, which I had never expected to leave, and which I loved and to this day, admire.

My brothers were more than ready—actually eager—to support my decision, once Walter and Msgr. Philip Kenney, our longtime family advisor in spiritual and social justice issues, had made a trip to San Francisco where I was studying. They wanted to make sure, firsthand, that I hadn't caught Hippie fever. After all, I was living just a block from Haight Ashbury. My brothers also happened to be in the midst of negotiations to purchase the Royal Coach Motor Inn chain, based in that area. While Walter was at the table negotiating the acquisition of a hotel chain that would enhance the future of the business, Father Kenney and I were dealing with some hard questions that would affect my future. It was important for me to listen to my own responses. The adage, "How do I know what I think until I hear what I say?" applied.

Walter's meetings were successful. He wanted to leave me feeling the same way. Of course, he could not resist saying they made the trip because he was afraid I'd run off with a priest. Those fears were allayed when they had found me in the parish hall at Sacred Heart Church on Fillmore Street totally immersed in a weekly discussion that my colleagues and I held with a group of minority teenagers. They were really teaching us, and we were inspired.

I would, indeed, marry a priest three years later, but they need not have traveled that dramatic number of miles to "save" me.

Left to right: Sr. Annunciata (my father's cousin, Jean Dunfey);
Sr. Ann Francesca (my mother's sister, Annie); Sr. Catherine LeRoy (me);
Sr. Ann Francesca (Mary in habit worn in Hawaii); Sr. Marie Francesca
my mother's sister, Mamie); Sr. Francesca (Kay); Sr. Julie Francesca (Eileen);
Sr. Marguerite Joseph (my mother's aunt, Ellie). circa 1962.

With arrival gates on ground level, security held fast to rule that no one could go out on the tarmac, that is until my brother, Walter, pleaded with the officer to allow only the immediate family to greet our SND sister home from her mission—in Hawaii! The door opened and all 31 immediate family burst onto the runway with the siblings and my mother on the steps. 1963

CHAPTER 19

1969

East Coast Meets the Midwest on the West Coast

In 1968–1969, Father Jim Freiburger had been facing his own decisions, although I knew nothing about him or them at the time. A diocesan priest from Dubuque, Iowa, he attended the University of San Francisco's summer school of theology. He was in a couple of my large lecture classes, but we had never really met. In our third summer on campus, however, we were both enrolled in a seminar on Teilhard de Chardin with only twelve students. Our first exchange was a request: "Eleanor, I'm going to a performance of Macbeth tonight, and I need a shirt ironed. I was wondering if you'd mind…" What? Did he know the skill set I had developed living with eight brothers? Well, I ironed that shirt in the sixth floor laundry room of our summer residence, Phelan Hall, where the sisters on my floor wasted no time teasing me for "taking in laundry."

The more significant exchanges Jim and I later had were about the course on the life and works of Pierre Teilhard. Dr. (Rev.) Norbert Wildiers, was the foremost scholar and personal friend of Teilhard. He was larger than life in physical, intellectual, and spiritual stature. Father Wildiers was our professor and two years later dubbed himself our "matchmaker!"

> An obscure Jesuit priest, Pierre Teilhard de Chardin, set down the philosophical framework for planetary, Net-based consciousness 50 years ago.
>
> Teilhard de Chardin finds allies among those searching for grains of spiritual truth in a secular universe. As Mario Cuomo put it, "Teilhard made negativism a sin. He taught us how the whole universe—even pain and imperfection—is sacred." Marshall McLuhan turned to Teilhard as a source of divine insight in *The Gutenberg Galaxy*, his classic analysis of Western culture's descent into a profane world. Al Gore, in his book *Earth in the Balance*, argues that Teilhard helps us understand the importance of faith in the future. "Armed with such faith," Gore writes, "we might find it possible to re-sanctify the earth, identify it as God's creation, and accept our responsibility to protect and defend it."
>
> —*Jennifer Kriesburg, "A Globe, Clothing Itself with a Brain,"*
> *www.wired.com/1995/06/teilhard/*

In the works of this Jesuit scientist-scholar, whose writings had been banned by the Vatican until recently, we discovered a message rooted in faith and optimism but undefined in any final way. Jim Freiburger, who would later become my husband, expressed Teilhard's influence on him:

> Teilhard changed my perspective of the universe in which we exist. He moves beyond the myopic institutional view of life based on a medieval theology. It was his vision that helped me be less constrained by Church culture and embedded rules. I had been searching, not for apologetic truths, but [for] underlying principles that guide us in life's decisions.

Jim's reasons for leaving the priesthood had been accumulating, one of the first coming when he was asked to assist a family whose children were arriving at school undernourished and very poorly clothed. His visit to the family home deeply disturbed him:

> Here were two loving but desperately poor parents who, in 1963, had a family of seven children, ages three-months-to-ten-years. The father was working menial jobs with scant pay. In the conversation that evening, the parents shared that they had been told in confession that they could not use birth control, but they felt another child would diminish the already dim future for their living seven.

Jim left the home of these good people recognizing that there was a "crack in his seamless adherence" to Church teachings. Frances Kessling provides a context for this era:

> When the advent of the birth control pill in the early '60s coincided with a major push for church modernization, there was widespread hope among Catholics that the reform-minded Pope John XXIII would lift the church's ban on contraception. After all, the Second Vatican Council had explicitly called for greater integration of scientific knowledge into church teaching.
> —*Frances Kessling "How the Vatican Almost Embraced Birth Control,"* Mother Jones, *May/June 2010*

In 1968, however, Pope John XXIII's successor, Paul VI, declared the Church's opposition to birth control in his encyclical Humanae Vitae. Jim realized he could not impose the Church's rules. He felt the Church's mission was to guide the faithful so that they could make their own informed, moral decisions based on Christian values, not Church regulations. Jim adds:

> When you place divinely appointed authority as the enforcer
> of the rules process, blind obedience can become the norm.
> Conformity prevailed when I grew up, and it was only later that
> I struggled openly with breaking those bonds of conformity.

Teilhard's thinking reinforced our aspiration to gather up the best of the past and embrace the future. It's worth noting that some sixty years after Teilhard's death, scientists and church leaders from around the world met at the Pontifical Council for Culture in November 2017 and "unanimously approved a petition asking Pope Francis to waive the "monitum" against Teilhard de Chardin's writings that had been in effect since 1962. We were not alone.

Staying or leaving—not the question

My mother did not separate those who stayed from those who left. Everyone was needed to serve, whatever their lifestyles. She expressed her support directly in a letter to her older sister, Sr. Marie Francesca (the sister whom my mother had replaced in the mill at age twelve, so that Mamie could enter the convent). When Auntie Mamie heard I was leaving the SNDs, she was, justifiably, distraught. As one of the most beloved leaders in the community, Sr. Marie Francesca looked to her four nieces to carry on the SND tradition. Now, the youngest was stepping away. With sensitivity and quiet assurance, my mother replied in a letter that ended:

> Mame,
> I am truly happy for Eleanor and have no qualms at all about
> her decision. I'm so thankful I have kept up with all this renewal
> because, as the mother of four nuns, I have to be prepared for
> four times as much change.

I was the first in my family to leave. In the twelve years that followed, each of my three sisters would make the same decision. While rules necessitated a process and the signing of papers of release from one's vows (religious promises of poverty, chastity, obedience), all four of us valued and sustained our bonds with the Sisters of Notre Dame. We had offered a combined total of 113 years of service to the community and its mission. When, as a wife and mother in 1992, I attended the thirty-fifth anniversary of my entering the convent, I came away recalling the understanding my mother had had thirty years earlier. I wanted to acknowledge her wise and prescient guidance that led me to that gathering:

Reunion

No longer are we those who left or those who stayed.
We have found our voices from the past
Unlocked, Recognized,
Affirmed through the fray—
Each one's story binding us anew to love and serve,
Named now simply, sister-friends
How good…!

The habits, they were "achanging!" Here I am with nieces, Linda, Catherine, Dianne, and Tish (hidden) at a family reunion in late 60s. In back, right: my mother and sister, Mary.

CHAPTER 20

A Whole New World—Not Only for the Sisters

There's no doubt that those years of dizzying growth, heady success, along with the time it took to try to keep up with it all, affected many families' lives, including Dunfeys'. The roles of husband (the "bread winner") and wife (the "child bearer and homemaker") still permeated much of society and, particularly, business culture. As the youngest in the family, I was just a teenager during my nephews' and nieces' childhoods. Then I was off to my many assignments as a Sister of Notre Dame. My relationships with my sisters-in-law was somewhat superficial, framed, and limited in the late fifties and early sixties to my meeting them encased in my starchy habit, all of us seated in stuffy convent parlors. Their kids wore their Sunday best, their behavior eyed closely by their mothers. Although we did not eat with our family, we did offer them cookies and a liquid my brothers dubbed "crepe paper water."

My mother understood the challenges her daughters-in-law faced: "Meeting up with a family like ours must have felt like meeting up with a baseball team in the locker room." Actually, at times, the latter may have been preferable. Some of my sisters-in-law were the only children in their families and several were not Catholic, yet they were expected to "adapt" to convent schedules, along with a host of other rules.

What I did not fully appreciate in those years was just how much each of my sisters-in-law looked after my mother, especially when all four of us daughters were in the convent. My mother was grateful, though, observing first hand, the challenges they faced and the long hours that absorbed their husbands in the ever growing family business: "It's harder for them raising even half the number of kids I raised," she would remark. "There are so many more demands on women than I ever had." When the years took a toll of some of my brothers' marriages, my mother reflected, "This is hard for everyone, but we can't judge. No one knows what goes on behind closed doors." She cherished her personal relationships with her daughters-in-law. Those bonds lasted and were noticeable especially at the family reunions, some which former wives continued to attend "because of Nanna D."

It was our sisters-in-law who also eased our re-entry when we left the convent.

Transitions
Catherine Marie (Kay), #1 daughter; Sr. Francesca

When my sisters Kay and Mary left the convent in the late 1970s, each experienced the welcome, help, and friendship our sisters-in-law extended. They provided wardrobes for my oldest two sisters (who thoroughly enjoyed modeling them and whose engaging ways became the added pulse of many social gatherings). They invited Kay and Mary to meet their friends and their friends' kids. The Hirshbergs are a part of that extended family of friends. Their daughter Nancy recalls meeting her first nun, and it happened to be Kay Dunfey:

> The four sisters were nuns, and of course, we were Jewish and grew up with Catholics but nobody liked nuns. The Dunfey nuns were the only nuns I really got to know, and they were really fun…
>
> Kay was wonderful…She had taught in Japan and brought us kids little statues—not of Christian saints though. Mine was a Buddha. She shared stories about world religions and how we should be accepting of other people's beliefs. I was probably in third grade at the time. Much later I realized that she lived her values as a world traveler, an educator, an optimist, a person who believed in the power of relationships to build community. I'm Jewish, but I held on to that little Buddhist statue, and I learned from her that Christ was about acceptance.

Nancy's memory of my sister was Kay's genuine acceptance of people. That acceptance was on display in a letter from Kay two years earlier. She participated in a research institute focused on representing Christianity in a greater spirit of openness to the Japanese people the missionaries were serving. Kay relayed a salient point made by Father Spae, secretary general of SODOPAX, the official link between the Vatican and the World Council of Churches:

> The Protestant missionaries came not drinking, not smoking; then the priests came not marrying; after them, the sisters, not going out in public. It's no wonder many Japanese equate Christianity with a totally negative view of life. To a people influenced by the very tolerant outlook of Buddhism, therefore, we are a katai (harsh) people.

Father Spae respected Kay's intellect and charism. He invited her to meetings in Geneva, "an awe-inspiring trip," she reported, to a "truly international city." Nancy Hirshberg understood this fun nun. Kay was, indeed, the life of any party, but she was also, as Nancy reflected, "the embodiment of Martin Buber's philosophy, the idea that you magnify life by building meaningful relationships with others."

Mary Frances, #4; Sr. Ann Francesca

"For it was Mary—Mary, grand as any name can be..."
                                                    —*popular Irish song*

It may have been a "grand old name," but when "our Mary," weighing in at twelve pounds (although older sister Kay would keep adding a few ounces when describing Mary's birth) arrived as the #4 Dunfey and the second girl, she imparted new meaning to that popular Irish Catholic girl's moniker: radiant, buoyant, exuberant, and candid, to name a few. Mary loved long lists of adjectives and words and used them to weave a story like no one else we knew. Her teaching assignments brought her to South Boston, Honolulu, Exeter, San Francisco, and Baltimore. When she left the convent in 1975, she remained in DC as a liaison for the National Historic Preservation. She did not simply do the job; she enveloped it. My brothers offered the helpful advice that there were too many words in her job title: "You'll never fit that on a business card, Mary." They purposely created so many versions of the title, that even after her ten years in that position, I had to double check that I was writing it correctly. But Mary loved words, so that was not a problem for her.

The words of her colleagues offer a glimpse of my sister. One described a number of employees, mostly forty-somethings and mostly men, who were quite pleased with themselves that they had moved up the ladder of success. They considered themselves quite sophisticated and accomplished. Mary, however, related to the person beyond appearances and titles. Robert J. Jones said of his colleague:

> "Mary was the first person to introduce herself and hold herself out as a friend at my new job in June 1981. Our organization was in a state of confusion with a major event coming up in a few days, but Mary made time for me on that first day and beyond. I learned I could always count on her daily "Top of the morning," and after greetings were exchanged, we might share a family story or two. She treasured her family more than anything, except maybe, her independence...

I recall memories as if they happened yesterday. That's because Mary gave you something of herself, not just a vapid exchange of words, but wisdom understanding, and humor or whatever you needed to make you feel better. I hope we made her feel better, too.

In 1976, Ken Knox, the associate director of the Neighborhood Reinvestment Corporation, was responsible for conducting a workshop for the city of Birmingham, Alabama. Knox was tasked with bringing together people with "quite different perspectives" to find common ground. The goal was to "build a local housing program, thus 'turning around' a deteriorating neighborhood." Among the sixty people Ken describes as "captured" for this two-day workshop held about a hundred miles from Birmingham were several militant neighborhood residents, a dozen bankers, city officers, and several colleagues to help with "crowd control." Mary Dunfey was sent to the workshop to assist Ken.

> This was one of my first experiences with Mary. I wondered how this smiling, quite pleasant, talkative, former nun could hack it in such a diverse group of people already gathered into enemy camps on the bus we chartered to take them to the sessions. It seemed that nobody trusted anybody else, while our job was supposed to elicit commitments and reach agreements on how to proceed in the establishment of a non-profit corporation that would address serious housing issues in the deep South.
>
> To my surprise, very little hostility ever surfaced and as time passed, I kept waiting for the proverbial shoe to drop. Then I noticed how groups of people were always gathering around Mary. Were they listening to her wisdom? Not really. They were listening to her stories! She was teaching me something by being herself. Everybody needed and enjoyed humor and good conversation, and this was the perfect medicine to break the tension.

Underlying the more obvious "pleasant, engaging" traits, Mary was an intelligent debater, a voracious reader, seasoned and mature. When it came to moving issues forward, she could advance the agenda with tact—a smile and a tale.

Mary did love her independence and would respond with her favorite one-liner to those who inquired if she was married: "No. I'm an unclaimed treasure." She was.

*"Who can say more
Than this rich praise,
That you alone are you?"*
—*William Shakespeare,* Sonnet 84
(found in one of Mary's collections of quotations from her readings).

Eileen, #9 (after four boys!), Sr. Julie Francesca, Eileen Robinson

My sister Eileen left the convent in 1982, a few weeks after our mother died. It was yet another transition from her life in Notre Dame where she had served in Exeter and Rye, NH; Old Town, ME; and Wellesley, Tyngsboro, Brighton, and Needham, MA. Eileen was a reading specialist, parish minister, superior, and principal, dedicated to providing children with a strong foundation of reading in the primary grades. When she left the convent, she wasn't looking for a special love, but she was in the right place to find it—close to home, our family homestead in Hampton Center at Lamie's. The Isles of Shoals cocktail lounge, located downstairs from my mother's apartment, was perhaps the only popular spot for nightlife outside the summer season, when Hampton Beach establishments gave it some competition. Teacher by profession, entertainer by talent, Charlie Bradshaw, with his heart-thumping, finger-pounding piano talent, played to standing room-only, or rather, dancing-room-only, audiences every weekend. Eileen was enjoying an evening with her childhood friend, Estelle, and both loved to dance. Someone else in the tiny lounge that night had enjoyed ballroom dancing for years. Paul Robinson was a recent widower whose son had coaxed his dad to join him at Lamie's that evening. Eileen felt a tap on her shoulder and looked up to see a tall, handsome man with a shock of silver hair. "May I have this dance?" Eileen said "yes" to the dance and, within a year, to Paul's marriage proposal and then, for twenty-seven years, to their loving companionship.

Eleanor, Sr. Catherine LeRoy, Sr. Eleanor Marie;
Eleanor Dunfey-Freiburger

I should have known the law would catch up with my multiple identities. Years after I left the convent and had become Eleanor Dunfey-Freiburger, I needed to get fingerprinted, part of the process of joining a bank board. Arriving at the Manchester police station, I was directed to a sliver of a room off the lobby. Sargent O'Rourke checked my card, asking, "Any relation to the Dunfeys over on the Seacoast?"

Figuring on the usual *I-know-Walter-or-Jack-or-Jerry*, I anticipated what I thought would be his next question: "Do you know one of my brothers?"

"No. I had one of the sisters in school."

"Oh, then—Sr. Ann or Sr. Julie? They both taught in Exeter."

"No. I had Sr. Catherine LeRoy at Bishop Fenwick High in Peabody, Massachusetts."

My shock filled the closet-sized space: "Well, you're looking at her!"

His shock spilled out the door.

Here I was getting fingerprinted to prove my identity, and the person fingerprinting me knew me as someone else. We talked of the early days at Fenwick (I was among the teachers who opened the regional high school in 1960) until I ventured to say that the receptionist might be wondering why it was taking him so long to get my fingerprints. I headed out the door, laughing all the way to the bank (board meeting).

CHAPTER 21

The Sixties: Go West and North, Young Men

The sixties served up a counter culture jolting the venerable traditions of most religious, educational, and social institutions that had held fast to paternalistic rules, rituals, and behaviors far beyond their original intent and usefulness. Business was no exception. It was also an era for businesses to wake up to personal and social responsibility; to step up to the plate and become more civically engaged. There was more than a nudge to expand one's business philosophy and entrepreneurial spirit. It was also the decade that the Dunfeys caught the winds of change. My brothers flew with it.

1959—The Carpenter Hotel, Manchester, New Hampshire
At the cusp of a new decade and two years after I had entered the convent, my brothers began a new venture thirty miles west of Hampton. It held a new array of risks and opportunities than those Lamie's had presented a mere five years earlier. The fledgling Dunfey Family Corporation purchased the Carpenter Hotel in Manchester, NH. Jack, Bud, Bob, Walter, and Jerry, bought the bankrupt operation from the Rines family. At twelve stories high, the hotel, located on downtown Elm Street, was the tallest building in the city at the time and definitely presented itself as the tallest order of business to date for the Dunfeys.

"It was tough convincing the bank to sell at first," says Jack. Word of the young, inexperienced, upstart Democrats had spread: "We must have had just about the lowest possible reputation if even the banks did not want to turn a bankrupt property over to us," he mused. Nonetheless, the bankers were finally convinced, probably by my brother Bob who was not known to give up—or in—easily. After the reams of papers were signed and the trio of new-owner brothers went into the bar off the lobby to order drinks, the Carpenter Hotel's new manager, twenty-six-year-old Walter Dunfey, offered the toast: "So—now what do we do?"

Fly by the seat of your pants. At the Carpenter, the young upstarts did soar to new heights—like opening Dunfey's Top o' the Town lounge on the twelfth floor. With vision, savvy, hard work, and wit, an eye for similarly motivated employees, and a willingness to take risks, they quickly turned the property around. They engaged vendors who had gotten to know and trust them at Lamie's. They upgraded rooms and essentially provided people with a new, inviting place to stay and play in Manchester. Modest as this further reach into the hotel business looks in hindsight, it was no small challenge for the Dunfeys.

In keeping with the spirit of the sixties, the Carpenter also offered a venue that expanded exposure for the family's increasing involvement in New Hampshire's political life. It was in the Carpenter Hotel lobby, in 1960, that John F. Kennedy announced his candidacy for president of the United States. That moment was commemorated by the 1961 unveiling of a plaque, overseen by brother, Ted Kennedy.

The Eastland and Congress Square Hotel

In 1961, my brothers also set their sights northward, to Portland, Maine, where they purchased another property—the combined Eastland and Congress Square Hotel located in the heart of downtown Portland, it was the largest commercial (as opposed to resort) hotel north of Boston at the time, with 750 rooms and a significant senior resident population, mostly located in the two-hundred-room Congress Square Hotel. The two hotels were connected on several floors. With this location also came an impressive group of Democratic Party leaders. Senator Edmund Muskie, Senator George Mitchell, and Maine governor Ken Curtis could all trace their early offices and campaigns to the Eastland.

"We built a twelve-story addition with a swimming pool on the top floor, and tore out more rooms for a new lounge, 'Top of the East,' and added another elevator." Jack remembers the Eastland as "fantastically successful." Financially, politically, and socially, the thriving property would give the Dunfeys yet another opportunity for creative ventures. Ranking high on that list was the grand opening of the Hawaiian Hut at the Eastland. Dave Wong, owner of the most famous Chinese restaurant in the Boston area, China Sails, went all out to help the Dunfeys make the themed restaurant possible, "lending" us his #1 chef, Sonny Ng, to assure the venture would succeed. Sonny Ng's eighteen-year-old wife, Bik Fung Ng, soon followed from Hong Kong, thanks to the efforts of Senator Bobby Kennedy, which led to the Ngs' naming their child Robert Kennedy Ng. Bik felt adopted by "Mother Dunfey" so she also re-named herself: "Bik Fung Ng Dunfey."

Jurgen Demisch became regional manager responsible for several hotels including the Wayfarer, the Carpenter in Manchester, and the Eastland in Maine, "whose boiler system was so old," he said, " you could never ever sell enough rooms to pay the oil bill. I spent a lot of time shutting off lights and turning down thermostats." Dunfey hotels were not "cookie cutter" in design. With no two alike, Demisch reflects: "At day's end, it was the service that had to be distinctive. Employees had to be single minded about how to treat guests, run restaurants, and work together. That was the company glue when none of your hotels looked alike."

The Dunfey Family Corporation Left to right: Jack, Jerry, Bud, Bob; front center: Catherine (Kate), Walter.

Manchester, New Hampshire, The Hotel Carpenter, the Dunfey Family's first hotel purchase in 1959. The hotel was in bankruptcy, 1959. Portland, Maine, The Eastland 1960.

John F. Kennedy opened his campaign for president of the United States, in the lobby of the Dunfey Family's Carpenter Hotel. Dedicating the plaque memorializing that occasion are Senator Ted Kennedy with my brothers, Bud, left, and Walter. June 2, 1961.

Bob Dunfey giving last-minute update to presidential candidate, Senator Bobby Kennedy on East Coast campaign trail while Govenor Ken Curtis and Senator Ed Muskie look toward guests arriving. Eastland Motor Hotel, Portland, Maine. 1968

On the campaign fundraising trail from Portland, Maine to Nantucket, Massachusetts. Left to right: Senator Ed Muskie, Jack Dunfey, Senator George Mitchell. 1970s.

Patsy Takemoto Mink, the first woman of color and the first Asian woman elected to Congress, participated in the passage of much of the 1960s Great Society legislation, and was an early critic of the Vietnam War and worked tirelessly for women's rights, equality and justice. Here, Mother Dunfey welcomes Congresswoman Mink to the opening of the Hawaiian Hut, first of its kind Polynesian cuisine north of Boston. The Hawaiian Hut became a popular spot in downtown Portland's Eastland Motor Hotel, purchased by the Dunfey Family Corporation in 1961.

CHAPTER 22

New Hampshire Democratic Party— Roots and Wings

For the Dunfey Family Corporation to become "fantastically successful," as Jack had described the Eastland in the 60s, the management structure as well as the buildings needed an upgrade of sorts. First of all, Dunfey positions had to evolve and be defined: Jack, president and treasurer; Walter, director of operations of the Carpenter Motel and Wayfarer; Bob, manager of the Eastland; Jerry, director of operations at the Hampton Beach restaurants, Lamie's and the Meadowbrook Motel at the Portsmouth, New Hampshire rotary; and Bud, overseeing personnel matters, operating the real estate and insurance offices, and emerging as a significant voice in New Hampshire Democratic politics.

Bud's history in New Hampshire politics dated back to the early fifties at the University of New Hampshire, when he wrote his Master's thesis, "A Short History of the Democratic Party in New Hampshire." Although "short" may be an accurate description of the party's actual influence to that point, such research was deeply grounded in the fascinating history of the state. Bud (known as Bill in some political circles) established the UNH chapter of the Young Democrats with a core group of his peers. His personal commitment required a voice that called for a strong two-party system in the state. For the many—and there were and are many—who only caught glimpses of Dunfeys escorting the Kennedy brothers around New England in the sixties, an op-ed column that ran in the *Manchester Free Press* on October 3, 1963—some seven weeks before President Kennedy's assassination—offers a far more accurate description of the connection and early experience of "Dunfey and the Democrats":

> This week former Democratic National Committeeman Bill (Bud) Dunfey was in Washington as a guest at a presidential reception, and reportedly he will be offered a top post on the White House staff…Earlier this week we listened to a conversation about this elevation of Dunfey to the rarefied air of the White House staff and one person said, "Boy, what a lucky break for Dunfey, he sure fell into it this time." Now there's a real chuckle…he fell into it. Nothing could be a wilder under-estimation of the truth, and

159

to prove it we must go back to 1950 when Bill transferred from Miami University of Ohio to the University of New Hampshire.

That was a-way back before the Dunfeys were the New England Hiltons of the hotel business and they were still in white aprons toned with mustard as they cooked cheeseburgers for the students (at UNH) in Durham...

That was before there were any Gov. Kings or Sen. McIntyres, and being a Democrat was admitting you were something between a beatnik and a bomb-tosser.

The op-ed continues with an eye to Bud Dunfey in the state campaign headquarters of those days, as election returns came in: "[Democratic] candidates then looked like individuals who should have been cared for rather than voted for...Somehow you wanted to go in and rescue Dunfey, that nice clean-cut fellow..." Only through the long, frustrating efforts to build a credible roster did the Democrats produce some "firsts" for New Hampshire: a Governor John King and a Senator Tom McIntyre.

The *Press* concludes:

It would be over-simplification to say that Dunfey built the New Hampshire Democratic party by himself, but he was there for twelve long years...If Bill Dunfey becomes a member of the White House staff, he certainly won't be "falling into it." He pulled himself...and the Democratic party...all the way by his teeth.

Bud did not go to the White House, but he did go to the United Nations as a citizen delegate during the Carter Administration, when Andrew Young was named UN ambassador from the United States. It was an appointment aligned with Bud's priorities—ahead of the curve on issues and behind the scenes in action. His major focus for his UN term as citizen delegate was Zimbabwe, Namibia, and Mozambique, "not exactly household names to most Americans (at the time)," reported free-lance writer Eileen McEachern, in the Rockingham Gazette. Over the counter at the store in Lowell, my dad had introduced us to the larger world. That larger world would be Bud's concern when he addressed the UN General Assembly from the same platform as the Pope and Castro with a statement on apartheid in 1979. In October of the same year, Bud's presentation focused on "Foreign Economic Interests" stating, "It is the desire of my government to work with other governments represented in this chamber toward our common goals—the independence of Zimbabwe and

Namibia—the elimination of apartheid…" On November 8, 1979, Bud made another major address to the General Assembly on Zimbabwe and Namibia. Once again, Bud was educating us all, planting the seed of what would be our thirty-year anti-apartheid commitment. He attuned us to complexities in that larger world, even as we put down roots in Massachusetts, New Hampshire, Maine, and Vermont, raising families, growing the business, and engaging in New England politics. As it turned out, Democratic politics on a national scene would come to New England's doorstep.

Arriving at Grenier Air Field, Manchester, NH, the day before the national election would make John F. Kennedy, president of the United States, Bud was JFK's New England presidential campaign manager.

Dunfey family at Inaugural of President John F. Kennedy, 1961. Seated left to right: Mrs. Robert (Shirley), Mrs. Roy (Ruth), Mrs. Paul (Rita), Mrs. Richard (Audrey), Mrs. William, (Ruth), Mrs. Walter, (Barbara), Mrs. Gerald (Barbara). Standing: Robert, Sr., Mrs. John (Joan), John P. (Jack), Mrs. Catherine A. Dunfey, Paul, Sr., Richard, Sr., Bud, Walter, and Jerry.

My mother (left center) first met Rose Kennedy in 1968 at a dinner to raise the funds to pay off the late Robert Kennedy's campaign expenses; she knew other of members of the Kennedy clan since her son, Bud, served as JFK's New England campaign manager.

CHAPTER 23

1962

The Wayfarer: New Vistas Economically, Financially, Politically

On the afternoon of June 24, 1962, the tenth anniversary of my father's death, I stood with my mother on what would become a distinctive symbol of welcome for the newly-opened Wayfarer Inn in Bedford, New Hampshire. A carefully crafted wooden covered bridge offered pedestrians a heightened view of the adjoining historic John Goffe's Mill. Only the water slapping the rocks in the brook below broke the silence of an extraordinary moment: the dedication of one of only three hotels (the other two Sheratons in South Portland, Maine) that the Dunfeys would build.

My mother smiled and reminisced about the groundbreaking on this rural property, a year earlier:

> Until your brothers brought me up here to a turkey farm, Eleanor, I had always been open to their dreams and ventures. But that day, it was a different story. As we balanced ourselves on those rocks down there, Jack talked of intersecting highways, a motor inn designed to blend with the natural setting—and even a covered bridge. All I could see were turkey feathers, and really, I thought they were out of their minds. On that day two years ago, I wondered what Dad would say.

Now, those intersecting roads were all in place, the precarious rocks still holding fast below, and we were standing together on that covered bridge. The smile on my mother's face contained only a hint of her pride and excitement. The Wayfarer was a dream come true for many, but especially for our resilient mother, who had trusted, albeit a bit warily, her sons' most daring venture yet. With the major addition of a Convention Center in 1966, and especially with its covered bridge, The Wayfarer became the showcase and backdrop for the first "First in the Nation" Democratic Primary. Major newspapers, such as the Boston Globe and Washington Post and all the major networks and their senior correspondents, like CBS's Walter Cronkite and Mike Wallace, set up shop initially at the Carpenter Hotel and then moved to The Wayfarer in an icy New Hampshire January. NBC's John Chancellor, Tom Brokaw, and their entourage, along with loyal local politicos supporting one of several Democratic presidential candidates, gathered around the huge hearth in the dining room and the expansive bar in the lounge, shutting out the effects of winter, but offering spectacular scenes of the falls at John Goffe's Mill. My sister Kay described the waterfall in Wayfarer brochures as a "view that had waited 200 years for windows to watch it."

Another scene to watch every four years was the raucous exchange peppered with jokes and razzing, the targeting of one another's Democratic Primary candidate preferences. Spirits which might otherwise be as frosty as outside temperatures gave way to the self-deprecating, underdog humor of New Hampshire Democrats, who often had reason to feel "down and out."

In fact, actual "winning" was almost as rare as a mild New Hampshire winter. That truth came to me years later when my friend Donna Theobald and I, each with two children between twelve and seventeen, stood together in tears in the Wayfarer Convention Center as the results of yet another election were announced, this particular one for a Congressional race in which John Sununu Jr. defeated my cousin Joe Keefe. Through her tears, Donna said, "Eleanor, do you realize our kids have never been to a victory party?"

That pretty much summed up what it meant to be a New Hampshire Democrat at the time. But not completely. The winning would come. Call it resilience; call it hard work; call it tenacity, purpose, or perspective: New Hampshire politics, for the most part, remained a civil exercise even among those whose opinions differed. That kind of respect—even begrudging respect—made it possible for people with differing political opinions to disagree vehemently before an election, but then work together on mutually beneficial legislation.

Such respect even yielded the unexpected: friendships! In 2017, Brad Cook, of the law firm Sheehan, Phinney, Bass and Green, reflected on a homegrown lesson in state history and business:

> When people retain their civility, it can bring mutual opportunities. In a small state like New Hampshire, especially in an earlier era when the population was smaller, politics was less combative, and candidates had "opponents," not "enemies." Participating in public affairs could lead to meaningful business and lifelong personal relationships.

Cook describes a key example. Following the death of Senator Styles Bridges in November 1961, Tom McIntyre ran unopposed for the

Democratic nomination to fill Bridges' unexpired term in the U.S. Senate. Republican Perkins Bass was supported by a number of Sheehan, Phinney, Bass, and Green law partners, including moderates like Bill Green and Kimon Zachos. Bass ultimately won the nomination and faced McIntyre in the general election. During the campaign, McIntyre ran on a platform supporting President John F. Kennedy's proposals for federal aid to education and medical care to the elderly under Social Security. In the special election on November 6, 1962, McIntyre defeated Bass by a vote of 117,612 to 107,199. He was the first Democratic senator to be elected from New Hampshire since Fred Brown's election in 1932. Cook continues:

> McIntyre's campaign was run largely by the Dunfey brothers, who owned hospitality businesses in Hampton and Manchester. During the campaign, the Dunfeys and the Sheehan attorneys, although on opposite sides, got to know, like, and respect each other. After the election, the Dunfeys hired Bill Green and the firm to represent their hospitality empire, which grew to include the Wayfarer in Bedford, Parker House in Boston, and hotels in New York and in many cities of the world. Their business kept several attorneys in the firm busy for most of their careersin the '60s, '70s, and early '80s...This story shows how disparate parts of life can lead to relationships, business opportunities and economic progress, if only people retain their civility and take advantage of mutual opportunities.

Starting in 1984, and through my thirty years at New Hampshire College/ Southern New Hampshire University, I would observe, firsthand, the civility and astuteness of Kimon Zachos who served as chair of the board of trustees, and Bill Green who became chancellor during a critical era in the history of the institution.* He was also a director of our family's educational non-profit, New England Circle/Global Citizens Circle. Bill survived much good-natured teasing about his Republican leanings. With humble roots grown strong in Jewish, Greek, and Irish households, and a humor that kept political, educational, and business challenges in perspective, we all forged ahead, together accomplishing so much more for our respective institutions than we ever could have without the benefit of one another's often divergent viewpoints.

---

* Bill's oversight, strength and extraordinary tenacity helped save the college, and he was instrumental in identifying Dr. Richard Gustafson as president. Gustafson went on to build on that foundation and serve for seventeen years guiding its transition from New Hampshire College to Southern New Hampshire University.

Those relationships deepened and lasted. The willingness of progressive Democrats and moderate Republicans to work together led to Republican Governor Walter Peterson's appointment of Bud, a UNH alumnus, to the University of New Hampshire's board of trustees. And when Justice David Souter, a Republican, was nominated to the United States Supreme Court, Bud testified before Congress in support of his nomination. Bud knew and admired Justice Souter, who served under our brother Dick, Chief Justice of New Hampshire's Superior Court.

The Dunfeys' political involvement and focus on social justice had been served up and dished out early on, around the dinner table and over the counter, making us incurable, strategic optimists, ready for

PORTSMOUTH HERALD
September 19, 1990

Dunfey adds his testimony for Judge Souter

By Bob Mitchell
Herald Washington Bureau

WASHINGTON — New England lodging magnate William Dunfey lined up with supporters of Supreme Court nominee David Souter Tuesday during a long day of testimony from critics and fans of President Bush's choice for the High Court.

Dunfey, founder of Dunfey Hotels, now Omni International Hotels, told the Senate Judiciary Committee in a brief statement late Tuesday that he served with Souter for five years during the early 1980s on the board of overseers at Dartmouth Medical School.

DUNFEY NOTED his background as a former state chairman of the Democratic party and said he was aware of Souter's ties to the state's GOP establishment.

"In our work together, David Souter earned my complete respect, just as his distinguished career as a judge has won the respect of the people of New Hampshire," Dunfey said.

A Rye Beach resident, Dunfey testified with a mixed panel of Souter supporters and foes as the committee's confirmation hearings moved toward conclusion.

Earlier, a group of New Hampshire lawyers and former colleagues of Souter in the state attorney general's office praise the nominee's open-mindedness and fairness in a joint appearance before the committee.

"In our work together, David Souter earned my complete respect, just as his distinguished career as a judge has won the respect of the people of New Hampshire."
— **William Dunfey**

The witnesses included Steven McAuliffe, president-elect of the New Hampshire Bar Association, and Rep. Chuck Douglas, R-N.H., a conservative lawmaker and former colleague of Souter's on the state Supreme Court.

Opponents included several leading feminists and abortion rights advocates, including Kate Michelman of the National Abortion Rights Action League, National Organization of Women President Molly Yard and Eleanor Smeal of the Fund for the Feminist Majority.

"We consider placing Judge Souter on the Supreme Court to be too great a risk," Michelman said.

the long haul that leads to long-term constructive change. Perhaps that's why a Leo Kanteres and a Walter Dunfey so easily found common ground on social issues. When the New Hampshire Democratic Party created the Dunfey Kanteres award in 1987, Will Kanteres, Leo's son, was asked to bring to life some memories of Walter and Leo.

First, he made it clear that the award represented the "hard work of hundreds of people who helped build a progressive Democratic Party in what was an extremely Republican state: men and women like Harry Makris, Maria Carrier, Mary Louise Hancock, Jean Wallin, Madeline Gladu, C. Arthur Soucy, and on and on."

Leo and Walter had street smarts and personal charm, and they knew about real life poverty, too. Will says:

> They shared a strong gut feeling for democratic ideals, having learned lessons about social needs firsthand—the Dunfeys from watching their parents struggle financially in the early years— and my father learning about healthcare issues and disability rights by caring for his older brother who suffered from Muscular Dystrophy. Back then "handicapped accessibility" meant that Leo carried his brother on his back up the three flights of stairs at Manchester's Lincoln School.

Walter and Leo turned out to be the fortunate ones and they proudly used whatever clout they had to become the original "Yes We Can" Democrats.

Leo Kanteres' first "classroom of the world" was on school stairways. The Dunfeys' was over the counter at the store in Broadway's Acre. Both sets of experiences were reality checks about the effects of the Great Depression, of World War II, and of discrimination due to race, ethnicity, and disability. So perhaps the reporter's description of our brother Bud's pulling up the Democratic Party "all the way by his teeth" wasn't such a stretch, after all. Like the Kanteres family, and like many first-and second-generation immigrants, they had been schooled in temperament and pulling-by-the-teeth tenacity, as Bud describes:

> My father was an optimist…He would not let me be crushed by the pervasive economic fear that gripped my world…At 6 a.m. I walked with him the one mile across the Merrimack River and into the slum neighborhood to open "the store." It was a sleepy journey for a nine-year-old with Dad talking the whole time.

Bud continued the relay of that optimism. Our cousin, Joe Keefe (named for his uncle and Dunfey cousin Joe Keefe, killed in WWII), describes how: "For more than thirty years, if you were a Democrat—running for the state legislature or for president of the United States, Bud was your advisor, strategist and mentor." In his remarks made at the New Hampshire Humanities presentation of the William Dunfey Award to Ambassador Andrew Young in 2013, Keefe noted the key quality of Bud's politics:

> His interest in politics was always but a means to an end. The end being a more vibrant, more just community—be it here in New Hampshire, or in our nation, or in the larger human community. Bud's partisanship was never personal, always civil, always practical and always about higher ideals. So, he worked continually across party lines, building bridges of trust."

The family's kind of politics was shaped early, but in the sixties, countercultural shifts in politics and the economy showed the urgency for that same inclusive philosophy to be translated as well into our family's evolving business. Properties such as the Carpenter, Eastland, and Wayfarer stood as testaments to the ways that growth, new markets and destinations, and economic potential needed a wake-up call. To build on the strength and wisdom of the old, the brothers needed more than just each other to assure the progress and spirit of the new.

Breaking ground on the first hotel built by the Dunfey Family Corporation. 1961.
Catherine Dunfey does the work as her eight sons supervise: Left to right, Roy, Jack,
Paul, Bud, Bob, Dick, Walter, Jerry.

"A scene that waited 200 years for
windows to watch it," writes my sister,
Kay, about this scene in a *Boston Globe*
supplement about Dunfey Hotels. 1963

Built in keeping with historic covered bridge architectural design and direction, the pedestrian walkway provided entrance to the Wayfarer dining room over the brook below the original John Goffe's Mill, opened as a gift shop.

The good citizens of Wentworth, NH, would not let the historic, pedestrian Wayfarer covered bridge, be wasted. After demolition of the Wayfarer, they moved the bridge to its new home. 2017

Who ever said Walter Dunfey did not look up to William Loeb?

Walter, looking down this time, not wanting to miss President Johnson's remarks to NH Governor John King.

Above: When I took St. Mary's, Lynn, MA, senior class to Washington, DC in 1965, Senator Tom McIntyre invited us to his Senate office. Later, he sent a note to my mother with this photograph: "Your daughter would have undoubtedly made as good a politician as she is a nun..." My record in the latter might reveal what would have happened had I chosen to be a politician. None of my 11 siblings ran for elective office, preferring to serve behind-the-scenes.

Right: My brother, Justice Richard Dunfey, was surprised as were the rest of my brothers, to find himself the subject of a positive op-ed column in the Manchester *Union Leader.*

An Editorial

Giving Young People Perspective

The other day Superior Court Justice Richard Dunfey made a suggestion before the Belknap County Law Enforcement Assn. that one way to prevent juvenile delinquency would be to hold classes, even at the grade school level, at court sessions throughout the state.

This newspaper feels that Judge Dunfey has come up with a worthwhile suggestion.

JUDGE DUNFEY

All too many children do not understand the full ramifications of the law, what it is like to be in trouble, and the consequences of foolish actions.

Some parents will oppose that suggestion on the grounds that such a procedure would bring their "darlings" into too early contact with the unpleasant aspects of life. This newspaper doesn't consider that a valid objection. Life is made up of many ugly things. But, it does contain more beauty than ugliness.

If you give children a more realistic view of life from an early age and show the ugly aspects as well as the fine ones, you thus prepare them so that future experiences are not so overwhelming.

We would hope that more school systems in New Hampshire would take up Judge Dunfey's suggestion and arrange for all classes to spend some time in a court room.

William Loeb
Publisher

Top left: My brother, Bud (known in political circles as Bill) making the rounds of pollsters, reporters, commentators during the New Hampshire Primary at Dunfey's Wayfarer Convention Center. Bud catches up with Sander Vanocur, NBC commentator. 1972.

Top right: John Chancellor, Anchor, NBC Nightly News and my brother, Jerry in 1972. The First-in-the-Nation Primary, broadcast from Dunfey's Sheraton Wayfarer Convention Center, Bedford, New Hampshire.

Walter Cronkite, CBS News Anchor, with my brother, Walter, and Jim Cote, Wayfarer manager, enjoying a rare sunny February morning before the opening of the New Hampshire Primary.

CHAPTER 24

Wooing Executives

The Dunfey brothers' strategic optimism now translated to identifying executives whose intelligence and experience would advance the business while being a "fit" with company values. Saying they were lucky in those searches is an understatement. Several of these long-term Dunfey alumni sat together at the Parker House sharing "war stories" over Boston cream pie one afternoon a few years back.

Norm Dugas says he considers himself fortunate to have learned the business from a family that puts people first. He adds, "They were just plain good at stealing executives." And every executive ever "stolen" has a story about how it happened. Norm first laid eyes on the Dunfeys in January of 1961. He knows the day and time exactly because it was in the midst of a whiteout blizzard, the kind of storm that just does not happen in Washington, DC, especially not during the President's Inaugural Ball. "It wasn't just any president; it was the Dunfeys' president—John Fitzgerald Kennedy—the first and only Irish Catholic to hold the office."

At the time, Norm was general manager of the Key Bridge Marriott. All eight of my brothers, their wives, and my mother were staying there. In later years, the Kennedys and Dunfeys tempted many New England reporters to draw close parallels between the two families, especially likening Catherine Dunfey to Rose Kennedy.

"Oh, I should never be considered a 'Rose Kennedy,'" my mother would say in all sincerity when our religion, Irish heritage, family size, progressive politics, and business success would garner more headlines. "Rose Kennedy suffered a mother's greatest sorrow—having to bury not only one, but three of her sons. There is no comparison possible."

On the snowy eve of John F. Kennedy's inauguration as president of the United States, no one could have imagined the loss of two more Kennedy sons. It was a new day, a new vision, offering new hope in America, and after an exhaustive and exhausting campaign, the whole New Hampshire delegation was celebrating and staying at the Key Bridge Marriott.

It was Norm who wrestled chains onto the "wagon" and made five white-knuckled trips back and forth from the hotel to the inauguration banquet through almost impassable streets upon which the beleaguered city department of transportation was pouring loam and clay rather than salt or sand. My brothers were so impressed with Norm that they hired him that day. Bob asked him, "Mr. Dugas, would you like to come to Manchester, New Hampshire, and run our Wayfarer?"

Norm said, "You bet!" The rest is best researched in Portland, Maine, which is where Norm actually started out because the brothers had just acquired the Sheraton-Eastland Motor Hotel that year. Norm had a steady hand, which the hotel desperately needed, and during that Inauguration Day blizzard he had already shown that he could survive Maine winters. Indeed, Norm Dugas's hand steadied not only the Portland property but every assignment he received in his career as a Dunfey executive.

Paul Sacco adds his personal follow-up: "The first person I met associated with the Dunfeys was you, Norm. I was just a whippersnapper then and you wanted a salesperson. I got the offer but didn't accept." Now Norm is listening intently. "Yeah," he quips, "You actually wanted money." Undeterred, Paul continues, "But in March of 1972, when the Dunfeys took over the Sheraton Hyannis, which became known as Dunfey's Hyannis, Walter Dunfey was part of the takeover team. He saw me and said, 'We bought this hotel just to get you.' Of course, it wasn't true," Paul says, "but it was a nice thought."

Jim Stamas's saga would match the others. "In 1973, the Dunfeys were going into the expansion model and they started looking around and hiring some of us. I came to the Dunfeys to be in charge of HR functions," says Jim. "Working for them was challenging and fun; also tough in the right ways. They'd say, 'Tell me what you're going to do, and then do it.'" Their philosophy, Jim says, was a simple but profound trilogy: "Each individual property manager's mission is to satisfy the customer, the staff, and the owner." Jim later founded Boston University's School of Hospitality.

Mary Carella had never considered a career of her own. She credits her Dunfey experience with inspiring that ambition and giving her a chance when women were not typically promoted or given positions of responsibility in business. "They never closed a door and…here's the kicker, they let you run with the ball if you said you could, even if you had never done it before. They took a group of very young, mid-management 'kids' and empowered us to be successful…If you worked hard, you would be successful. Period. Man or woman…oh yes, they were way ahead of the curve on that one, too!"

Behind the scenes, my mother cheered on the role that women were increasingly assuming in the business: She commented in an interview: "A former waitress is now manager at the Sheraton-Meadowbrook, and a former hostess is now an area manager. I think women can and should be in the business world." The "area manager" my mother referred to was Evelyn Gillespie, who had started out as hostess, become a Wayfarer table host, moved to a front desk position and on to be named first a manager, then general manager. Evelyn's long, dedicated career was shortened by serious sight issues, but she was a successful and respected Dunfey colleague.

Bud deserved much of the credit for paving the way for women in the company (and in politics). Carella, who went on to found her own marketing firm, considers her own path: "Here it is almost thirty years after my first day of eleven years with Dunfey...Like many others, I went on to be successful. That's not so unusual, except that when I took the job at Dunfey as a secretary, I had no intent to turn it into a career. But I left with one: a young, female vice president."

The pool of good people being cultivated revealed the need and opportunity. Acquisition of new properties throughout New England would offer an expanding talent-pool of new opportunities to build careers in hospitality with the Dunfeys and beyond. Louise Hirshberg earned her degree in retail from Boston's Simmons College, then she moved back to New Hampshire and applied her learning to the Carpenter Hotel in Manchester. She thought the rooms were a bit dog-eared.

"Bring me a proposal," manager Walter Dunfey told her.

Next thing she knew, she had a position as purchaser and interior designer for Dunfey Hotels. "Nice that I was independent. As long as I wasn't losing money, I could do what I wanted. They didn't tell me how to decorate." When Louise took over as manager of the Wayfarer's Goffe's Mill gift shop, she asked her boss, Jim Cote, what was expected of her: "Make me look good!" Jim quipped. Louise succeeded in making her boss, as well as Dunfey properties all over New England, "look good." Her qualifications looked so good that a "headhunter" identified her as an excellent candidate for buyer in the Epcot project. There, Louise turned designers' dreams into reality at Disney World.

Company archives overflow with decades of award ceremony programs highlighting the appreciation for and accomplishment of employees. In a photograph of one such award presentation, managers and Dunfey executives congratulate a long-time dishwasher at one of the hotels. He's accepting a certificate of achievement for having taken advantage of a company scholarship for culinary school. The Dunfey (no-interest) Educational Loan Fund was another initiative meant to encourage aspiring employees to further their education and professional development.

Jack's announcement at the end of the sixties, at an annual meeting at Lamie's, was a significant indicator of the shape and delegation of duties to come: "We continue to place great emphasis on our growing management training program. We have fifty-one new candidates in our eight-month program who will be available for active management roles next June." Just three years earlier, Jack had proudly announced that "sometime soon, the first eight trainees for the brand-new management program will be enrolled."

Bob, (center back) and Jack Dunfey along with managers from left to right: Jim Cote, Norm Dugas, Gene Soles, Paul McGaunn, and Evelyn Gillespie, pore over expansion plans for the Wayfarer Convention Center. 1965

In 1966, NH's first major convention center, designed by award-winning architect, Donald Jasinki, connected the main building to the Brookside Convention Center addition.

Dawn on the Irish Coast*

Ó t'anam an diabhal! But there it is,
The dawn on the hills of Ireland.
God's angels lifting the night's black veil
From the fair, sweet face of our sire-land.
Oh, Ireland, isn't it grand, you look
Like a queen in a rich adornin',
And with all the pent-up love of my heart
I bid you the top of the mornin'!

For thirty summers, a stór mo chroí,
Those hills I now fix my eyes on.
N'er met my vision save when they rose
O'er memory's dim horizon.
Even so, it was grand and fair they seemed
As the landscapes spread before me;
O, Ireland! don't you hear me shout?
I bid you the top of the mornin'!

Now fuller and truer the shoreline shows
Was ever a scene so splendid?
I'd almost venture another voyage,
There is so much joy in returning.
Old scenes, old songs, old friends again,
The vale and cot I was born in.
O, Ireland! don't you hear me shout?
I bid you the top of the mornin'!

*"This song describes an Irish emigrant's feelings on returning to his native home. It was written in 1877 by John Locke (1847–1889), a Fenian activist, exiled to the United States. He entitled it 'Dawn on the Irish Coast' but it is also known as 'The Exiles Return', 'Morning on the Irish Coast' and 'The Emigrants' Anthem'. It was inspired by a friend's account of a brief return visit to Ireland."

—*The Jim Carroll and Pat Mackenzie Collection, County Clare, 2015*

When my sister, Kay recited the above poem from memory, our Irish cousins joined in; they had memorized it in school.

CHAPTER 25

The Isle of Ireland

"O, Ireland, up from my heart of hearts, I bid you the top of the mornin'!"

From Boston back to Ballyferriter

When I was eighteen, my mother and I traveled on board the Dutch SS Nieuw Amersterdam ocean liner to visit my grandmother's birthplace, Ballyferriter, Dingle, County Kerry, Ireland. Such a voyage was so unusual in 1957 that twenty-seven relatives and friends waved us off as we left Boston Harbor. We were the first in our family to return to the "old country," and we did so thanks to correspondence that kept relatives connected through years of separation. Those exchanges dated back to 1901, in the aftermath of my grandfather's burial at sea. My young uncle, Jack, traveling with his father, arrived alone in Cork Harbor and was met by cousins who would care for him. The missives exchanged between Ballyferriter and relatives in Boston/Lowell were filled with sadness, combined with pleas that the cousins send Jack back to his mother and family in America.

More optimistic letters filled the years between the early 1900s and 1957. These led to my mother's and my visit. We arrived in the late summer's chill and a very early morning's darkness to find a blaze of light shining on a collection of rosy-cheeked faces smiling expectantly through the fence. We knew this cluster of cheerful, post-midnight souls had to be related to us. Sure enough, a chorus of lilting Irish brogues rang out from behind the fence: "Is that yourself, Catherine? Is it yourself, Eleanor? Ah! Glory be, 'tis, 'tis!!" Correspondence took on greater significance and increased frequency after that visit.

A decade later, in 1968, my brothers were sensitive to the fact that our mother was in her mid-seventies (considered "old" in that era), and they wanted to take her back to Ballyferriter. They felt that this first trip for all twelve, would be the highlight of my mother's life. Unfortunately, the timing was just before convent rules changed to allow nuns to travel with their families, so my mother, brothers, and four teenage grandsons (!) replacing the four sisters, made the trip that turned out to be a turning point in our family's ties with the Isle of Ireland.

When the Dunfeys rolled into the tiny hamlet of Ballyferriter, their arrival was greatly anticipated. One of our cousins, then ten years old, recalled, recently, what it was like waiting with the "whole village. It was as exciting an event to us," she said, "as was the 'Star Wars' crew's arrival to film 'The Last Jedi' this year (2016)!" That first of many family trips to the Dingle Peninsula—and more specifically to Ballyferriter, Ventry, Bailagisha, Dunquin, and the Blasket Islands—awakened our deep Irish roots. It expanded our aspirations to reach beyond borders, not only of our New England business and the States, but within Ireland itself.

From Ballyferriter to Belfast

The "Troubles" in Northern Ireland burst into the headlines on January 30, 1972. That day would become known as "Bloody Sunday." In the Bogside area of Derry, Northern Ireland, British soldiers shot twenty-eight unarmed civilians during a protest march against internment. Thirteen young men between the ages of seventeen and forty-one died immediately; another boy died four months later. The news shocked the world. My brother Walter, along with our cousin, Jim Keefe; Vin Dunn, a lawyer; and businessman Leo Kanteres, realtor and honorary Irishman for the duration, traveled to England where they sought out Bernadette Devlin, "a fiery young member of British Parliament from Ulster [the name of the six counties that comprise Northern Ireland]." Bernadette spent an hour with the four businessmen, thanked them for their concern, and told them to "be sure to contact John Hume, a Catholic member in the Stormont [Ulster]."*

In Belfast, the four did just that. They met at length with John, the beginning of a lasting bond with John and Pat Hume that would shape our family's relationship with Northern Ireland. John expressed his conviction that if there was to be peace in Northern Ireland, the United States had to play a major role "because there is no one else." He was convinced that leaders like Tip O'Neil and Ted Kennedy needed to raise public awareness of the "Troubles." Walter promised to contact both, and he did so. However, Senator Kennedy's first attempt, a phone call to reach Hume, was ill-timed. Kennedy perhaps forgot the five-hour time difference that meant 9:00 p.m. in Washington, DC was 2:00 a.m. in Derry. John added that the regular rash of threatening late-night calls didn't help his mood either. "Hello! This is Ted Kennedy—" the voice said when John answered.

"Ya—and I'm J__ C__." Hume hung up on the senator. Kennedy asserted his identity again in a second call, in more exasperated tone,

* Forty-five years later, Bernadette Devlin joined the 2017 Global Citizens Circle to South Africa as a mentor to the Social Change Initiative fellows from Belfast, Northern Ireland.

according to Hume, who admitted it took a third try to convince him that United States Senator Ted Kennedy was, indeed, on the other end of the line. The relationship that grew over the following years proved crucial for Northern Ireland's peace prospects.

Joe McQuaid—assigned by his father and boss, B.J. McQuaid, to one of his first interviews for the *New Hampshire Sunday News*—sat with Walter and reported that the businessmen's goal of the trip was "more than just meetings with people whose names had become familiar to a world watching in horror at the bloodshed. Walter and his companions went to listen." They returned to the States having heard what they should do:

> 1) Don't be like some Americans who have come, made promises to us, and then have "never been heard from again." They cried, "Our children are being gassed every day after school…"
>
> 2) Tell Tip O'Neill and Ted Kennedy that if Americans really want to make a difference, they need to connect and work with John Hume, the young community activist and moderate leader from Derry.

Fast forward to a November 2017 *Guardian* op-ed by Seamus Mallon, deputy minister of the non-violent political Social Democrat Labor Party (SDLP) founded by Hume. Mallon opines:

> The Hume/Kennedy axis and an Irish government committed to peace and justice was a powerful team. Skilled practitioners of the art of politics can clearly define their objectives and remain aloof from all distractions that would essentially weaken their resolve.

President Clinton has called John Hume "The Irish conflict's Martin Luther King." My brother, Jerry, had brought Hume's name and work to the attention of Coretta Scott King, and in 1999, Hume would receive the Martin Luther King Award. That award, John said, was even more meaningful and personal than the prestigious Nobel Peace Prize he received along with Ulster Unionist Party leader, David Trimble in 1994. The staying power of John Hume's singular, concise purpose, merits our attention and remains relevant in pursuing conflict resolution. He would call it principled compromise:

> To bring about a solution where Irish people of different traditions can build institutions of government to provide for lasting peace and stability on this island, and for new harmonious relations with Britain itself.

Staying at it…

After returning from Northern Ireland, Walter's natural next step was to update all of us and begin what would be the long road partnering in peace efforts. We were now reconnected with our Irish relatives in Ballyferriter, Dingle. The family realized that we could not celebrate our Irish connection merely with songs and toasts. The economic hardship of those who shared our precious heritage was intertwined with and affected by the "Troubles" in the north of Ireland. As long as the people there suffered, the Isle of Ireland could not prosper as it should.

Bob, in particular, had found his life's mission among the rubble of age-old monastic structures in Ballyferriter/Co. Kerry, where he saw and felt the effects of the struggle in Belfast through the eyes of the family's close cousin, Celia, born and raised in that city. She had come to Ballyferriter in 1952 as the bride of a Kerryman and schoolmaster, my mother's first cousin Doncha (Denis) O'Conchuir.

My brother Bob was so drawn to those deep family roots on the Dingle Peninsula that he built a home within view of my grandparents' birthplace, Bailagisha, so that my mother would be able to welcome Irish relatives as "neighbors" rather than merely be a visitor in their homes. Our cousin, Donchà (Denis), helped choose its Irish name, Feorann, which means "edge of a verdant bank on a mountainside, a sandy level on the edge of the sea." Each summer Bob invited my sister Mary, who had left the convent in 1976, to look after Feorann and welcome family, friends, and (thanks to Bob's generous spirit) many friends of friends. No one was better suited to welcome anyone and everyone. My sister Kay said of her younger sister: "Her intense interest powered almost every first encounter into sincere friendship." Mary made her mark along the narrow strip of road leading to the village, walking—or more accurately, sauntering—the way our father had sauntered along the boulevard at Hampton Beach each summer's night, stopping to chat and making a half-hour's stroll into a two-hour excursion. Her love of storytelling, singing, and colorful jokes made her a favorite patron in the pubs, especially with Paudy O'Se (Paudy O'Shea), a Kerry football star whose establishment was a center of Ventry sports and social life on the Dingle peninsula. Mary was so known and loved in that corner of Ireland that if a Dunfey visited before summer, someone would invariably inquire: "… and when is Mary comin' home?"

The Dunfey family story is replete with tales of strengthening bonds from Ballyferriter to Belfast over forty years. Peace activists in the North including Martin O'Brien, May Blood, and Jackie Redpath, made certain that we met and included a broad range of community activists from all sides of the peace process. In 2000, the family was recognized for reconciliation efforts on all sides of the conflict. Jackie Redpath spoke for the communities:

> We wish today to honour a particular clan, a particular family. Their forbears left Southwest Ireland in the nineteenth century from the hamlet of Ballyferriter in Dingle, County Kerry. Their children rediscovered their roots and from the late '60s have re-engaged with the island of their origins.
>
> They introduced us to Irish America with an impeccable sense of balance, a willingness to take risks, always pushing at the edges, but never losing their sense of fun.
>
> We looked for something to sum up their achievements in Northern Ireland. It was quoted at Robert Kennedy's funeral, which we know will have a particular meaning for the family: "A man (or a family) does not show his greatness by being at one extremity but rather by touching both at once [Pascal]."

The award was a specially commissioned globe in Waterford Crystal, which is on display in the Ballyferriter Heritage Centre (The creation of such centres throughout Ireland was an initiative of the American Ireland Fund's mission to advance peace, culture, charity on the Isle of Ireland). The centre in this village was originally the schoolhouse both my maternal grandparents attended. The museum was dedicated to my mother in 1985.

The Dunfey family receiving recognition by the communities of Belfast for their contribution to peace. Left to right: Ian Jamieson, Great Shankill Partnership; Angila Chada, Springboard Opportunities; Joe Stewart, Greater Shankill Development; my brother, Jack; Baroness May Blood, Greater Shankill Partnership; Martin O'Brien, Committee on the Administration of Justice; my brother, Bob; (front row kneeling) Jackie Redpath, chief executive, Greater Shankill Partnership. Belfast 2000

Coming home…

> *There are many Kerry men who say there are only two real*
>   *Kingdoms—*
> *The Kingdom of God, and the Kingdom of Kerry.*
> *The Kingdom of Kerry contains Killarney of the lakes, Tralee of*
>   *the Roses, and Listowel of the writers.*
> *The County is distinguished by a gossamer-like lunacy which is*
>   *addictive but not damaging.*
> > *—John B. Keane poet, playwright, pub owner*

True to their word, our Irish relatives would be with the family of Dunfeys when death claimed several of my brothers and sisters, beginning with Mary, in 1989. "Bring them home to us. We'll look after them." And we did, laying Mary and soon after, Walter; our nephew, Philip; and, in 2016, Bob. They are at rest in the Kingdom of God—and Kerry. The ancestors my siblings are laid to rest with did not know the Ireland we in later generations have come to cherish. Those who went before us had inherited the deleterious effects of Penal Codes, extreme poverty, and the Great Hunger of 1845–1850, when Ireland's population declined in the millions due to deaths from starvation and disease, coupled with mass emigration to North America and England. A Quaker's handwritten account describes the "deplorably destitute" victims they discovered when bringing food to the Dingle Peninsula: "There were daily scenes of accumulated wretchedness."

Now, a new generation of the family visiting their Irish cousins sing in local pubs and saunter along well-worn paths; they bike (at their own risk!) and hike along the ridges of the Three Sisters' graceful sweep of peaks that lead all the way to Sibyl Head, turned "Star Wars" site where crews filmed scenes for "The Last Jedi." The cousins even survive riding backwards in rental cars, nose-to-nose with tour buses in the frequent "traffic jams" on the Conor Pass, more accurately called "no Pass," as whoever is unlucky enough to be in the smaller vehicle, has to roll it backwards to the lookout, to allow the larger vehicle—often a tour bus—to pass where the road widens at a spectacular scenic look-out rest area.

Reunion

In 2010, our O'Connor cousins welcomed a hundred descendants of the O'Connor clan to Ballyferriter for a first-ever reunion. A number of Dunfeys, including my husband, Jim and me, joined with scores of relatives, most of whom we had never met. During the four days of celebration, we took advantage of a sunny June morning to visit the Great Blasket Islands, a short boat trip out of nearby Dunquin Harbor. That crossing was uneventful—far different from earlier ones we had made when the boat was tossed around like a child's toy in the waves. On those trips, I had wondered if we would see our ancestors in the great beyond before stepping on the Blaskets. I understood then why the islands had been permanently evacuated in 1953.

We had no such concern on this brilliant June morning. Some thirty tourists scattered along the paths and into cottages whose walls echoed with oral accounts of literary treasures like Mauris O'Sùlleabhàin's *Twenty Years a'Growing* and Peig Sayers's stories. All of these treasures and more have been devotedly preserved in Dunquin's stunning Great Blasket Island Museum, whose towering floor-to-ceiling window keeps watch over that jewel of nature. (And yes! An O'Connor cousin was involved with building and overseeing that landmark; and another cousin, at the helm of his boat, ferried us to the Great Blaskets that morning.) I made room next to me for an elderly gentleman, dressed in his Sunday best—suit, tie, and cap, with shoes that evidenced many paths traveled. My genial seat partner offered a gracious hello and shared that, since the age of four, this had been his annual pilgrimage from England, adding that he considered these summers his "coming home."

We disembarked, a euphemism for leaping onto a loosely-anchored, floating ramp. The slightly bent gentleman beside me had no trouble. The ramp, appeared to recognize that footstep and stood at attention, its annual duty to welcome the wayfarer home. He tipped his cap and thanked me for having made room for him to sit on the narrow slip of the boat bench. Then he disappeared up the wide, grassy slope with a pace that was impressive considering the sturdy suitcase and the eighty-two-years he was bearing. The encounter had left me as curious about this man as I was about the views beyond the curve.

In her memoir, *The House on the Hillside*, Felicity Hayes McCoy describes the scene that awaits those who travel to Great Blasket Island:

> When you reach the island you…climb a high, grassy road that leads to an abandoned village. The half-ruined houses, built of field-stones, cluster together against the Atlantic wind. Some are built so closely against the hillside that their roofs are on a level with the stony green fields.

Jim and I circled around the ribbon of pebbled paths to one of those inviting stone cottages tucked into the craggy hillside. Swaying on a clothesline like flags in a light breeze were original hand woven wraps, bonnets, mittens, and scarves, a sure sign the weaver knew well the fickle extremes of weather on this westernmost coast of Ireland, which people call the "last stop before Boston."

The cottage with its freshly painted, bright blue door and window frames appears from the lower lanes the size of and scene on a commemorative stamp. I noticed the same gentleman, now comfortably situated in a more suitable chair, next to the artisan and her clothesline of wares for sale. They were speaking with two women, apparently seasoned hikers whose layers of clothing and boots were designed for whatever the weather might dispense.

Looking to satisfy my curiosity, I inched my way into polite hearing distance with Jim at my side. The gentleman was responding to some conversational thread about the urge to return to one's homeland. We'd learn later that the women, who lived in Australia, had spent years planning this return home to Ireland. The gentleman continued: "I have an unusual story about coming home to Ireland."

He then shared that, some twenty years earlier, on his annual trip to the Blaskets from England, he had made his customary visit to St. Vincent Church in Ballyferriter. It was a weekday morning, so he was surprised at the number of people gathered inside. There were local folks for sure, but there, in the first several rows, were at least fifteen businessmen. He inquired about them and was told that they had come "all the way from America" to attend this memorial for their friend whose family roots are Ballyferriter. "To think they came all this way to bring their friend home! I've never forgotten it."

I stood in stunned silence, recognizing that this gentleman had just described my brother Walter's memorial service, held exactly twenty years earlier. Walter's request was being honored. Close to twenty-five friends and family, along with many Irish cousins had, indeed, fulfilled his wish to "come home." The gentleman, I later discovered, was the highly respected Great Blasket writer, Ray Stegels, author of *Next Parish America*. He was more stunned than I when I told him the rest of that story.

President Eamon deValera welcomes the Dunfey family to Ireland. The clan celebrated Catherine Dunfey's birth-day in Dublin with a host of Irish cousins and more than 20 young bagpip-ers (middle photo) with their rousing welcome *in* the main lobby of the Gresham Hotel. 1968

FALL 1968

THE WAYFARERS CLUB

Private Line

PUBLISHED EXCLUSIVELY FOR MEMBERS OF THE WAYFARERS CLUB BY *The Dunfey Family*
Editor: Norm Dugas, The Wayfarers Club — Hotels and Motor Inns of New England
Hampton, N. H. 03842

DUNFEYS VISIT WITH PRESIDENT DEVALERA IN IRELAND

Eamon deValera

Dunfey Clan — left to right, first row — Richard, Jack, Mrs. Catherine, President DeValera, Jerry, Bob and Walt. Next row — Paul, Roy, Ricky and somewhere in the next row — Bob, Jr., and David.

Over one hundred and fifty relatives, new and old friends, gathered at the famous Gresham Hotel in Dublin, Ireland, for a gala birthday party in honor of Mrs. Catherine Dunfey's 74th birthday on Wednesday, August 14, 1968. The birthday party was one of the many highlights of the ten-day trip to Ireland by the Dunfey Family. When they arrived in Dublin, (Continued p. 5)

Mrs. Dunfey and a few of the 35 boys of the Crumlins Boys Pipe Band from Dublin, Ireland who will be on tour in the U. S. during the Holidays and will appear at the Sheraton-Eastland, Portland.

Harvest Hospitality

It's harvest time and, once again, the Dunfey Family (Hotels and Motor Inns) extend our warmest welcome and offer the best of the season to our traveling Wayfarers.

From Portland, Maine to Hartford, Connecticut, each of the Hotels and Motor Inns is putting forth a special effort to make your stay with us more enjoyable. Don't be surprised at check-in if you're offered to "help yourself" to a bright red Macintosh apple displayed in an antique cart in Sheraton-Yankee Drummer, Auburn or drawn a glass of fresh, tart cider from a keg in the lobby of the Sheraton-Lexington, or offered a complimentary cigar during your stay at Sheraton-Tobacco Valley, Windsor.

Make it a point to join the other Wayfarers at your table in the Tavern Dining Room and ask your hostess about our Special Harvest Cocktail and enjoy a hearty Harvest Dinner prepared especially for our Wayfarers Club members (with our compliments!)

Come and join with us in this traditional season of hospitality.

Four NH Businessmen Meet Top Ulster Leaders

THE NEW HAMPSHIRE SUNDAY NEWS, MANCHESTER (N. H.) — Sunday, February 27, 1972

LOOKING like an Irish pub proprietor himself, Manchester businessman Walter Dunfey reviews notes taken on his trip to England and Ireland last week.

By JOE McQUAID

Four New Hampshire businessmen, three of them Irish-Americans, flew to England and Ireland last week with hopes of meeting some of the principals involved in the continuing strife in Northern Ireland.

By the time they left Dublin's Shannon International Airport last Monday, they had met with Bernadette Devlin, toured the embattled Bogside section of Londonderry, chatted with Republic of Ireland President Eamon DeValera, and had an impromptu meeting with IRA leader Joe Cahill.

THE LUCK OF the Irish must have been on the side of Dunfey, James Keefe and Leo Kanteres (an honorary Irishman for the trip) from Manchester and Atty. Vincent Dunn of Concord.

In a five-day trip they were able to see and do what would ordinarily require several weeks or perhaps months' time.

The goal of the trip, however, was more than just meetings with people whose names have become familiar to a world watching in horror the bloodshed that besets Northern Ireland.

For Dunfey and the others the determination was to "see what we, as Irish Americans, can and should do to help."

THE ANSWER to that query came rapidly and, Dunfey said, was repeated time and again "by just about everyone we talked to."

"They told us to try and get a fair press for them," Dunfey recalled. "They said Britain controls the world press and only their propaganda gets out."

Dunfey said the New York Times, for instance, has been covering the Northern Ireland situation from its London bureau.

THE CHIEF RESULT of their trip, according to Dunfey, was a determination to form a New England group of concerned Americans to help the Irish. While Dunfey said "the least difficult thing for the IRA to get now is

THE MEETING at Shannon Airport with Cahill, the wanted man perhaps most feared and hated by the British and Ulster Protestants, was the frosting on the cake for at least one of the group.

"I nearly dropped my teeth when I saw him," Walter Dunfey told the Sunday News this weekend.

Dunfey, vice president of the Dunfey Family chain of New England hotels, was the leader of the New Hampshire group, if only for his many close relatives in Ireland.

money," he and the others did not discount a drive for contributions here.

Dunfey said he will be working with the American Committee for Ulster Justice, a New York based group of Irish-American Catholics. But he also said the Irish the group met had unkind words for such American groups.

"THEY TOLD US the others had come and made promises and then left Ireland and were never heard from again," Dunfey said.

The trip itself sounds more like a fairy tale than fact, Dunfey admits. Arriving in London on a Thursday, the group sought out Bernadette Devlin, the fiery, Marxist-leaning member of British Parliament from Ulster.

After several hours delay, Dunfey and the others went to Parliament. While waiting for Miss Devlin, they caught sight of the Rev. Ian Paisley, a right-wing Protestant involved in the Ulster turmoil.

The New Hampshire group had an hour's talk with Miss Devlin, who thanked them for their concern and told them to contact John Hume, a Catholic M.P. in the Stormont (Ulster Parliament).

THE GROUP flew to Dublin Saturday, had a three hour "bull session" with relatives and political reporters, and then drove to "Derry" as Catholics call the predominantly Roman Catholic Northern Ireland City.

Dunfey said his relatives "said three masses for us in Dublin on Sunday. They were scared for us."

In Londonderry, the group met with Hume whom Dunfey described as a "real moderate, everyone says that."

Hume wanted the group to meet with the families of the 13 people killed during the now infamous "Bloody Sunday" demonstration a month ago.

"Hume said just talking with us would give these families a real lift," Dunfey recalled. "But British troops were outside and we certainly didn't want to start an incident. Hume understood."

Dunfey and the others were told to "stick around for the 3:30 'matinee.'" At that time, young children in the Bogside go near the barricades the Catholics have erected to protect themselves by the numerous British troop searches.

"THE KIDS, and they are just little kids," Dunfey explained, "toss stones over the barricades. There's nobody on the other side. It's still the Catholic neighborhood. Anyway, at 3:30 in come the British troops. They lobbed gas, tear gas and nausea gas, over the barricades."

The New Hampshire group "got a taste" of the gas, being only 100 yards from the barricade. Dunfey said the people of the Bogside walk around with handkerchiefs over their mouths.

"It happens every day at 3:30 and 7:30 p.m.," Dunfey said. "One woman stood in front of a building, right where the people were murdered on Bloody Sunday, and said 'get them to stop gassing our children. They gas them twice a day.'"

Dunfey was able only to talk on the telephone with Republic of Ireland President DeValera because the group was leaving Monday noon for Boston.

"He also thanked us for coming," Dunfey said.

AT THE AIRPORT, the group met Cahill, who stepped out of the airport crowd and told them of his appreciation for their coming.

Cahill has a price on his head and it may have been that luck of the Irish that kept Dunfey and the others from the middle of another incident.

Last week, southern Ireland began a crackdown on IRA leaders. One of those arrested was a prime link between the IRA and their American supporters.

It was quite a trip.

Northern Ireland

Recipients of the
Global Citizens Award,
Community leaders,
(now Baroness) May
Blood, the Shankill;
Liz Groves, the Falls
Road, inspired cross-
community and other
participants, including
Martin McGuinness.
Boston. 1997

Marjorie "Mo" Mowlam, with Colm O'Comarum, Irish Institute, Boston College;
Deidre O'Dwyer, student editor, The Harvard Crimson; at a 1999 Circle, "Northern
Ireland: Next Steps" moderated by Kathleen Townsend Kennedy. Mowlam,
member of English Labour Party politician, served as secretary of state for Northern
Ireland when Good Friday Agreement was reached. She took a particular political
risk by going inside the Maze Prison when it became clear that the peace process
would only succeed with the backing of the prisoners. Mo Mowlam's signature was
her style as well as substance. Mowlam was the hyperbolic manifestation of New
Labour's "popular touch" says Maria Dalton in "The Toss of a Wig and the Belfast
Agreement." *The Irish Times.* April 5, 2018.

Senator George Mitchell was first introduced to the Isle of Ireland at my brother, Bob Dunfey's family home, Feorann, in Ballyferriter. When the Senator was appointed as Chair of the Northern Ireland Peace Talks, Bob introduced him to the Protestant and Catholic community activists, many whom we had been working with since 1972. Left to right: Bronagh Hinds, Ulster Peoples College; Inez McCormack, UNISON Northern Ireland; Liz Groves, Falls Community Council; Baroness May Blood, Great Shankill Partnership; Monica Mc Williams, co-founder Women's Coalition; my brother, Bob, founder of GCC; Senator George Mitchell; Alan McBride, WAVE Trauma Centre; Caroline Wilson, National Union of Students; Sandra Peake, WAVE Trauma Centre; Joe Stewart, Greater Shankill Development Agency. Washington, D.C. 2000

Ulster Democratic Party and Progressive Unionist Party leaders: Left to right are David Ervine, Billy Hutchinson, David Adams, Gusty Spence, Joe English and Gary McMichael, Circle discussion leaders, "Principled Compromise not Compromised Principles" 1994.

Sinn Fein leader, Gerry Adams and James Carroll, syndicated columnist, author, and frequent GCC moderator, discuss former IRA members working for peace. The Boston Circle was held following President Clinton's granting a visa to Adams who has renounced violence and declared the "drive for peace is now a 'central part' of Sinn Fein's existence. 1994

Self-confessed former IRA commander whose embrace of peace led to his appointment as Sinn Fein's chief negotiator in the talks which led to the Good Friday Agreement. McGuinness transitioned to politics and served as deputy first minister for ten years. My brother, Jerry, and I, pictured with Martin at a GCC program, *The Irish Peace Process*, moderated by Kevin Cullen, *Boston Globe* columnist. 1995

Martin O'Brien, Northern Ireland, social justice advocate and peace activist, honored at Notre Dame College. Left to right: Jeanette and Bob Dunfey, Martin, Eleanor and Jim Freiburger

Ballyferriter, Dingle, County Kerry

Doncha O'Conchuir (Denis O'Connor), preserver of archeological treasures on the Dingle Peninsula, advocate of Irish language learning, longtime Ballyferriter school master, and first cousin of my mother, Catherine Dunfey. Doncha personified one of his favorite reflections that "heritage is the sum of our resources for living." We Dunfeys, and countless others, have been enriched by his life and work.

My son, Joel, with Doncha, pausing to relflect on the bench built in memory of our ancestors, our siblings and nephew, and the many others who found their way "home" from down the lane in Bailagisha or from distant lands.

1985   2016   2016

In 1985, Bob and Walter Dunfey participate in the dedication of the Ballyferriter Heritage Museum in honor of our mother, Catherine Dunfey. Thirty years later, in 2016, Sophia and Emily Freiburger, and Simon, Willem, and Jackson Eisl pose in that same place in honor of my mother and their great grandmother. The building was originally the schoolhouse both my maternal grandparents (O'Connor and Manning) attended. My mother's first cousin, Doncha (Denis) O'Connor was school master for years.

No trip to Ireland is complete without a visit to cousin, Lìle's, cozy cottage tucked in a hillside over Dunquin Harbor—especially as a wild Irish rain waters her garden. The Irish describe it thus: "Ah, now; there's a mist about!" Left to right in each other's warmth near the turf fire—are cousin, Lìle O'Connor; my oldest granddaughter, Sophia Kay Freiburger, and me.

Our grandsons, Jackson, Willem, and Simon Eisl spending time with Celia, Doncha's wife, in the O'Connor family Ballyferriter homestead where her son, Aodán, family photographer and archivist, cares for his mother. 2016

In a favorite Dingle pub known for real Irish music, Fergus O'Flaherty, master of many instruments and gifted tenor, hushes the room with his rendition of the "Town I Loved So Well." Our cousin, Líle, has played her concertina there since she was fourteen years old. Around the table, our family adds our own Slàinte. 2016

The goal was to hike to Sibyl Head, scene of Star Wars filming of the Last of the Jedi in 2016, by way of the Three Sisters on the Dingle Peninsula. Our grandchildren and their parents celebrate at the site with their seasoned guides, cousins Máire and Josie. All were looking for "Luke," but the only one to greet them was a self-appointed, genial "Irish security officer."

Feorann
with apologies to Mauris O'Sulleabhàin's
"Twenty Years a' Growing"

These twenty years a'growing
a verdant bank by the edge of the sea
a homestead not of brick
but of the heart, for everyone to
take away and cherish forever.

These twenty years a'giving
by one who measures happiness
through what he shares, not what he gains,
the one who made our heritage come alive
brother to all—Bob.

These twenty years a'knowing
walking, biking, meeting, greeting
seeing the twinkle in an eye,
the raising of a glass—sláinte!
the lilt of a song—roots.

These twenty years—growing, giving, knowing—
Go raibhmaithagat (thank you).

for Bob
by Eleanor, 2002

CHAPTER 26

NOVEMBER 1968

All the Way to Boston...
All the Way to the Parker House

"...heaven by hotel standards..."
—*Mark Twain, Parker House resident, 1877*

In the years we were securing our roots on the Isle of Ireland, my brothers were also continuing their journey in the hotel universe, looking to buy the country's oldest continuously operating hotel. It had traditions spanning more than a century, and it was located in heart of the city where America was born. But in 1968, like so many other crumbling traditions, Boston's Parker House was dying. Fiscally malnourished for decades, it had lost hundreds of thousands of dollars for six straight years. The Grande Dame of New England hostelries appeared tattered, torn, and depressing. The talk in Boston was not about her future, but about when the Parker House would be demolished to make room for a new office building in the prime business district across from City Hall.

That talk stopped in November, 1968. There had been rumors the Dunfeys were buying the hotel and would spend millions to restore lost glories and add new ones. By early December, a formal announcement confirmed the rumors. My brother, Jack, the forty-four-year-old president of the Dunfey Family Corporation, told the Boston Globe: "We are now the owners of the Parker House...We will never tear it down or tamper with any of the traditions that made the hotel famous." The announcement conveyed a seamless transition. But it actually wasn't. The deal was almost dead before it saw daylight.

The real story

"Harvey Parker had come down from Maine in the mid-1800s with a few dollars in his pocket," my brother Jerry muses, "and eventually established the historic Parker House." The Dunfey brothers came down from Maine, New Hampshire, and Vermont in December of 1969 with a mixed bag of Dunfey Quality Court motels—the Eastland and Carpenter Hotels, the Wayfarers Club, the Sheraton franchises; a growing reputation for reviving dying hotel/motel properties; a flare for creative additions such as Dunfey Mini-Vacations and Cracker Barrel Lounges; and an assortment of billboards around New England with their "Come-As-You-Are" messaging.

Though it was only fifty miles away, the Parker House was a world away from a fried clam stand—the Dunfey's first profit-making venture on Hampton Beach, New Hampshire, twenty-two years earlier. Gary Hirshberg, a teenager in 1968 and a close family friend, had seen the Dunfeys work incredibly hard for years. "They were always on. A hotel means 24/7. Then, they just inhaled and bought this gigantic property. To us, the Parker House had mystique." When Gary later decided to start Stonyfield Farm Yogurt, he turned to Walter for advice: "Walter had probably never even eaten a cup of yogurt in his life. But he was astute. 'This is going to be incredibly hard work. Are you ready for that?' I knew we were because I had seen it. I'd absorbed it. I got that from watching them, especially with the Parker House."

This latest venture was certainly not based on the current profit margin. My brothers could not afford to exhale. At that time, the Parker House was in the estate of the Sherrard family, a well-known New England hotel name. However, they were in tough shape. "They hadn't made payroll in three weeks," says Jack. "Suppliers hadn't been paid. When we bought the hotel, we agreed to take on the debts as well. We had to do it fast. But two days before closing, First National Bank of Boston backed out."

My brothers were in an impossibly tight spot. Simply put, they needed the dough. A decade earlier, they had finalized the purchase of their first hotel, The Carpenter, in Manchester, New Hampshire, which was also in bankruptcy. After that purchase was finalized, Walter had raised the toast: "Now what do we do?" Jack and Bob could hear the echo of that question/exclamation once again as they looked for a way out of what seemed like another "no way."

One idea: They knew, respected and had worked with Wallace "Wally" Hazelton, President and CEO of Depositors Trust Corporation (Casco Bank), Maine's largest bank. Bob suggested calling Wally. Jack was dubious, but Bob was determined: "We called the bank out of desperation the day before the scheduled closing," Jack says. "The only reason Wally was still there after five o'clock on a Friday was that he had called a board of directors meeting." Wally heard Bob out and said he'd call back after he discussed the situation with the directors.

"Bob and I sat staring at the phone for what seemed like an eternity," Jack recalls. "I became more and more incredulous by the moment, with Bob, more tenacious, never once wavering." And Bob was right. "We were lucky. Wally was a real spitfire and believed in us. The next morning, he chartered a plane, flew down Francis Finnegan, his VP, who handed us a check for half-a-million dollars. An additional 2.5 [million] was promised if we could make the deal before the end of the year."

With Bob's characteristic behind-the-scenes grit, he and Jack made the deal, enough to pay vendors and back salaries in time for Christmas. After the Parker House takeover, Bob and Jack negotiated with every one of the vendors, from oil sellers to grocery suppliers: "We had forty attorneys in one room at a long conference table," says Jack. "We made a deal that they would take fifty cents on the dollar for all debts owed."

Jerry had stopped by the Parker House Revere Room for breakfast on what could have been that fateful Friday. Employees were on duty as usual even though they hadn't seen a paycheck for three weeks. A seasoned waiter greeted his early morning customer and was noticeably surprised to hear Jerry say, "Things are looking tough now—I hear." Gathering up his pride and professionalism—all that sustained him as he headed into the Christmas season without his pay—he replied, "Yes, sir. That's right. But there's a new day coming, I'm sure of it. There'll be a new day."

News of the Dunfey family's purchase of the Parker House traveled much more quickly and satisfyingly than room service orders the following day. Jerry returned for breakfast on Sunday morning and was greeted by the same waiter who, this morning, was hardly able to contain his joy within his crisp uniform: "Oh, sir," he managed: "I didn't know who you were yesterday morning. I had no idea."

Jerry's firm handshake, broad grin and characteristic "How're ya hittin' em?" greeting with a slap on the back, conveyed Jerry's own emotion:

"Well, you did say that there was 'a new day coming' didn't you?"

"Yes, sir, I did, but honestly, I never believed it could really happen."

The brothers appeared to believe in their ability to resurrect the historic landmark into the gem Mark Twain had described while a resident at the Parker House almost a hundred years earlier in 1877:

> With a local newspaper in hand and puffing on a large cigar, he
> observed to a reporter: "You see for yourself that I'm pretty near
> heaven—not theologically, of course, but by the hotel standard."
> —*Susan Wilson, Heaven by Hotel Standards*

To celebrate what every one wanted to believe was the hotel's "new day," the Dunfey family invited all employees and their families to a holiday party in the Parker House ballroom. My mother enjoyed giving each employee's child a present; each family also received a turkey for the Christmas holidays. She welcomed all the families to the famed four-teenth-floor rooftop ballroom—until then off limits to employees unless they were working a function there. A new era had indeed begun at the Parker House.

Some things would stay the same, though. The famous Parker House rolls would continue to accompany every entrée. Even that item had its legendary history: It is said to have originated almost 130 years earlier when a young pastry chef flew into a fit of rage while making dinner rolls when he supposedly heard that his sweetheart, a maid in the hotel, had been accused of stealing a dowager's necklace. Angrily, he hurled several fists full of risen dough into the oven where they baked, crisp outside and soft inside, in the folded shape pressed tight by his clenched fist. When the Dunfeys took over the hotel, my mother, without the benefit of the recipe or a good throwing arm, told folks it would be her job to make the rolls every morning.

The Parker House takeover was a leap like no other for the Dunfey Family Corporation. It raised expectations exponentially: How could a family with just ten years experience in the hotel business—in the sparsely populated northern New England states—make it in Boston? Well, for one thing, the Dunfey family and their talented executive team did not con-sider "hospitality" an industry. Hospitality translated to people—custom-ers, employees, owners—and it was people who had informed the Dunfey business philosophy from the get-go.

Bud expressed it this way: "Every winter morning a couple of us had gotten up in the dark and walked the two miles to the store with our dad… We learned a lot in that store, but most of all we learned how to meet peo-ple. It was a natural part of our growing up. What better training could hotel people have?" One commentator described the trajectory this way: "The Dunfeys' path to Parker House began when the twelve started to work, which was soon after each learned to walk!" All of us remember our dad's daily wake-up call at 5:30 a.m. "Get up! You're missing the best part of the day!" He could put a positive spin on a bleak morning; his ease with humor and song was contagious and helped make hard work the butt of jokes, rather than a reason to quit.

Before the ink was dry on the Parker House purchase agreement, Fred Jervis once again assumed a critical role focused on personnel. Integral to its turnaround and in order to get the full sense of that historic landmark, Fred met not only management, but listened to and spoke one-on-one with doormen, bellmen, chefs, front desk staff, dishwashers, and housekeepers, recognizing their critical importance to the heart of the operation. Fred was not about "focus groups." He was about focused, personal interaction, giving employees a hearing and a voice. He then did what Fred did best: he worked with each level of management to translate what he had heard into sensible, viable action plans.

Our oldest brother, Roy, had inherited a large dose of our father's zest for living—what one Boston ad describes as a "tourist's zeal" for the city. He was retiring from the Mosler Safe Company in Hamilton, Ohio, at a time when the family needed another diplomat in addition to Bud, the practiced negotiator. An incurable optimist in all seasons, Roy would advance the ambitious plans to assure Dunfey Hotels became a stand-out operation. Paul Sacco says that Roy joined the band of brothers as ombudsman for the company and later for Omni Hotels. "He was the most loved person—kind, gracious, genuine," according to Sacco. "The truth is that if you put all the brothers together, you would come up with Roy." He remembers working side by side with Roy. "He treated me like I was his boss, even though we all knew better." Roy and his wife, Ruth, settled into an apartment in the Bosworth Building of the Parker House.

My brother Jack says he learned to rely on Roy to handle all grievances. "If there were any complaints whatsoever, whether it was in Maine, or later in Paris or London, Roy would handle them." Mike Deitemeyer, president of Omni Hotels at the time, put it this way: "The role Roy played as an ambassador and ombudsman lived on as the Dunfey Family Corporation expanded, although now it takes many individuals to do what he did by himself."

From clams to Parker House rolls—a
most unlikely journey from Hampton
Beach, NH, to Boston's most famous
hotel. Left to right: Bob, Jack, Mother,
Walter, Jerry, Bud. Don't miss longtime
employee, "Dewey the Doorman" smiling in the background.

Taking over the Parker House a few
weeks before Christmas meant that Santa
was one of our first guests. Here, along
with my mother, they celebrate with all
the families of Parker House employees in
the elegant 14th-floor ballroom, off limits,
up to that time, to staff unless they were
working a function there. 1968

A "toast to Harvey" Parker. Dunfey brothers, from Left to right: Jerry, Bob, and Jack, Walter, toast Harvey Parker during the 120th anniversary celebrations at the Parker House in 1976.

Parker House Rolls

Yield: 2 dozen rolls

Ingredients

1/2 cup scalded milk
1/2 cup boiling water
1 tsp. salt
1 tsp. sugar
1 tbsp. butter
1/2 yeast cake dissolved in 1/4 cup lukewarm water
3 cups bread flour, or enough to knead

Method

Place milk, water, salt, butter and sugar into mixing bowl and mix well. Add yeast. Then add flour until it is stiff enough to knead. Cover and let it rise to double its bulk, shape into balls, put into buttered pan and cover. Let it rise in a warm place again to double its bulk. With the floured handle of a wooden spoon press the balls through the center, almost cutting in half. Brush one half with butter, fold the other half over and press together like a pocketbook. Let it rise again and bake in a hot oven (400° F) for 15 minutes. Brush the tops with butter after baking.

According to Mother D. her "job description" at the newly acquired Parker House was to make the rolls each day! Here's the recipe from Susan B. Wilson's *Heaven by Hotel Standards*.

Elma Lewis, the "matriarch" of Roxbury, and founder/producer of the Black Nativity, was her community's champion convener, mover, and shaker. Here she receives thanks from the #1 champ, Muhammed Ali, and the #1 convener, Jerry Dunfey, after they received the annual Elma Lewis School of Fine Arts award.

Another cultural icon, Malcolm X, then known as Malcolm Little, was a busboy at the Parker House during the time of the Pearl Harbor invasion
—Susan B. Wilson, *Heaven by Hotel Standards*

"During a stateside sojourn of several months in 1912 and 1913, Ho (then called Nguyen Tat Thanh, or simply Ba) worked as a cook's helper and pastry chef at the Parker House...."
—Susan B. Wilson, *Heaven, By Hotel Standards: The History of the Omni Parker House*

The Parker House   (of the 1880s)
By Morgan Llwelyn

Was it ever
gentler, warmer, more glowing?
Beyond knowing, now,
the days when Dickens walked these halls,
sheltered by these walls;
brushed his teeth and washed his face in
Parker House s porcelain basin.

New life enters
old bones sweetly,
restores neatly
patinaed luster
with a tender
feather duster.

Eased and cosseted,
charmed and pampered, guests
unhampered by Eighties madness
forget sadness.

The metal dragons of Tremont Street
are floors below; slain
at their feet.

Author and poet, Morgan Llywelyn, often stayed at the Parker House and became a family friend. We discovered this personally-typed poem after one of her visits.

A Hundred Thousand Welcomes!

From Lowell to Hampton; from Vermont to Maine, and beyond, Jerry cycled. In 1968, his "itinerary" led him to the Parker House.

Finally a moment to sit down and toast to the opening of the Parker House "Eat and Drink at Dunfey's Last Hurrah": Left to right: Jack, Paul, Walter, Roy, Bud, Bob, Jerry. 1971

CHAPTER 27

Restoring a Classic

The fiftieth anniversary of the family's purchase of the Parker House is this year, 2018. It is also Eddie Cotto's fiftieth year as an employee, although only forty-nine have been recorded, because Eddie started when he was fourteen. The senior bell captain recalls a Parker House from the time when TVs were still black and white, the rugs were worn, creditors were knocking on the door, and a full orchestra still played in the main dining room for ten diners:

> When the Dunfeys took over the financially ailing hotel in 1968, they renovated it and eventually returned it to profitability…They were a caring people…They learned through trial and error—and were fortunate to be there as other major Boston events of the '70s, like the Bicentennial, the Tall Ships, [and] the successful conversion of the antiquated Quincy Market area into a major tourist destination converged to buoy the local economy. In that prime location on the Freedom Trail, the Dunfeys put the Parker House on the map again.
> —*Susan Wilson, Heaven by Hotel Standards*

"First of all," says Jerry, "Eddie was right. We really were learning by trial and error. We had reason to be nervous." Often during those early years, Jerry recalls, "We faced up to the possibility of failure. By 1971, we were questioning how wise it was to pump another million into the care and feeding of the sixteen-story Parker House that had an endless appetite for cash." At this very juncture when the company was mortgage-stretched, Aetna Life and Casualty purchased all the outstanding stock of the Dunfey Family Corporation, which, at that time, operated twelve hotels and motor inns in five New England states, including the Parker House. In announcing the acquisition, Aetna's CEO, Olcott D. Smith, said: "The Dunfey group of properties adds a new and profitable dimension to Aetna's corporate development program…at the same time, Dunfey's management expertise will give Aetna added capability in this growing field." Aetna recognized a potential win-win situation. Paul Gagnon was key to coordinating the affiliation with Aetna, which had great respect for the Dunfey Family Corporation's ability to rehabilitate and revitalize failing properties.

With Dunfey helping Aetna by transforming the five inns of their national Royal Coach chain and Aetna providing much needed capital, it was, indeed, a timely, win-win situation.

Infusion of cash, initially from Aetna, provided the impetus for refurbishing the main dining room and renaming it "Parker's," and for turning the basement floor of the hotel into a new kind of dining experience, whose theme was "Dunfey's at the Parker House: Eat and Drink to the Last Hurrah." In her book *Heaven by Hotel Standards*, Susan Wilson, Parker House historian, describes the background of the name: "In 1956, Edwin O'Connor had written The Last Hurrah, a thinly disguised version of the life of Boston's most legendary mayor, James Michael Curley."

Now patrons were welcomed into a turn-of-the-century atmosphere created by walnut paneling, Edwardian framed mirrors, gay nineties light fixtures, and a brass railed bar, along with photographs of famous guests including the Kennedy family, House speakers "Tip" O'Neill and John McCormack, Ho Chi Minh, and Malcolm X. With its charm and its stories, Dunfey's "eating and drinking spot became the most Boston room in Boston," according to one reviewer. The grand opening party included the kickoff celebration of another book, *Johnny, We Hardly Knew Ye*, this one published after JFK's assassination. Its authors, Dave Powers and Kenny O'Donnell, two of Kennedy's closest friends and advisers, attended the kickoff.

The 'oops' factor

Behind the scenes of grand celebrations and successes, there were day-to-day realities. Among other responsibilities, Roy took great pride in his role as ombudsman, AKA guest relations director, and sent a handwritten note "from a Dunfey" to each customer who submitted a complaint about any of our properties across the country. Depending on the level of criticism, he also typically would enclose a gift coupon, ranging from a free cocktail to a complete two-day Dunfey Mini-Vacation hotel stay, as a gesture of goodwill.

Some letters he received were quite creative which tickled his refined funny bone. At one corporate meeting, he particularly relished reciting the following note, which he had committed to memory: "Fear not. The Loch Ness Monster has been found. Last night at your Last Hurrah restaurant in the Parker House, it was served to me and my guests in the guise of a bouillabaisse. But give the little critter credit. He didn't go down without a fight." As you might guess, the author received a phone call from Roy, a monster-size apology, with an unequivocal admission of the guest's ingenious, if disconcerting description of the complaint. That gentleman received a Dunfey Mini-Vacation, a special all-inclusive weekend stay at a Dunfey property.

Roy's handling of that justifiable criticism reflects the policy regarding the company's response to mistakes. Own them. Rectify them. Use them to learn and always try to move on with a side of laughter. That kind of approach carried over, if only partially, when it came to criticism about the treatment of a long time Parker House housekeeper. In 1981, Jeremiah Murphy, columnist at *The Boston Globe*, got a scoop about the horrific way a sixty-three-year-old housekeeper was treated when she could no longer fulfill her requirement to clean sixty rooms. The details of his column describe a cruel disregard for the degree of labor required of this house-keeper, especially in the face of her longevity in the position and her declining health.

It so happened that in a New Hampshire rectory on that November twenty-first, the morning the column was published, the pastor of a parish was preparing his Sunday sermon when he read about the shameful behav-ior at a Dunfey-owned hotel. He included the tale as part of his message to the congregation. A friend of the Dunfeys who attended the Sunday service in that parish immediately alerted my brother, Walter, about the sermon, in which the priest bemoaned the fact that such a public family, whose parents had brought them up in hard times and who knew what it was to be poor, would treat employees so insensitively. Imagine, making the almost blind sixty-three-year-old lady clean sixty rooms, thus assur-ing she would not be able to work the two years that remained until she reached retirement age. The Dunfeys had surely forgotten where they came from and that was a pity. End of sermon.

Walter's ire heated the telephone wires as he talked to Bud in the adja-cent office in Hampton and Roy and Jim Stamas at the Parker House. An investigation began immediately—revealing the newspaper got some key facts wrong—but *The Boston Globe* took three months to print a retrac-tion. They persevered in demanding accuracy, although as Walter and Bud reported, "[We] felt we were on a dead-end street." Finally, on February 22, 1982, the *Globe* published a retraction:

The Boston Globe

MONDAY, FEBRUARY 22, 1982   Telephone 929-2000

It took three months, November to February, and a number of meetings, each increasingly exasperating. Jim Stamas remembers it all in detail because, he says, "I had never seen Jack lose his cool, but I could tell it was taking all his self-control not to explode. Finally, the retraction was published correcting the discrepancies between the original column and the facts: The housekeeper was not 63 years old with the hope of working two more years in order to qualify for retirement. The woman was 72 years old and already entitled to full retirement. Neither was the housekeeper required to clean an outrageous number of rooms—60 a day. Her contract stipulated she do 16 rooms, but under a special arrangement with the Parker House, she was allowed to do 10 rooms a day.

Walter shared the retraction with the priest-author of the sermon. To his credit, the pastor clothed himself in a wardrobe of humility, stood up on Sunday morning, March 1, 1982, three months after the original sermon, and read parts of Walter's letter from the pulpit, with all of the original errors corrected. The priest then went a step further, rendering his own classic apology to Walter in a handwritten letter:

> Dear Walter,
>
> I was glad to hear from you recently so you could set me straight regarding the November column of Jeremiah Murphy. Your letter was very well documented and gave me the true picture in a very nice manner. I appreciated that and made a public apology at Masses this past Sunday. I told them about your policy of allowing employees to work after age 65 if they can successfully fulfill their duties. Further, that you have rewarded many of them with fully paid trips to Ireland.
>
> I further elaborated that that is the Dunfey family I knew when they went to St. Patrick's Church (Hampton Beach) early each Sunday morning led by their father, LeRoy, and mother, Catherine. They would all receive Holy Communion and then rush back to their "C St." restaurant to serve breakfast and later in the day, clams and hot dogs.

> Lastly, I promised the parishioners that, from now on, I'd stick
> to explaining the Bible—instead of columns in the *Boston Globe*...

Roy, Walter, and said priest added the exclamation mark to that experience—laughter—at Walter's quip about the price they would have paid had our mother ever thought they knowingly allowed such treatment of any employee. After all, it was our oldest brother Roy's job to make sure the company lived up to our parents' expectations.

What my brothers and my mother were not surprised about were the verbal, political darts and cartoons that found their way into print. Humor served well in those situations. When my mother was described by another reporter as a "domineering matriarch," she, and every one who knew her thought the moniker hilarious. In fact, my mother changed her self-assigned, favorite title up to that time, "Chairman of the *Bored*," to "Your mother, the *Domineering Matriarch*."

1969–1971: buildings, people, and Boston's civic life

As the company's director of corporate public relations and marketing, Jerry played an integral role in the hotel's transformation: from menu tests to room designs; from upgrading systems to developing marketing plans. The Parker House had been described as having waited like a grande dame standing in the doorway...She needed to be treated with the deference due a landmark in a landmark city. At the same time, Jerry saw the need to apply that same deference to Boston's diverse populations, who were also waiting for doors—and not just employee-entrance back doors—but the front doors to open and welcome diverse talent and contributions.

Representation was crucial. The civic challenge of electing the right candidate to represent the city in Congress would not be easy. National shocks from three assassinations, an increasingly unpopular war in Vietnam, a long overdue civil rights movement, and the exploding, divisive busing issue that would define Boston nationally, fractured relationships and fed the fury. Jerry recalls:

> The president and chair of the Portland, Maine, NAACP, in which I held membership, had introduced me to Ken Guscott, president of Boston's NAACP. I invited him to the announcement of our Parker House purchase. Within a few months, Ken came to my office one day and urged me to stop what I was doing to go with him.

When my mother noticed a Want Ad in the newspaper, she couldn't resist applying for a job. Perhaps she wanted "out of the kitchen" instead of making PH rolls!

He hurriedly escorted me to a meeting room on the mezzanine (which Coretta Scott King would later dedicate as the Martin Luther King room). To my surprise, I saw nuns, priests, and a standing-room-only crowd of a more diverse group of people than I had yet seen in Boston.

There, in the front of the packed room, Attorney David Nelson was speaking. He would be the first Black candidate from Massachusetts to run for Congress. (Republican Edward Brooke of Massachusetts was the first African American to be elected to the Senate in 1966.) And his opponent was Louise Day Hicks, already well-known for her divisive rhetoric and platform.

Jerry went back to his office and, within an hour, received a call from Joe Oteri, asking him to go over and join the campaign. "I got my marching orders and they changed my life at the Parker House." Our nephew, Rick Dunfey, also got his marching—or more specifically, climbing—orders:

> In the summer of 1970, my uncle Jerry volunteered me, a rising college sophomore, for his pal David Nelson's primary campaign run for U.S. Congress from our Boston district.
>
> In racially-charged, overwhelmingly white Boston which had always struggled with integration efforts, newly-imposed forced busing of public school children had raised simmering tensions and lowered discourse. David was the runaway underdog in a primary field with the likes of vocal anti-busing advocate Louise Day Hicks and voice-of-reason newcomer Joe Moakley.
>
> My main duty was to help David get on the ballot by getting a required quota of residents to sign his nomination papers. This meant going house to house—or, in my case, with predominantly Irish-Catholic South Boston as my assigned turf, going mainly from three-decker to three-decker.

Volunteers were provided with a stack of postcard-sized info cards with David's credentials. He possessed one huge asset in local Irish-Catholic enclaves as a so-called Triple Eagle: he was a graduate of Boston College High School, Boston College, and Boston College Law School. "When the card with that side showing was handed first to voters, they eagerly reached for my ballpoint pen," according to Rick.

On the other side of the card was David's photo, a close-up candid of him leaning back in a chair, talking into a phone receiver tucked under his chin. "When the side showing that image was seen first," Rick noted, "reactions were mixed, at best."

> One hot evening, an older Irish-American woman stood in her third-floor tenement doorway and stared at that photo on the card. And then stared at me, repeating that process five or six times before looking up and down at me: "Are you Black?" she asked in a bewildered manner. It wasn't faulty lighting. She just couldn't make the connection: Why would I be working for someone who didn't look like her and me?

Rick admits he's not sure what "spilled out" of his mouth, but something "clicked with her. She took my pen and signed David's nomination papers. I learned in that moment that a ballpoint pen can be a transformative weapon."

David Nelson lost his bid, but that campaign opened a door to action for many, including Jerry. He had learned how to serve more than turkey sandwiches over the counter at the store on Broadway. He remembered the "different tone" of remarks on the other side of the counter when the only Black family in the neighborhood walked by. Later, when "pushing clams," generating marketing strategies, or backing certain political candidates, it was natural for Jerry to act according to the civic lessons we had all seen our dad live. My brothers' embrace of the Democratic Party's progressive social causes was rooted in the post-war-and-Acre in Lowell.

Crises outside the front door

Boston was experiencing the strains and scars of these realities. And the Parker House was situated in the hub of Boston's Hub. More than a decade later, Art Jankhe, in his feature, "The Liberals' Santa Claus" (*Boston Magazine*, December 1984), looked back at the Dunfeys' influence during those turbulent years, the late sixties and early seventies. He assessed the family's handling of its financial and political "power." The article refers to the Dunfeys as the "Santa Claus of future liberalism," hosting fundraising events for local, state, and national candidates for political office.

The specific event to which Jahnke makes reference was a fundraising cocktail party for three women, one running for the governorship of Vermont (Madeleine Kunin); one for U.S. Senate from Maine (Libby Mitchell); and one for U.S. House from New Hampshire (Dudley Dudley). The author's claim is that the Dunfey's wealth, formidable skills as businessmen as well as their enviable network of friends in high places, helped launch and ignite the campaigns of New England elected officials and those candidates whose values mimicked their own.

There was truth to that claim, and our family's political involvement did reach beyond New England. My brothers were unapologetic. With self-deprecating humor, they embraced efforts to advance progressive policies. They were advancing women to leadership positions in the corporation and were equally engaged in encouraging, mentoring, and supporting capable and progressive women and minorities in politics. The Parker House was a natural, elegant center for hosting fundraisers. Doris Bunte, a Black state representative from Roxbury, whom Jerry supported in all seven of her campaigns, recalled fifteen years of Dunfey's work with Black groups such as the NAACP and the Elma Lewis School of Fine Arts. "Whenever we wanted to accomplish something, Jerry was here" says Bunte, "and he wasn't just here for the good times. He was here all of the time."

1968: Do "something"

In 2018, fifty years after the country's immeasurable triple trauma of assassinations starting in 1963 with President John F. Kennedy, Mike Barnicle describes the experience. He speaks of the "Culture of the country, completely altered...":

> That year (1968) was a calendar that bled. The wounds came on a daily basis. Martin Luther King had been killed in Memphis, cities burned and by Tuesday June 5th when Bob Kennedy was shot in a kitchen at the Ambassador Hotel in Los Angeles more than 6000 American soldiers and Marines had already died in Vietnam in a war that was carving a wound in the American soul that has not yet fully healed all these years later...
> —*Mike Barnicle, "What I Saw on RFK's Funeral Train 50 Years Ago Today,"* The Daily Beast, *June 6, 2018*

The sixties had bequeathed its radical upheaval and national trauma to us. A total of sixteen children were left behind when these three leaders were killed. Adding the thousands left behind from racial conflicts and the war, people were left with a sense of helplessness added to grief. At such times, we look for something—anything—to do. The Dunfey and Hirshberg families would, thankfully, be given that "something to do."

In the summer of 1968, Coretta Scott King had even more responsibility than she'd had before the tragedy that shook her, her family, the nation, and the world on April fourth. She was now looking for a place where she and her four children could start to heal, to play, and to escape the attention of the nation. She hoped for a quiet place where she could begin writing what would become her book, *My Life with Martin Luther King, Jr.*

It so happened Earl Graves, assistant to Robert Kennedy and later, founder of *Black Enterprise* magazine, was close to both the King and Dunfey families. He knew Walter and his wife, Barbara, had a cottage on Lake Winnipesaukee in New Hampshire. He was aware that each family had four children, some of whom were close in age. Earl called Walter and Barbara, and they extended an invitation to the King family to use their cottage that summer as a hideaway of sorts.

Three decades later, in a feature on the King family's New Hampshire 1968 summer vacation, *Concord Monitor's* Eric Moskowitz, describes some of the memories Dunfeys and Hirshbergs recall. Jerry Dunfey spoke of the great concern for the safety of Coretta and the children. "In a period of national turmoil, conservative publisher William Loeb had taken to printing names such as King and Kennedy in Communist red on the front page of the *Union Leader,*" Jerry said.

"William Loeb was a powerful force in the state," Walter Jr. added. "He wanted to out the fact that the Kings were somewhere in New Hampshire, and he knew my father had something to do with it." Security was heavy; thirteen-year-old Walter and all the kids had strict orders not to reveal the children's identities to anyone.

Life stories evolve from such invitations. This one includes a homey cottage, a bunk house, a small boat called "Putt-Putt," a lovable black lab named Inky, a diving raft for swimming, and a collection of Irish and Jewish kids—Dunfeys and Hirshbergs. It may sound like the makings of a September school essay: "What I did on my summer vacation." The Hirshbergs had five children (since when did Jewish folks have more kids than Irish Catholics?), best friends and neighbors of Walter and Barbara's four Dunfey offspring.

A photo reflects the fun of that summer vacation, surrounded by Dr. King's "dream" of "prodigious hilltops of New Hampshire." Here were his children with other kids—black and white; Catholic, Protestant, and Jewish—discovering what they all had in common.

Kid fun—diving off the floating raft, learning to water-ski, boating around the lake, and stopping for ice cream and burgers. But there were tense moments, too, Walter Jr. admits—for instance, one afternoon when he stopped for some fuel: "The guy came out, unhooked the hose, but when he got to the boat and saw four black kids, he said: 'You're going to have to go someplace else to get fuel. We don't sell fuel to colored people.' He might have said the 'n' word—not sure":

> I'd worked at the marina, bailing out boats after rainstorms, etc. I knew the owner and went right up to his shop. I remember being so mad that I had a hard time telling him what had happened. He walked down to the fuel dock, went to the pump and grabbed the hose. The attendant got up to say something but I'm not sure if he did before the owner turned to him and said, "You're fired." The owner then stepped down onto the transom, (stern), of the boat, smiled at the kids, made friendly, light-hearted chitchat.
>
> I was following him back up to the shop to pay when he asked me if the kids were who he thought they might be, (or some thing of that nature). I froze. I'm not sure I heard my father's, mother's, or Coretta's voice, or all in unison, saying, Don't tell *anybody* who the children are! He then asked if they were Martin Luther King's kids, and I just stared at him. He smiled, rubbed my head and said, "Don't worry—your secret's safe. Be careful out there."

One of Walter, Jr.'s indoor responsibilities was to get everyone into their bunks at night and then turn on the radio. "The King children would kneel by the bunks and pray for each other, their mother, and their father, and that the police would find the person who had killed their father."

The King children set out on their daily lake adventure with Walter, Jr. at the helm. 1968.

Even in that quiet hideaway, reality found them. One night, a news alert crackled through the cloth covered speakers: "Scotland Yard has caught the man who shot Dr. Martin Luther King, Jr..." The kids exploded and ran down to the cottage. "Mommy, Mommy—they caught him. They caught him!"

Stories, like this recollection from that summer of '68, need to live on, a legacy passed from one generation to the next. Oh, we know there are family stories of foibles and failures, of material things; of misunderstandings and hurts. What kinds of stories will our children have to tell? What lasting lesson was learned from that "summer vacation"? Perhaps, the importance of invitation, of offering a safe space in time of need; of making time for the simple things: a Putt-Putt and an Inky, too. Years later, Gary Hirshberg, who was fourteen-years-old in 1968, recalls meeting Mrs. King: "The first time I reconnected with her after that summer, was in 1977, at the Parker House dedication of a meeting room to Dr. King. The first thing she said to me was, 'I remember Inky and I remember the little boat that you guys drove me around in, called Putt Putt.' I couldn't believe it. I didn't even remember those little details."

CHAPTER 28

1971

Mother of the Bride at age 76

The twelve years between 1968 and 1982 yielded more firsts for my mother—especially 1971. She enjoyed visiting Vermont, where Jim and I were teaching, he at Burlington High School and I at South Burlington High. His apartment was in the North End and mine downtown near the University of Vermont. We had decided to spend time getting to know each other and had begun to develop a mutual network of colleagues and friends. Months earlier, Jim had signed the official papers that released him from his priestly duties. I was with him at the meeting. Now we were ready to move on.

But wait: The Auxiliary Bishop in Manchester, near the end of our meeting, gently requested that we get married "privately."

"Get married privately?" I said. I could feel long pent up tears filling my eyes. For more than a year, we had fulfilled every jot and tittle of the process after each of our decisions to leave the priesthood and religious order. We knew how serious the decision was. We did not want to leave the Church. In fact, at that time, we were still thinking that the Church would continue to evolve with Pope John XXIII's inclusive vision. We might even be among a generation of married former priests and nuns serving increasing numbers of people and new needs.

I confess that was more my thinking than Jim's. He was much more realistic—and he was right. After a year and a half, here we were in front of this very kindly, well-meaning representative of the Vatican, adding one more instruction: "Don't go public."

"How do we possibly think of our marriage in private terms?" I countered. "My family is probably the largest, most public family in the region. We want to have our families at our wedding in Burlington," I sputtered.

"Burlington?" "Vermont?" the bishop questioned. "You want to get married in Vermont?"

"Yes." We explained we were both teaching high school there, were active in our parish, and had a thriving community of friends.

That was a whole different situation. Another jurisdiction! The bishop picked up the phone and called his counterpart in Burlington. Within ten minutes, Jim and I had an appointment to arrange our wedding. Manchester's well-intentioned auxiliary bishop had avoided an awkward moment, and my mother would be "off the hook": She would have a son and a priest named Jim, finally satisfying my grandmother's wishes! My mother and my family and Jim's parents and his family could be with us at the wedding—finally, a legitimate exception to some rule.

When I told my mother about the meeting, she was thrilled, of course, but also a bit wistful: "It just seems sad that the Church can't encourage those who may want to leave but still want to serve." She would echo that opinion later about the sons and daughters of former priests and nuns. "I'd say there are many who could make the Church proud!"

Reason to celebrate

At age seventy-six, my mother found good reason to celebrate, claiming another "first": mother of the bride. She had already witnessed eight sons getting married—some more than once. Jim survived a bachelor party that defies description, thanks to my brother, Walter. From all I've described about Walter, the reader may understand why I won't commit that event to writing. Jim would commit—in more than words—not only to me on our wedding day. He also inherited the Dunfey clan, most of whom he had come to know during the previous year and a half.

My oldest sister Kay's arrival from her assignment in Rome, days before the wedding, sent us on a last-minute shopping trip just in time to take advantage of the annual sale at Priscilla's of Boston (designer of Grace Kelly's wedding gown). There, for a few weeks, expensive samples were marked down to $6-$30, rivaling even the famous Filene's Basement prices. Kay would be my maid of honor, her elegant gown and her very presence "priceless."

On the sunny afternoon of August 7, 1971, Jim, his parents, and his best man, his brother Tom, walked down the aisle together as I followed with my oldest brother, Roy, who would later describe the relationship that made his being by my side at that moment so significant:

> Of the many blessings that have come my way, none is more unique than that "special" relationship that exists between two siblings who never lived together.

My other ten siblings, their wives, and children joined the Freiburger family—all six siblings, their spouses, and their children, from Iowa. The sum of our merged "immediate family" totaled ninety, and we had, of course, made room for a few mutual friends. I doubt that this gathering would have met the well-intentioned New Hampshire bishop's requirement that we marry in a "private" ceremony. This total of invitees for a wedding was about as "private" as Dunfeys and Freiburgers could manage. We celebrated the public sacrament which calls on the "community present" to support the couple setting out on the journey of married life. They did.

The gowns, hairstyles, and music morphed after the seventies, but our choice of seventies ballads reflected a moving on from the previous decade of upheaval to a new moment of optimism. We resonated with the Carpenters' "We've Only Just Begun," the Seekers' "There's a New World Somewhere," and John Denver's "Today," the last verse celebrating, "Today is my (our) moment and/ Now is our story/ We'll laugh and We'll cry and We'll sing."

It was not in song lyrics, however, but in "Markings," the memoir of Dag Hammarskjold, the United Nations' second secretary general, that we found a reflection on optimism concise enough to fit on our wedding invitation and a year and a half late later, the announcement of the arrival of our first child:

For
all that
has
been –
Thanks
for
all that
will
be –
yes

design: Naomi Rousseau Sullivan

Msgr. Phil Kenney, Dunfey family spiritual and social justice advisor. Left to right: My oldest brother, Roy, and sister, Kay; the bride, Eleanor; and groom, Jim; and Jim's brother, Tom Freiburger. Cathedral Chapel, Burlington, Vermont. 1971

Mother of a bride at age 76, my mother counts another first—a daughter getting married—after eight sons. August 7, 1971

True to the 70s, the Carpenter's "We've only just begun" sends us "on our way," 47 years ago.

"For all that has been—Thanks. For all that will be—Yes!"
By December of 1972, I was at yet another doctor's appointment, two weeks overdue to deliver a baby, with my mother as my easygoing, highly experienced adviser. While I went in to the examination room, the lovely midwife thought to make conversation with my mother in the waiting room:

"Is this your first grandchild?" she asked.

"No, not quite," my mother responded, with her winsome smile. "It's my thirty-fourth." Understanding the shock on the midwife's face, the seasoned grandmother continued: "But it's very special because it's the first from a daughter." The exchange probably left the friendly midwife even more bewildered. Afterwards, my mother laughed as she shared the conversation with me, and perhaps my response of laughter started my labor. My mother's thirty-fourth grandchild, Joel Dunfey Freiburger, finally arrived. Two and a half years later, Maria Catherine, grandchild #35, was born on her due date at 6:30 a.m.

Jim's parents lived in Iowa, and although we spent two weeks each summer with them on their farm, we were fortunate to have my mother close by through those first ten years of our parenting experience. We needed all the help we could get: "How to Parent" lessons hadn't been a part of our curriculum, in college, the priesthood, or the convent.

"Were all women nuns before...?"
During the seventies, a number of priests and nuns were making decisions about their futures. My three sisters would choose to leave. Just how many former colleagues spent time in our home before making their decisions struck me when, one noontime, in the midst of my spreading mustard and relish on our kids' hot dogs, five-year-old Joel casually asked: "Mommy, were all women nuns before...?" He did not say before what and I didn't ask, but the question was certainly understandable. Except for his Nanna Dunfey, almost all the women he had met in his young life had had some association with a religious order!

Those years of on-the-job training as a parent reminded me of my own upbringing. Until that time, I had never considered the way my mother raised us. I had always seen only my dad as the activist, the exemplar of civic life. Insight woke me up to what should have been obvious to me all along.

A mother's example: "Look after one another"
My mother's example, Jack reminisced, showed us what "social justice" looks like. She would never have heard that term in those days. She lived

it, though. I began to consider what Jack said and started to appreciate how right he was. Whether it was the way she treated our mentally disturbed neighbor who would cry out slurs, fortunately indecipherable, or her taking in and caring for a neglected child who was just four years older than I, my mother walked the talk of social justice in her everyday life.

Perhaps the greatest influence on me was her friendship with another neighbor, Mary Smith, who lived two blocks down Fifth Avenue in Lowell. We walked by her home every time we went to St. Rita's Church or Hall—which was often. Her son John, about twenty when I was seven, was wheelchair bound. Whenever he was on his porch, which was also often, we stopped to visit and saw up close the challenge of physical control that cerebral palsy inflicts. I had never heard of that condition. I didn't understand its cause; I just saw its effects. What did make a lasting impression, though, were the effects of our frequent visits. I saw pure joy on John's face when my mother appeared, usually with four or five of us in tow. He would gather up all that involuntary motion in his arms, legs and head, and clearly what he most wanted to control: his grin. John and his mother, Mary, were not hidden away out of sight. We knew them well and saw our mother interacting with joy and respect, friendship and quiet assistance. Through special efforts, the Smiths were even able to rent a little cottage right near us on Nudd Terrace at Hampton Beach.

My mother's lesson was not lost on us. Thirty-five years later, I would meet Harold "Laddie" Holt, a forty-two-year-old man who was equally challenged by cerebral palsy. His family had devised a way for him to communicate via a typewriter placed on the floor, so Laddie, with a pointer on

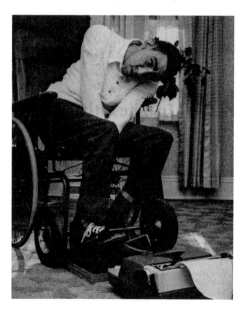

A thriver, not merely a survivor, of a birth that left him unable to control his body except for one foot, Harold "Laddie" Holt, his mother, Hilda, and family, inspired change as well as hope: Copies of each of Laddie's two books, *As I Am*, and *In the Other Fellow's Shoes* were placed on every U.S. senator's desk by Senator John Chafee (Republican, R.I.) before the vote on the Americans for Disabilty Act. 1991

the toe of his right foot—the one part of his body over which he had some control—could type.

By the time I met him, Laddie had a closet full of paper rolls with verses he had punched out on that typewriter, countless rolls of his thoughts, his dreams, his notes to those he had met as he tooled his wheelchair down to Sabin's Point in Riverside, Rhode Island—his memos and muscles fueled by honesty, humor, and optimism. Together, he and I unpacked these verses, and the scraps took the form of two books: *As I Am* and *In the Other Fellow's Shoes*.

Laddie went on to win United Cerebral Palsy's prestigious national award for his service and his book that year of 1981. At the time, our family managed the Shoreham Hotel in Washington, DC, so my brothers arranged to host Laddie's mother, Hilda Holt; his sister and brother-in-law, Ruth and Bob Livingstone; as well as two daughters; my mother; my son Joel (age seven) and daughter Maria (almost five). Both of them knew Laddie well, having accompanied me to several of my home visits with the honoree.

While we all recall with sheer delight the national award dinner and presentation, it was our arrival at the Shoreham that claimed first place in our later stories. My brothers had sent a limousine to National Airport for Laddie and guests. With all of us plus our luggage, there was no room for the bulky commode, a necessary item on Laddie's list. That afternoon, anyone watching the slow-moving DC traffic would have noted a late-model limo with a commode bungie-strapped to its roof, making its way to the swanky entrance of the Shoreham Hotel. We figured that was a first for the limo—and for the hotel.

The arrival was unique and successful. But the first day's luncheon, planned for twelve of us in a side room off the lobby, almost didn't happen. Laddie's mother, Hilda, took me aside and said she planned to feed Laddie in their room "because, you know, Laddie can't control his saliva when he eats, so he drools. I don't want him to embarrass the children." Embarrass the kids? I could empathize but had to convince her that would not be the case. "Hilda, the kids make a mess at meals. They won't even notice; they're so excited." I asked if she would please consider trying out the arrangement just for that luncheon, and if it was uncomfortable, then by all means, we would make other provisions.

Who was embarrassed at that lunch? Not Laddie. I was. Maria and Joel sat on either side of Laddie, who was at the head of the table. Just as dessert was served, Maria called down the table to me: "Mommy, you lied to me about Laddie."

Oh, no. I could see the smile start to curl on Laddie's lips. "Really?" I asked cautiously.

"Yes. You said his body doesn't work, but it does." She was right. When I had introduced them to Laddie two years earlier, I had "prepared" them by saying, "You're going to notice that Laddie's body doesn't work, but his mind does." Now, seeing Laddie eyeing me and laughing out loud, I replied as casually as possible: "Well. It doesn't. Does it?"

"Yes, it does. He can chew his food. He can blink, and he can kick my leg!" Laddie's "kick" replaced the "pat on the shoulder or back" when you tease a friend. He did not have control of his arms, but he had one leg twisted into control, and that worked just fine to let folks know he was totally involved in a conversation. Maria was right, of course, and I learned a key lesson that day: a child describes a person by what they can do while an adult often describes people by what they can't do. After that lunch, there was no question: Laddie sat at the head of the table with Joel and Maria beside him for every meal during the next three days.

Thanks to U.S. Senator John Chafee (R-RI), a copy of each of Harold Laddie Holt's books was placed on the desks of all ninety-eight of his Senate colleagues when the Americans with Disabilities Act was voted into law nine years later, in 1990. Laddie had proven, in more ways than one, that the spoken word is not always the only word, or the last word.

In 1988, Jerilyn Asher, longtime Global Citizens Circle director, wrote to Laddie Holt after she and her fourteen-year-old daughter—who lived with cerebral palsy—read *As I Am*: "Every time a severely disabled person tells his or her story in poetry or prose,(s)he gives courage to all other physically challenged individuals who dared not to dream or hope... I read this book with my daughter who, though intellectually bright, is severely physically disabled. Several days later, Jennifer wrote this poem to Laddie":

> *I am me. To be me is not always easy*
> *It means being alone a lot*
> *And sometimes being very lonely.*
> *It means having people laugh at me and stare.*
> *It means watching the other kids run and play*
> *When I long to and can't.*
> *But it also means having people around me*
> *Who love me so much that*
> *They would fix me if they could.*
> *And since they can't, they hug me a lot*
> *And give me books to read by people*

A lot worse off than I am
People who can laugh through their tears
Which gives me hope.

Harold "Laddie" Holt died in 1997 at the age of 63.

Remembrance *by Eleanor*

"I will show you a way out of no way," *Deuteronomy*
He who could not talk to be understood
    found a way to speak his mind—through gesture, eyes, and the
    voices of those who loved him
He who could not hold a pen in hand
    found a way to use a pointer on his shoe
    to write his words of humor and wisdom across the years and into our hearts
He who could not walk
    found a way to blaze new trails for wheels—and new paths to understanding
He who could not be independent physically
    found a way to forge independence in will and spirit.
We who may feel there is "no way" at times, go from here today knowing—
    Thanks to Laddie—we, too, can find a way out of our "no way."

With our parents' examples of what social justice looks like, the Dunfey family took its next leap. Social justice concerns had been listed on every business meeting agenda over the years. According to Social Justice and Educational Equity (www.wascd.org, accessed 08/10/2012) social justice "is the way in which human rights are manifested in the everyday lives of people at every level of society." We understood it as what we owe one another as human beings. Early on, the centers of our "everyday lives" had been around the kitchen table, in school, and over the counter: eating, serving, listening, arguing, playing, teasing–and learning. We belonged. What did we glean from those centers of our daily lives? A measure of security. An ability to communicate. A confidence to risk. A hefty dose of humor, and most of all, trust.

We also knew early on that not everyone enjoyed those same rights and privileges. "We had been given much," my mother often said, and "much would be expected of us."

Each August, we visited Jim's parents, his six siblings and their families in Asbury, Iowa. Their award-winning soil conservation farm gave testimony to stewardship of land better than any text book or course. Environmental justice in action. More cousins, too, to add to farm adventures and life bonds.

CHAPTER 29

1974

A Circle of Global Citizens (GCC)

"The Dunfeys were forerunners in diversity and social justice…their pioneering efforts with New England Circle and their commitment to inclusion made us better managers."

—Mike Dietemeyer, "Dunfey alum," former President of
Omni Hotels and currently President and CEO,
Interstate Hotels and Resorts

From success to significance

"Hold the credit," my brother Jerry and I say when it comes to what we do. Being #11 and #12 in the clan, we realize that we get kudos for accomplishments that were really the work of our other eleven siblings. Jerry calls it the Dunfey Credit System. "So often I get complimented for something Bud or Jack or Kay actually did all the heavy lifting on," Jerry muses, "and I realize that were I an only child, that couldn't happen. It's because I am 'one of the Dunfeys involved in restaurants, hotels, politics, service, social causes, and especially, Global Citizens Circle.'"

John Cole, who wrote materials in the early years of the Circle, put it this way in 1974:

> Much of the Dunfey business system, including New England Circle (now GCC) travels over a private wavelength. Each is expected to fill in for the other. Usually, one speaks for all, and it matters little to the others which one does the speaking. No one is expected to get individual credit for a job whether they helped complete it or not.

Traveling that same "wavelength" forty-five years ago, my brothers shaped the style and mission of what became the family's singular initiative. Each sibling had, over the years, been drawn to involvement in politics, education, human rights, social justice. We had enough brothers and sisters to cover multiple local and global causes. Regular communications from each of us were intended not only to inform the rest of the family, but more so, to persuade the rest of us to support a cause or candidate. Even while still in religious life, we "sister nuns" were always included in conversations—except those about financial support! We all had a sense of being equally engaged in one another's causes. The sum was definitely greater than its parts.

Jerry expresses it this way: "Although we were more than gratified with our business achievements, it has been the 'Circle' which has continued to give us meaning—a real sense of fulfillment." As the youngest of the family, I have thought of it as "nudging us from success in business to greater significance in our world." We continue to experience the Dunfey Credit System and believe that the commitment to Global Citizens Circle is the most fitting tribute we can pay to our parents. They were the ones who, in their lives, guided us through counter service to public service.

In 1971, thanks to the infusion of cash from the Aetna deal, we had not only renovated the Parker House into a classic hotel, we had added a popular politically-themed pub, The Last Hurrah. The Aetna sale also provided opportunity to explore new ways to address many of the issues on our social justice agenda. We certainly did not have answers to the assassinations of three of our nation's leaders, the Vietnam War, the deeply rooted racial injustice, the government scandal here at home nor either Northern Ireland's "Troubles" or South Africa's apartheid regime. But we, like so many other concerned citizens, had burning questions. Searching for solutions in our own circles—silos of religion, politics, business, education—was equivalent to sharing versions of our already strong opinions. We needed to listen, talk, and question—to build trust despite differences of opinion. Where better for a big clan steeped in hospitality (and strong opinions) to start than by setting tables of diverse, intergenerational dialogue to expand that circle of family?

1850s: The Saturday Club at the Parker House

The Parker House archives provided a model for such exchanges. The Saturday Club, comprised of "mid-nineteenth century literati and intellectuals," had gathered in that historic hotel starting in 1855. Such notables as Emerson, Hawthorne, Holmes, Dickens, and Lowell spent the last Saturday of each month "hosting festive roundtables" engaged in "poetry readings, impassioned discussions, and book critiques," writes Susan Wilson in her history of the Omni Parker House, *Heaven by Hotel Standards*. These distinguished citizens also probed issues of their day, and moved to bold action. Booker T. Washington led the group's last gathering in 1902.

Seventy years later, New England Circle (now Global Citizens Circle) would revive the honored tradition, incorporating the even deeper inspiration of our parents who welcomed to their table people of all backgrounds.

Although somewhat word smithed since 1974, the original mission statement conveys the heart of the Circle's purpose: convening "diverse groups of concerned individuals... building trust...leading to sustainable action." The fundamental conviction of the founders (my brothers) in 1974 continues to be our priority as we look toward our forty-fifth year:

> Our Mission
> Our purpose is to assemble diverse groups of concerned individuals for discussions of social, political, literary, and educational topics; our goal is to exchange challenging ideas and opinions that can lead to constructive change in our lives, our nation and our world.
>
> —*Jack, Bud, Bob, Walter, and Jerry Dunfey, founded 1974*

Appendix 2 includes more specifics about GCC including stories, social media links and selected images. Issues in our cities, nation, and world are topics the Circle addresses. Our first 150 program titles and discussion leaders are also listed on the website: globalcitizenscircle.org.

The way it works

If the owners of the Parker House invited politicians, activists, educators, business people, and others to dinner and discussion, most would come. That kind of invitation might not even be unusual for certain people. But what they might be surprised to discover is the mix of participants at their tables. Offering discussion leaders no honorarium made it possible that every Circle be free, allowing wide representation of people and opinions. A realtor might not have the opportunity for dinner conversation with the executive director of a homeless shelter; a manager of a Dunfey hotel might not have the chance to sit and talk with a community activist or college student.

Lew Feldstein, former president of the New Hampshire Charitable Foundation, co-author with Robert Putnam of *Better Together*, and long-time GCC director, writes:

> So you sit down at the table and every single person has a story to tell...The idea is simple: Get as many people as possible to invest in the idea we are each part of a community and that our differences add distinguishing marks to the common life we share.

There was speculation regarding the motives of the Dunfeys in holding these types of gatherings at the Parker House. One longtime Boston political pundit's take: "I think it's marketing for the hotel...It brings important people in, and that's good for them as liberal power brokers…." After all, we were known, quite accurately as progressive Democrats. We needed (and still do need) to listen to that criticism and be certain the Circles were geared to inclusion and not simply an echo chamber. Gary Hirshberg thinks of it this way: "They [the Dunfeys] were earnestly trying to find a way to have genuine dialogue…The Circle is a correction to their own partisanship as well. It's a great experiment, and we need it more than ever now."

Frequent questions about the Circle
"How do you find diverse invitees?"
Simple: we look for them!

Find the people who are not usually "at the table." Enter: Hubie Jones, one of the original Circle participants and now a GCC director emeritus. Jones was a local leader of the civil rights movement and a social change agent in Boston for decades. He had met Jerry in 1970 when Jerry decided to support David Nelson's race for Congress, not only financially but by making the Parker House available for campaign events. Jerry's first meeting with Hubie Jones, then the executive director of the Roxbury Multi-Service Center, was not about politics or civil discourse. It was about furniture. "We're renovating the Parker House and have some really good furniture. Just wondering if your clients could use it. If so, we'll get it over to the Center." Done. The furniture was delivered, but that was just the beginning of a shared social commitment and friendship.

Within days Jerry followed up. Hubie saw the reason:

> He wanted me for the same reason he sought out others who fill those tables: he wanted to make the Parker House dense with possibility. He knew the human capital he could gather, and how in turn, people needing a 'lift' could benefit from networking with some otherwise inaccessible people."

Jerry's approach to searching out participant diversity became our modus operandi.

"How do you create an atmosphere that respects each invitee?"
Sarah Holden's description of her experience at a Global Citizens Circle event answers one "how":

> I must comment on the graciousness of the evening. That you introduce each of your guests was particularly noteworthy; the stars among us did not diminish the lights of the rest of us...

Luyanda Mzumza, South African pacifist and refugee scholarship student at Southern New Hampshire University, expressed the respect he experienced at the first of his several Circles, both in the way people listened to his comments as well as the tone and reply discussion leader, CIA director, William Webster, expressed.

Luyanda wrote, "I felt dignity as a human being, a dignity I had never before experienced." That kind of atmosphere has to be a priority in planning every Circle. My mother's, "Be sure you treat everyone like a guest in your own home" was simple but worthy advice.

As our agenda of pressing issues and financial realities grew (especially when the family moved on from the hotel business) we used a variety of venues to hold our programs while still focusing on inclusiveness and the tradition of introducing each participant, whenever possible.

"How do you decide what issues to address?"
Our mission's singular focus on diversity of participants has yielded a store of issues facing our communities. The Circle was founded in the midst of upheaval in the aftermath of war, assassinations, and the overdue civil rights movement. Critical issues abounded. In the early seventies, we felt the urgency, for instance, to listen to a historian educate us on presidential impeachment. Henry Steele Commager was that issue's most highly respected voice and a life-long crusader for civil rights. Dr. Commager asked to return to the Circle because of the "diversity, intelligence, and participation of the guests."

Issues have no borders
We did not set out to establish a non-profit, educational forum regionally, nationally, and internationally—nor had we ever dreamed of someday owning the Parker House when we were "pushing clams" at Hampton Beach. But combine the rising tide of issues, the discovery of the Parker House archives, the business success the family had enjoyed, and it was not a big leap back to the "dinner table" as a way to break open some silos, including our own. I consider it our family's "continuing education process."

We could bring critical world issues and their spokespeople to our tables of conversation with a grocery store owner from Dorchester or a community cooperative director from Contoocook. And we could listen, engage, learn and then act.

Details of Northern Ireland's Troubles, for example, traveled home with Walter as early as 1972. Walter and Bob championed that cause. South Africa's pernicious apartheid system would become a Global Citizens Circle priority in 1981 thanks to Jerry's early commitment to that beloved country.

And Jack touched down on almost every continent in his human rights work, keeping us informed on many levels, especially through his work securing prisoners' release in Cuba and Central America. Walter joked, "Jack spends his vacations in prisons around the world." True. The human rights' work he was involved in succeeded in the release of eighty-seven prisoners. Other siblings and GCC directors brought to the table special causes and people, many of whom had also suffered from their government's injustices. Then we, and a cohort of dedicated volunteers, would work together to make the programs and follow-up happen through mentoring and connecting participants and issues, often face to face "linked in" efforts always behind the scenes.

Arnold Hiatt, president of Stride-Rite footwear company, opened a day-care for children of employees in 1971, years before it became a more frequent practice. That initiative is only one example of Hiatt's embrace of corporate social responsibility. His leadership to this day in fighting financial corruption in electoral politics, is another of the reasons for his being honored with the GCC award. Here he leads the table discussion with co-host (top center) Emmanuel College President, Sr. Janet Eisner, SNDdeNamur.

CHAPTER 30

What We Owe: Our Time to the Young

"I do not plan to give a speech; I turn to you and ask: Why aren't children really important?"

—Graça Machel, South Africa's First Lady,
Global Citizen Award recipient, Johannesburg, South Africa.

"I think one reason is that children 'take time.' Often adults and those in power don't take that time…"

—Maria Freiburger, Americorps volunteer teacher
in Jackson, Mississippi, GCC delegate.

"We have a powerful potential in our youth, and we must have the courage to change old ideas and practices so that we may direct their power toward good ends."

—Mary McLeod Bethune (1875–1955)
"First Lady of the Struggle," educator, advisor to
President Franklin D. Roosevelt on African American issues.

While children were sorely affected in Boston's busing crisis, and Northern Ireland's youth were in the line of fire in the "Troubles," other corners of the world were experiencing a school-age generation of young people testing their voices and suffering for it. In South Africa, for example, on June 16, 1976, two children, fifteen-year-old Hastings Ndlov and twelve-year-old Hector Pieterson, were killed by police while protesting "Bantu" education (which conveyed the connotation of "deplorable") in Soweto, South Africa. Only Hector Pieterson made news because a photographer caught the horror on camera, and that picture stunned the world.

In September 1977, thirty-year-old black activist, Steve Biko, died in police custody, after six days in detention and twenty-two hours of interrogation—handcuffed, manacled and tortured. Biko is remembered because journalist, Donald Woods, tenaciously investigated and exposed the murder of the articulate and charismatic leader of the Black Consciousness Movement.

And the young will lead them

In the mid-eighties, I did not go to South Africa. South Africa came to me and my family in Manchester, and then to Global Citizens Circle, in the person of a pregnant refugee, a scholarship recipient at New Hampshire College (now SNHU). Two weeks after winter term began in January of 1986, a colleague asked, "Eleanor, do you think you could find a home for a refugee student who's here on scholarship from South Africa? Her name is Tshidi. She arrived pregnant. Staying in the dorm is obviously not going to work out." Still not quite grasping the question's implications, I said, automatically, "Sure. I'll try." Right then, I had an inkling that our family just might be growing by two very soon. After all, Tshidi's flowing African dress would not conceal her secret into the semester. She would need an answer as soon as possible.

The answer came swiftly. My husband Jim was fine with the idea; Joel, an eighth-grader had only one hesitation: "You know I'm not that good with newborns," he admitted. He put up with a lot of teasing about that later when we told Tshidi, but that night he was more than satisfied when I assured him the mother was coming with the baby. Maria, a fifth-grader, was ready before the conversation ended. She was planning where the cradle would fit in her room and suggesting we move in another mattress for her to sleep on, so Tshidi could have her bed. It was late January. Tshidi would move in several weeks later.

I met Tshidi in my office the following day, and she confided: "I can't believe I actually came. My husband and I felt I might lose my scholarship if it was discovered I was pregnant, but we felt I should still come." And so did the baby! Tshidi gave birth to a healthy girl, Mpho' (meaning "gift") at Catholic Medical Center in Manchester on a sunny April morning. We were at the hospital soon after we heard the news but were told that only the "immediate" family could visit. "We are the immediate family!" The somewhat perplexed nurse allowed us in. Jim's decision to put pink balloons on our front lamppost did leave a rather reclusive neighbor even more perplexed about "immediate family." After a few days, he made his way across the yard to Jim and in a whisper commented: "I didn't know Eleanor was pregnant!" Jim's answer might be the reason we did not see the neighbor until summer: "Oh," replied Jim adding, "—and—the baby is Black." Actually, in the eighties, aside from the large international population at New Hampshire College, the state was traditionally "lily white." That perception surfaced even a decade later when Maria, then a junior at the University of Notre Dame, was being interviewed for a volunteer stint in Kenya: "So," one interviewer queried: "What makes a student from "lily white" New Hampshire, think she can relate to African children in Kenya?"

Maria said, afterward, that she even surprised herself with her response: "Well, New Hampshire may not be very diverse, but just come to our house," and then she told the story of Tshidi and Mpho; and Virginia and her baby, Victoria Maria, who were the next to live in our home. End of interview. Maria went to Kenya to work with school children that summer of 1996.

A decade earlier, Tshidi was providing all our family with a new lens on geography. It brought places like faraway "Soweto" (short for "southwest township") into our consciousness. "All of a sudden, Soweto seemed like it was next door," Joel commented on June 10, 1986, when the tenth anniversary of the uprising was being remembered in the news.

The price they paid

"They change their sky but not their soul who cross the ocean."

—Horace, The Odes

"I must leave or they will kill me."

Tshidi was not exaggerating. Twelve-year-old Hector Pieterson had just been killed by police. The teenage Tshidi describes running home from school and sobbing the news to her mother, Mama Sophie.

Thousands like Tshidi's teenage school friends would be rounded up after that protest against the imposed and inferior Bantu education. She was transferred from a refugee camp in Swaziland (where she and her husband, Eddie, met) to Tanzania, where she served as a counselor for refugees. She was later sent to military training in Libya and after that, given the option to take courses in Zimbabwe. During the same time, she and Eddie married and had a son, Rungulane, and then a baby girl who died of a virus at eight months. Before the age of twenty-five, this young couple had experienced the loss of a child, and separation from their parents, siblings, and country. Being torn from families in such a violent way left the physical and emotional scars of the evil apartheid system on them and their families. It was another kind of "Great Hunger." But they were, above all, survivors.

And the young did lead them…

It was the tenth anniversary of that uprising which, with ongoing sanctions, is said to have been the ultimate blow to apartheid.

The young had led them but at a great price. Tshidi, now twenty-six and a mother of two, shared that, on the fateful day in 1976, they had been so naïve: "We were just school kids. We thought the protest would end in six or seven months, and we'd all go back home."

It did not happen in that way. Instead, ten years later in 1986, Tshidi was sitting in our dining room, her father no longer alive, and her mother holding out hope that she would live to see her oldest daughter again, as well as her grandchildren for the first time. Tshidi was nursing her baby girl, born while her husband and four-year-old son were still in a refugee camp in Harare—all still without a country. Weeks later, Tshidi's sunny personality and contagious laugh could no longer conceal her true feelings. Standing in our kitchen holding Mpho', her anguish poured out. She questioned all her decisions and wondered if she should have left South Africa in the first place. What would happen next? I would not find any words in that moment. We simply hugged with three-month-old Mpho' tucked safely in an iro, her mama's baby wrap.

I would recall that heartbreaking moment many times but especially twenty-five years later on December 5, 2013—the day President Mandela died—and "baby Mpho'," now twenty-six, was living with us once again, having come from South Africa after her mother's unexpected death at age fifty-two. It was now Mpho' who stood in the same spot in our Manchester kitchen, distraught at the loss of her mother, saddened in hearing that Madiba [President Mandela] had died, and releasing her own anguish over apartheid's destroying several generations of families through its evil system.

I could not comfort Tshidi in 1986 or Mpho' in 2013. I could only offer sentiments, however inadequate, when Tshidi's mother (Mpho's grandmother) Mama Sophie died of complications from diabetes, in Soweto—also too young—at fifty-nine. The reflection was written as solace to Tshidi, Mama Sophie's daughter. Now the words were a similar gesture to Mpho', Tshidi's daughter:

To Mama Sophie, 1998

...Darkness hovered o'er those years
Families flung far-apart(heid)
Wings only to flee a land
That would not root them in its segregated soil.

Those daughters and sons carried the burden of their story
Into homes and schools around the world.
Roots that had been ripped up and tossed across continents
Took hold anew, our larger human family enriched.

Sleep now, dear Mama, "Go well" to reunion and rest
You lost your children but they shared their stories—
Your seed sown and grown in the fertile soil of diversity
Formed families with roots and wings

...We will not forget the gift of life
You and all your generation gave to us.
We will not forget at what great price
That precious gift was purchased.

Together again but without a country, Eddie and Tshidi Muendane with their children in our home. Mbatha and Zoyi would complete the family before they returned to South Africa in 1998, as full citizens.

The apartheid system separated thousands of families such as the Muendanes. Tshidi and Mpho on left; Eddie and Rungulane on right.

With warm understanding, Harry Belafonte welcomes Tshidi Muendane, South African refugee and scholarship recipient in graduate studies at SNHU, to a Global Citizens Circle. On left, Nadine Hack; on right, Eleanor Dunfey.

My accidental double exposure of this photo shows two images: one of Mama Sophie Temba, Tshidi's mother, outside her home in Soweto; the other superimposes her image onto the photo I snapped later, of President Mandela's prison cell hundreds of miles away on Robben Island. The image speaks the truth: All South Africans were imprisoned with Mandela under apartheid.

"Do not seek to be 'African' leaders; be global leaders..."
—*Chief Emeka Anyaoku, Africa's Commonwealth Secretary*
General in conversation with South African emerging leaders

In the late seventies, before many had heard the word "apartheid," Jerry was drawn to the suffering of the non-white population in South Africa. Donald Woods, a trusted journalist of the imprisoned Nelson Mandela, exposed the police brutality that caused Steve Biko's death. Donald and his wife, Wendy, were ardent anti-apartheid activists whose life-long commitment to justice was the subject of several books, among them, *Biko; Asking for Trouble*; and *Cry Freedom*. In 1987, David Attenborough produced a film, drawing from all three accounts and titled, *Cry Freedom*.

In 1981, Donald and Wendy were Global Citizen Circle discussion leaders and educated participants with their firsthand stories of apartheid's continuing atrocities. The Circle could provide an open, respectful atmosphere for activists to share such stories and urge us to become more informed and involved particularly about the controversial and complicated issues such as sanctions. Apartheid was not only South Africa's issue. It affected the world.

A Circle in 1986 on Capitol Hill in Washington, DC on that subject exposed the continuing horror of the apartheid system. Global Rights leader Gay McDougal's initiative and coordination made that program possible. It was the first time I met Archbishop Desmond Tutu, considered now the "world's pastor" (but more comfortable just being the "Arch"). He was traveling the world, as were Donald Woods, documentary filmmaker, Sharon Sopher, and others, imploring countries and companies to divest themselves of all South Africa business interests as a deadly blow against the apartheid system.

The archbishop spoke his plea clearly and powerfully conveying that, Yes, companies who were still doing business or holding investments in the country might be providing jobs, and even perhaps housing and maybe even minimal health care. But not for people's wellbeing; only for government's self-interest and control. Apartheid was an evil system that did not allow its citizens of color to vote and left them powerless.

As I sat in that room on Capitol Hill listening to the Archbishop; my husband, son, and daughter were having dinner at our home in Manchester, NH, with Tshidi, and I was carrying a handwritten letter with a poignant plea of her own: "Please, dear Archbishop. Do not give up your efforts."

They started early and stayed at it
That same weekend, Archbishop Tutu blessed my brother and Nadine's marriage. My sister Mary (who was working in DC) and I were present.

Their involvement in South Africa grew. From township activists to stellar moral leaders like Nelson Mandela and Graça Machel, from the families of Albertina and Walter Sisulu, to those of Archbishop Desmond and Leah Tutu and Oliver and Adelaide Tambo; they were "on call" no matter the request. What is important, however, is not their pictures or any of our pictures with these great heroes who "started early and stayed at it" (the wording in the Global Citizens Award). What is important, rather, is what we all do behind the scenes; do what strengthens family ties, as Jerry and Nadine have done with the children and grandchildren of those remarkable leaders and countless others. We Dunfeys had received our marching orders from Northern Ireland's community activists in 1972: "Don't be like some Americans who have come, made promises to us, and then have 'never been heard from again.'"

In 2008, South Africa celebrated those who had supported them early and stayed at it. Then South African president, Thabo Mbeki, honored those he called the "stars of our national firmament." Citizens in the fourteen-year-old democracy had been invited to nominate a foreign national who, they felt, had "stayed with" South Africa during its long anti-apartheid struggle. South African exile, Luyanda Mzumza, had participated in several Global Citizens Circles in Boston. For more than a decade after his return to his homeland as a full citizen, and in his work with youth and the peace movement, he and Jerry continued to work on their shared causes. In 2008, Luyanda's letter led to Jerry's award: The Order of the Companions of OR Tambo (founder of the African National Congress, ANC) honoring those "who have actively promoted the interests and aspirations of South Africa through outstanding cooperation, solidarity, and support. Jerry and Nadine Hack, his wife and partner in all his global social justice work, especially in South Africa, accepted the award in Pretoria.

The Presidential Awards' ceremony took place at noon. Global Citizens Circle held a program that same evening in Walter Sisulu Square of Dedication in Soweto, with participants ages sixteen to seventy-five, in a lively conversation led by fellow award recipient, Chief Emeka Anyaoku, Africa's third commonwealth secretary general, a wise and humble conversant who was particularly impressed with the youth participation. The chief implored them not to aim to be "African leaders," but rather, "global leaders."

After a momentous day and evening, Jerry expressed feelings that summed up what must have seemed a moment when the impossible actually had become possible: "As out of this world as the presidential ceremony was, all I'm thinking about is the GCC program this evening. That was my 'real award.'"

Recipients of the Order of Companions of OR Tambo, Left back: Ronald Dellums, Jerry Dunfey and wife Nadine; Archbishop Emeritus Njongonkulu Ndungane and Chief Emeka Anyoaku. In front are Yashia Padia, on behalf of her father Chanderdeo George Sewpershad, Deputy President Phumzile Mlambo-Ngcuka, President Thabo Mbeki, Harry Belafonte, Reverend Frank Chikane and Linda Biehl. Note: *Amy Biehl's Last Home* by Steven Gish, 2018, tells the remarkable story of Amy and her parents in this 25th anniversary of the murder of twenty-six year old Amy Biehl, in the Ruguluthu Township, South Africa, two days before her return home. Her father, Peter, died in 2001

Alexandra Township's leader and activist, Linda Twala (second from left) in white shirt) pauses with GCC delegates for a time of reflection in front of an overgrown field which hides a mass grave of countless unnamed victims of apartheid. 1998

After almost thirty years in prisons—Walter Sisulu on Robben Island and Albertina Sisulu in countless home arrests and threats—both received the Global Citizen Circle award in Boston in 1991. In 1998, Sheila Sisulu, also imprisoned in the struggle, a courageous educator/activist became the first Black person to represent South Africa as ambassador to the United States. President Mandela appointed her to that position in 1999. Here she and her son, Linda (second row, middle) join in welcoming GCC delegates for a family picnic at a crèche across from their Soweto bungalow.

The eldest "Gogo" (grandmother or any elder) conveys her welcome in the universal language of a hug. Linda Twala, Alexandra leader, turned his own home into a rest home for Gogos and still, today, continues to dedicate his life and resources to the elders, many of whom had never traveled beyond Alexandra until 2017, when Twala brought them to Robben Island to see where their leader, President Nelson Mandela, lived in exile for 27 years. They could relate; they had been "exiled" in Alexandra without their freedom even longer. 1998

CHAPTER 31

1984–2013

"Where the world comes to mind..."

"Where the world comes to mind" was for a number of years the tagline for New Hampshire College/Southern New Hampshire University.

And the world had come to campus classrooms and our home, as well. Now, on a sweltering May afternoon in 1987, Tshidi made her way across the stage set up on the New Hampshire College sports field. My excitement and relief that she reached such a significant milestone was interrupted by a colleague sitting behind me in the rows of seats set up near the platform.

"Have you met Virginia from El Salvador?" she whispered loud enough for me to hear. "She's in her first year of the graduate program."

"No. I haven't."

"Oh—well, she's pregnant..."

Virginia and her newborn, Victoria Maria, were soon in our world—and home. With Tshidi and then, Virginia, came their fellow students, such as Gopal Nair, a Malaysian of Indian descent. An astute political thinker and social activist, Nair's intellectual gifts were surpassed only by his generosity, especially in assisting these two refugee families, who were his classmates.

My husband, Jim, taught graduate courses in organizational leadership, often in classes with students from ten-to-twelve countries. My world religions course frequently enrolled students representing every major world religion. For the following twenty years, I was faculty advisor for the Human Rights Association (HRA). In 2000, Esteban Lopez and his wife, Zelma, came to SNHU from Ecuador to pursue master's degrees in finance and international business. Zelma assumed leadership of the HRA with the active involvement of Esteban. They participated in several Global Citizens Circles, including one on nuclear disarmament, "Responsible National Security: Getting our Priorities Straight," at which then-U.S. Senator Joseph Biden was the discussion leader.

"Even more important than those programs," shared Esteban, "were the follow-up informal gatherings at the Dunfey-Freiburgers' home, where graduate students and undergraduates, international and American students, whites and minorities talked about their differing experiences an perspectives. We had opportunities to see the importance of human rights here and around the world—then try to take action."

It was also the human rights association that held candlelight walks each Martin Luther King "holiday" which every other state in the Union had embraced. Thanks to stalwarts like Lionel Washington Johnson, Arnie Alpert, Jackie Weatherspoon, Harvey Keys, Renny Cushing, Jim Splaine, and many others, as early as 1979, the twenty-year struggle finally succeeded in 1999. New Hampshire was the last state to adopt the holiday, and Martin Luther King III was invited to honor the occasion. It was his first visit back to the state since he was a young teen when his family was invited to a Lake Winnipesaukee cottage after his father's assassination in 1968.

In a way, all the courses Jim and I taught touched on human rights, particularly courses in corporate social responsibility (CSR)/business ethics/leaders and ethics, with regular opportunities to have discussions with pioneer CSR leaders like Joe Keefe at Pax World Funds, Gary Hirshberg and Samuel Kaymen at Stonyfield Farm Yogurt, Gerardine Ferlins of Cirtronics, and Colette Phillips, the visionary of Colette Phillips Communications, Inc.

In the "Greed is Good" era that permeated many companies, we discussed the "ethics of enough"—finding a moral compass (with help of principles, both one's own and those of friends and colleagues) as a way to set criteria for decision making. Often, we discussed the many people who started out with good intentions but lost their bearings as they rose in prominence and increased their wealth. How many fathers, it seemed, succeeded financially beyond their wildest imaginations, but left their sons legacies of fines and prison terms because the fathers had lost their moral compass. I began focusing on the theme, the ethics of enough. There were plenty of lessons about handling failure. Not so many about the moral challenges accompanying "success."

In 2001, at the height of the Enron scandal, President Richard Gustafson appointed me to the Christos and Mary Papoutsy Endowed Chair in Business Ethics.

Jim and I also taught in the university's international programs: he in Dubai and Greece, and I in Malaysia, where my students came from The Maldives, Pakistan, Yemen, Indonesia, and China. A number of these students transferred from SNHU program centers around the world to complete their studies at our main campus in Manchester, New Hampshire.

Eemaan Rameez, whom I taught in Klang, Malaysia, made her way to our home from the Maldives on a freezing January morning in 2002—her plans uncertain for months, given her father's great concern for her safety in America in the aftermath of September 11, 2001. He really wanted her to finish her studies in Australia where her brother was living. But Eemaan really wanted to come to the States. He relented when she assured him she would be "part of a professor's family." He trusted her. Eemaan graduated and worked several years in the Maldives' resort industry—even through the tsunami when she and staff helped save victims and moved out of their rooms to shelter their traumatized guests.

Eemaan would return to SNHU for her master's degree. Her sister and father stayed with "the professor's family" when Eemaan was selected as the graduate student speaker in 2009. She addressed the more than ten thousand guests at commencement, drawing on her experience in that tsunami and speaking of the resilience we need to survive the countless "tsunamis" that up-end each of us in our own lives. President LeBlanc acknowledged her father and sister during the ceremony: "They traveled almost nine thousand miles to hear Eemaan speak today." Being recognized so personally at such a grand event moved her father to tears. While staying with us, Eemaan's father had enjoyed his early morning ritual of stepping outside for a smoke in the driveway; then coming in to enjoy his cup of coffee, conversation, and some days, Jim's pancakes.

"America is nothing like what I see on CNN," he remarked one of those mornings, as he described watching the neighborhood come to life each day. This accomplished father, who had traveled extensively in Asia and Europe, mused: "Until I experienced what it is to be at 'home' in New Hampshire, I never really knew what America was like."

I was fortunate to have a similar experience—in reverse. In Malaysia, I was "looked after" by the families of students whom I had taught on our New Hampshire campus. On September 11, 2001, Jim (who was visiting me) and I were at dinner with the whole Victor family whose daughters, Cheryl and Stacey, and son-in-law, Gabriel, had become a part of our family in Manchester. The family had suffered the tragic loss of their twenty-two-year-old, only son, David, while Cheryl was in my course. The bond that started in sorrow, deepened during the dark days following September 11 and continued in happier times when their youngest daughter, Stacey, earned her degree at Boston University.

Throughout our tenure at SNHU, Jim and I had unique opportunities. When our mail was delivered on a June morning in 1987, for example, there was an invitation from the families of Visutham Tantivanich and Sirikiat Praphailong to attend their wedding at St. Catherine's Church, with the reception in the church hall. I put the invitation in with Jim's mail because I knew they weren't my students; he placed it in mine for the same reason. After a few futile rounds of that, we finally realized that the bride and groom-to-be were "Apple and Joe," graduate students whom we knew very well because Tshidi and Mpho' had moved to their three-bedroom rented home after living with us.

The church hall, at that time, was a place to sign up for soccer or Little League or hold AA meetings—but not for a wedding reception. Figuring this couple would probably have a small group of graduate-student friends joining them for the occasion, we offered them our lovely, small backyard. It wasn't until, two weeks later, after we suggested they "take over" our house for the occasion, that we realized they had already contracted with a caterer—for sixty wedding guests. Fast forward to August 7 (our wedding anniversary, as well) and right there, in our cozy yard, there were table places set for a sit-down dinner for sixty people. Both sets of parents, visiting from Thailand, and other relatives and friends helped transform the area into "Little Bangkok," without any problem understanding one another's languages as we followed decorating orders.

Making her way down the stairs from Maria's bedroom, the beautiful bride, "Apple," wore the gown chosen for the wedding ceremony at St. Catherine's Church. She then changed to her other bridal dress for the backyard reception. It was a perfect summer afternoon until the newly married couple drove down Belmont Street in a car adorned with ribbons and enough soda cans to call all the neighbors from their dinner tables. As soon as the newlyweds turned the corner, and the caterers had gathered up all evidence of the feast, the heavens opened to a rainstorm that soaked our "Little Bangkok," but not its guests. We were all inside watching the day's events instantly produced by a videographer, an amazing production for those of us whose celebrations had been recorded on 8mm film reels.

Expanding the circle of our family, collaborating with colleagues and students across campus, coordinating university-wide initiatives and programs that incorporated Global Citizens Circle, and advancing a service learning initiative—all those experiences showed me, firsthand, how much I could continue learning when and where the "world comes to mind."

When GCC could not go to South Africa, GCC went to Beyers and Ilse Naudé through Xolani Webster Moshuge and Robby Vanrykel, SNHU alums and former roommates on the soccer team, who were honored to present the Global Citizens award to lifelong anti-apartheid activists. In 1996, I met Beyers in Johannesburg for a lunch and when we walked into the lobby of the hotel, all five of the front desk staff, black South Africans, gasped and one asked: "Is it you, Reverend Naudé?" When he smiled they surrounded him and expressed their gratitude for his work. After their spontaneous and sincere words, I remarked to Beyers: "I don't think you need lunch! That had to be a lifetime's worth of nourishment!" He smiled again. "It was, indeed."

Before addressing 9,000 guests at the 2010 SNHU Commencement, Eemaan poses with her father and sister, Jim and me. Afterward, she "graduates" with a major in kid-fun with "fellow grads," Simon, Willem, and Jackson.

Top: SNHU graduate students and human rights activists from Ecuador, Zelma Echeverria and Esteban López, with then Senator Joe Biden when he led a Circle discussion on "Responsibe National Security: Getting Our Priorities Straight."

Middle: Martin, III's first visit to NH was as a young teen in 1968 when the King family spent a vacation at my brother, Walter, and sister-in-law, Barbara's Lake Winnepesaukee cottage. In 1999, he returned to celebrate the Martin Luther King, Jr. holiday in the state of New Hampshire. Martin, III, shares his and his mother's and siblings' journey after the assassination of his father. In 2005, Martin III, returns to NH, this time to address 1500 members of the SNHU and regional community, urging all of us to "Remember, Celebrate, and Act," to keep his father's dream alive.

Right: The JFK Library and Global Citizens Circle co-sponsored a discussion with Richard Butler, former head, UN team in Iraq, pictured here with SNHU Human Rights Association officers, Hieu Tieu, left, and Kimika Embree.

Youngest graduate, eighteen-month-old Mpho Muendane, held by her proud mother, Tshidi. Malaysian graduate, Gopal Nair (fifth from right) achieved excellence not only because of his intelligence, but also his generosity, friendship and care of refugees. A member of our extended family, Gopal also saw to the needs of El Salvadoran student, Virginia and her baby, Victoria, who lived with us.

Twenty-five years after living with us as a newborn, Victoria Maria and her mother, Virginia Melgar, return to Manchester to visit her "first address" and SNHU.

Students from eleven countries share their ideas and their cuisines with one another during a summer session of "Dr. Jim's" organizational leadership seminar in our backyard.

CHAPTER 32

The Jack Effect

Integrating world religion, business ethics, and civic engagement with my involvement in Global Citizens Circle kept me active in all the causes my brothers and sisters espoused. Working so closely made me appreciate each all the more. For more than four decades, Jerry and I have had a unique lens on the ages and stages of our relationship with each other and with our siblings. Above all, we both realize what an influence our brother, Jack, has had in leading our family and its business.

Whether it was Jack's pointing to Jerry with confidence when he asked him to take over major marketing and publicity positions, or by, as Jerry writes, "freeing me up to be a part of the Senator Ted Kennedy delegation to South Africa in 1985," there's no doubt that Jack was an omnipresent force in our lives. He did more than his share of "heavy lifting." In 1949, when our dad recognized the need for division of labor as the family business expanded, Jerry remembers a "kitchen table meeting" where our father asked Jack to "head up" the business and then went on to have Attorney Jim Donovan draw up legal papers. Soon, he also brought Johnny Fairfield into the business. Johnny spent more than thirty years in his role as family friend and trusted professional.

Jack is now in his ninety-fifth year, a remarkable milestone for any one, but especially for someone who survived a ski accident that broke his neck—at age eighty-eight. Jack was hospitalized for the first time in his life after that near-fatal injury—his emergency tracheotomy at age two didn't count as being in the hospital because the operation was performed at midnight on the kitchen table with our mother as nurse.

Jack grew as a leader, the risk taker, human rights advocate, philanthropist, and key business strategist—the president and CEO of Omni Hotels International. Other siblings and relatives have their stories of his confidential assistance at critical moments. He certainly has affected my life in many ways.

"Hey, Eleanor…," Jack beckoned to me to come into the kitchen—not to cook, though. It was December 1994, and we were at Boston College, at that moment in its catering kitchen, just before another Global Citizens Circle gathering with John Hume as discussion leader. Jack wanted to go over the introductory remarks we had drafted. This ritual had become an integral part of what you might call our professional relationship in the

Circle. Jack knew what he wanted to say; he would send me thorough notes, and after seven years of partnering him in this role, I had developed a way of writing remarks in his voice. It was natural. I knew my brother's style, and he would always take great care in going over the comments. At every stage and age, I was continually amazed with the way our sibling relationship evolved: I was once the five-year-old kid sister who sobbed if any one dared sing his song, "Oh how I miss you tonight," when he was in the Air Force. I grew to the seven-year-old sibling who questioned why I had missed him so much, when this veteran pilot-brother of mine took me in his PT-19, perched on Bob's lap in its two-seater open cockpit with Bob's arms as my seatbelt and did a few air stunts to add to the flight (fright).

I forgave him long before I was ten because he saved my life (and that of my parents, my brother and wife, Roy and Ruth; and their kids) the night our "Restful" cottage at Hampton Beach leaked carbon monoxide, and we all passed out. Somehow Jack pulled and dragged us out of there. All I recall was his piling us kids in the Packard with windows rolled down as he drove up and down Ocean Boulevard until we were revived. I'm glad he didn't have his PT-19 handy. That might have given him another idea.

By thirteen, I was Jack's sibling waitress, then one of his four sister-nuns; a confidante after the death of our mother in 1982 and the six deaths of siblings between 1989 and 1991. Along the way we had became close colleagues in Global Citizens Circle. Now here we were, back in the kitchen cooking up ways that might give people an appetite for getting involved in yet another cause close to our hearts: Northern Ireland's peace prospects.

Credit for the family's local and global engagement also goes to Jack. "Only through unanimous consent could we have founded Global Citizens Circle, especially considering that it required the five brothers to share the costs equally," Jerry acknowledges. "It was Jack's leadership that led us all to bring each of our important causes to the table."

Top: Eleanor in the window hiding my chicken pox but not my excitement to have my brother, Jack, home on furlough.

Middle: Jerry gets a listening ear in Jack.

Bottom: Headed to D.C., my brothers, Jack and Bob, invited to travel with the Hume and Trimble families to Oslo for the presentation of the Nobel Peace Prize to Northern Ireland leaders John Hume and David Trimble. 1994

Above: Jack was an official observer in the historic election of Nelson Mandela as president of South Africa. 1994

Top: Jack watched lines form into the horizon starting at 6:00 a.m. Polls did not open until 8:00 a.m. Thousands stood for hours inching forward in the heat of the day, an unforgettable experience of the patience of the masses who were voting for the first time, citizens of the country that had fueled its economic engine with apartheid violence on these same people. Strong young men carried their elders and the disabled to the front of the line. Here in the States, Tshidi and Eddie Muendane and hundreds of South African refugee students drove hours to the African Consulate in New York, to add their first-time vote. Finally, they had a country; they were citizens of South Africa. It will take decades to undo what an evil system created, but the resilience of South Africans persists.

Bottom: Session with Fidel Castro, during Jack's Human Rights visits, usually took place from midnight on with Castro holding court, but Jack could get the Cuban leader to listen and had great interest in Jack's background in the hospitality industry. Over a decade, Jack and his delegations were successful in obtaining the release of 87 prisoners, removal of landmines in Angola, and permission for food supplies to enter Ethiopia.

Bob and Jack, with Nelson Mandela, South Africa's President, and Graça Machel, Global Citizen Award recipient, 1998. Johannesburg, South Africa.

President Reagan appointed Jack Dunfey to the original Peace Academy (now USIP, the US Institute for Peace. 1982

When a young, dedicated translator/facilitator for many of Jack's human rights meetings between El Salvador's government and the FMLN (Farabundo Martí National Liberation Front) was arrested and jailed in 1989, she says she could have easily been "disappeared" like so many of the women she was imprisoned with. Following her release, Jennifer Casolo was a discussion leader for Circles at SNHU and in Boston. In 2014, she wrote: "Twenty-five years ago today, I was released from the El Salvadoran prison," Jennifer shares, "and I quickly learned how the greater Dunfey circle had moved mountains on my behalf meeting me at the airport in Miami and cradling me…cleaning me up! letting me cry, and telling me some of the calls made on my behalf. I am alive because I called my friend, Andrea, who had Jack's number…before cell phones, when finding someone was near impossible."

Jack snapped this picture of Harry Belafonte when the two visited an Angola orphanage for child victims of landmines. This tragedy was also brought home with Senator Patrick Leahy's raising our awareness as the Circle's discussion leader and advancing legislation in Congress.

US Senator John Kerry (and later Secretary of State) and Jack Dunfey, GCC founder, at a Circle honoring Congressman J.Joseph Moakley, Washington, D.C. March 15, 2001 who, only months before his death from leukemia, discussion leader addressing, "Making Community work: A Lifetime of Local and Global Public Service." John Kerry and Jack, who share Moakley's commitment to community and world issues, voice their admiration for their friend and public servant.

The American Ireland Fund's recognition of President Clinton's efforts in the Northern Ireland peace process. Clinton had appointed Jack as a delegate to the White House economic summit in Belfast. Jack's wife, Lisa, joins in the celebration.

Archbishop Tutu relaxes for his birthday weekend in Waterville Valley, NH, after receiving the NH Humanities Bud Dunfey Award, presented by Julie Dunfey, Bud's daughter.

CHAPTER 33

Full credit: Your lives are my life.

John Cole said the Dunfeys traveled on "their own private wave length." That same metaphor conveys the kind of communication my mother nurtured in relationships not only with family, but with employees, friends, and acquaintances. She was a confidante, fully present to each person—trustworthy. Kate Dunfey never sought publicity or "celebrity status" even when it was justifiably within grasp. She lived in a comfortable but modest one-bedroom apartment over Lamie's kitchen where the familiar aroma of fried clams wafting the hall reminded her of earlier, less affluent years, and she took great pleasure in inviting people—a few at a time—to dine downstairs, admitting, "It was a great treat to sign my name to the check rather than have to cook the dinner!" After forty years of serving meals in her kitchen, it's no wonder she relished that perk. Staff, especially the family of Crotty teens, loved serving her. Lamie's added her favorite lunch item to the menu: Mother Dunfey's peanut butter and jelly sandwich.

Kate Dunfey also had simple taste in jewelry. Once, while she was traveling to visit one of us nuns, her apartment was burglarized. She laughed telling us, "They didn't take anything!" The reason? When she traveled, she carried or wore her only jewelry treasure: a set of Mikimoto pearls from daughter, Kay, in Japan. Mother Dunfey accepted, appreciated and thoroughly enjoyed the perks and pleasures that came with her sons' success, but she did not need them to be happy.

My mother's response to our repeated urging that she write her autobiography had always been that she didn't need a book to describe her life because she could do it in one sentence: "I was engaged to your father on Labor Day and was in labor ever after!" We finally did persuaded her to write her memoir. True to form, she wrote it as letters to and memories of our dad, her mother, and the twelve of us. It was her way of extending the intimate "wave length" we each shared with her. "Your lives are my life," she said.

When my mother received honorary degrees from Merrimack and Emmanuel colleges, we were overjoyed. We had all gotten credit over the years for the work she and our dad did and from which we gained so much. Talk about heavy lifting (and labor!). She deserved those center-stage kudos. But she smiled them off in her self-deprecating way: "I got my education in

Our mother, enjoying the unlikely idea that she would be the first in the family to "earn" her doctorate! Left to right, my sisters, Eileen and Mary, and brother, Roy, smile knowing she "labored hard" for it.

Merrimack College's honorary degree recipients, Catherine Dunfey, chair, Dunfey Family Corporation, and Arthur Fiedler, renowned director, Boston Symphony Orchestra. 1969

the "College of Knowledge" (her favorite description when asked about her academic history) at the Lowell Boott Mills. Now she was adding, "but I'm the first in the family to receive my doctorate, alongside Arthur Fiedler, no less, even though the rest of you have spent years studying!"

"All I ask of you..."

My mother lived for thirty years after our father died. On March 25, 1982, Catherine "Kate" Dunfey quietly slipped away to join him. In a small frame on her bedside table a brief reflection conveyed her lifelong and final message: "All I ask of you is forever to remember me as loving you," an evening song by Gregory Norbert.

Hampton Center expanded on the day of her funeral to welcome many dignitaries and longtime dear friends and neighbors, hundreds filing into the service where the twelve children our mother ushered into this life would now usher her into the next. Granddaughter Gail, representing the thirty-five grandchildren, was moved by what her cousins had shared with her in preparation: "Each of us felt we were her favorite..." she reflected. Ambassador Andy Young, as I mentioned earlier in this book, called Mother Dunfey a "light—a Lady Liberty welcoming a world of diverse people."

And Marty Sepè was there, the Acre teen in the 1940s, the hardworking, witty practical joker who had endeared himself to my parents and all the clan. My mother would have loved to witness his arrival on a motorcycle, screeching into a sliver of an opening and swerving to avoid the hearse in the front of the Church. His tribute would be in action, not words. The mother of the family he had loved and hung out with and teased and worked with as a young man, was now Lowell City Police Officer Sèpe. He would lead the many cars of family and friends making the thirty-five-mile trip from Hampton, New Hampshire, to Lowell, Massachusetts, to lay Kate Dunfey to rest beside her husband, Roy, in St. Patrick's cemetery.

It was Kay, my mother's namesake and first daughter, whose inspired reflection conveyed the gift our mother was to each of her twelve children.

Mother,
To you we were never a collective.
We were, in a sense, each an only child—
Roy—Paul—Kay—Mary—Jack—Bud
Bob—Dick—Eileen—Walter—Jerry—
  Eleanor

Each a person
Understood as separate
Accepted as individual
Cherished as unique.

What do you take away with you?
You take twelve distinct dialogues:
Expressions of welcome, wit, and wisdom,
Of concern for each one's special needs,
Of support in each trial, each triumph,
Every aspiration.

And what do you leave behind?
You leave a legacy of laughter—
You leave memories with meanings
Known only to each one
You leave twelve lifetimes to respond
To all your years of dialogue
And best of all, Mother, you leave
Us one another!
Ours the serenity of those who face the
  future
With the knowledge life is good—
We have glimpsed beauty from high
  secret places
We have loved you and in knowing you
Loved God.

"All I ask of you is forever to remember me as loving you."

Before   After

Top left: Welcoming my sister Mary, second from right, returning for a visit from her teaching post in Honolulu, Oahu. Fortunately, the ban on nuns having their pictures taken had, by 1965, been lifted. Left to right: Eleanor, Eileen, Mother, Mary, Kay.

Top right: Left to right: Eileen, Mary, Mother, Kay, Eleanor before our 1978 family reunion at Wallis Sands, NH. We would post family pictures, always with "creative captions," on the walls as a welcome. The day began with all 12 and our mom with Fr. Kenney celebrating a liturgy of thanks. At noon, all the families—usually close to 90—joined the festivities.

Middle: All twelve gather in the morning for our mother's annual birthday-family reunion at Wallis Sands, NH. After a home liturgy of gratitude offered by Msgr. Phil Kenney, the 70–80 immediate family join in the celebration. 1979

Bottom: First reunion after our mother's death. The family's longtime Lowell friend and favorite "music man," Charlie Gallagher, knew every song the Dunfeys loved to harmonize. Around the piano singing *'Til We Meet Again*, are left to right: Jack, Paul, Dick, Kay, Eleanor, Bob and Walter. 1982

CHAPTER 34

"Countah Cultshah"

Parker House doorman Richie Aliferis knows every inch of School and Tremont Streets, as well as the comings and goings of every taxi, after welcoming and bidding farewell to thousands of guests in the past forty-one years. I think back to a conversation he and I had on the School Street sidewalk one blustery (actually, most are blustery) afternoon after a Texas family took over the Parker House in the late nineties. In his own inimitable Boston accent, Richie said, "Elenah, do I have a good story for you!" He went on to relate that a number of Parker House employees, himself included, were flown to Texas for a "seminah" on service. He couldn't believe that almost the entire session was about the Dunfeys and their "cultshah." He was thrilled that the new owners wanted to emphasize the Dunfey tradition again. "But," said he with his wide, impish grin, "They didn't need to fly me all the way to Texas to talk about the Dunfey family. I could've given the whole lectshah right here at the Pahka House!" Richie could probably also give a "whole lectshah" and more, on the Dunfey family's "countah cultshah."

A dozen—now more—Dunfeys to serve you

"A person is a person through other persons. We are bundled together in our humanity."
—*Archbishop Tutu's description of the African concept of ubuntu.*

The hard work, humor, harmony, and hospitality/spirituality of our parents made us the persons we are, products of their "countah cultshah." In business, classrooms, social causes, and social life, the names of extended family remind us of the diversity of that counter culture. They are the names of ordinary people who live extraordinarily well: Keefe, McGaunn, Beaupre, Cote, Sepé, Tutu, Kanteres, King, Cohen, Antonopolous, Zappala, Hirshberg, Ng, O'Brien, Redpath, Mandela, Sisulu, McWilliams, Hume, Young, Leland, Ellis…Muendane, Nair, Melgar, Victor, Rameez, Praphailong, and Tantanovich. They have grown and enriched our family circle along with so many others whose names are known only to us. One of my mother's favorite one-liners was, "I think your dad and I started the birth of a nation!" Maybe, too, my parents felt it was their responsibility to populate the "village" that it takes to raise a child!

What led the Dunfey family from clams to convents, to a Circle of Global citizens? Our parents. They lived ordinary lives extraordinarily well—mill workers, Kate and Roy Dunfey, who started out with an orchestra, a luncheonette, and a baby every two years, weaving a new fabric of family. They gave us time to love and space to grow. The world has changed so much in the hundred years since 1918 when their first son, Roy Francis, was born. What has not changed, though, and what our parents knew instinctively, is that people will always need to belong—to be invited, welcomed, included, respected. Around tables of inclusive, diverse conversations locally and globally, we continue to honor their lived lessons.

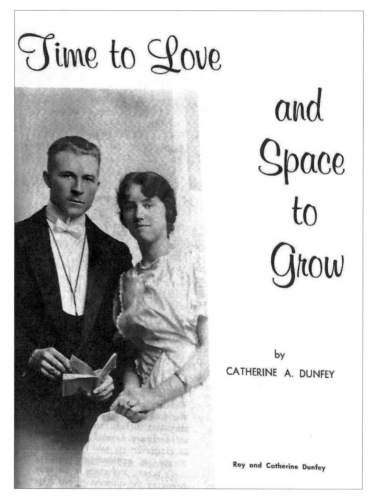

Focus Magazine
Sisters of Notre Dame de Namur
1966

The Dunfey family received the 1999 Irish International Immigration Center's Solas (Light) award. The ceremony was only months before the dawn of a new millennium, and just a few years shy of the one-hundredth anniversaries of my parents' births. Although I speak of my parents, the reflection honors all immigrant forebears from the many countries represented that night:

Reflection

Toward the close of the last century's evening, young women and men set ashore
The Irish, the Greek, the Italian—Lebanese, Canadian, and more.
They were part of a revolution, industrial at its core.

In the mills up the Merrimack River, their children worked morning 'til night
Through the warp and the woof, the sweat and the soot
They wove a new fabric of life.

Though their days could be viewed as dreary, the resilient echoes remain
In the song of their years, their smiles and their tears
With love, the thread that sustained.

The families prolific followed, most Catholic in propagation
"Twas the rule of the day," my mother would say,
"And with twelve, the birth of a nation!"

But the "nation" our parents gave birth to, was measured by welcomes, not size;
In our world there were Bouchers and Sepès, Antonopoulos, Mansurs, and Tighes.

The lesson they lived is quite simple: "There's a vast world outside your own door—
So be sure when you set your table—there's always room for one more."

Now we stand near the end of this century, setting forth for unexplored shores,
We're all immigrants of sorts, at borderless ports,
Global citizens birthing new lore.
Our parents' looms are not weaving, or shaping the next revolution
It's the bits and the bytes—the links, the websites
That are search engines forging solutions.

Yet we honor our ancestors' values, by linking our arms—and our web:
African, Asian, Dominican, Haitian
Weaving new fabrics of rich, diverse threads.

We can warm the hard and the software around tables and hearths of concern
Our work, song, and laughter will echo in the lives of the voiceless who yearn.

This award's a profound reminder, of all parents whose light showed our way—
They gave us the "top of their morning,"
Let us give them the "rest of our day!"
    1999

Acknowledgments

When you're the youngest of twelve children you know innately that you do very little—if anything—on your own. As the father of the twelve, LeRoy Dunfey also knew that. First and foremost, he counted on my mother, and when he wanted one of us kids, it was, "Hey...Dunfey!" We'd turn and he'd point to the one he needed.

In this journey of writing about my parents and their twelve children, I've called out many a "Hey..." and then pointed. I thank all those who responded so generously to what I needed at each step on that journey.

"Hey...each of you":

Kathy Mathis. After all the years of people nudging me to write the story of my family, you helped me at the outset to overcome my greatest block: finding and using "my voice." You were an invaluable mentor in that critical phase, and your interviews of "Dunfey alumni" and friends, as well as your genuine interest, gave me resources and confidence to assume responsibility for writing this saga. I am ever grateful for that invaluable launch.

Jerry Dunfey. I've pointed at you for as long as I can remember—in those early days probably trying to blame you for some sort of prank. But I learned early to count on you, and I would never have begun writing this story without knowing I could count on your memory, unlocking details others had long forgotten, and for providing long lists—all typed in your signature "cap style." You may be #11 to my #12, but you're #1 in my eyes; the source of my primary research and motivation.

Jack Dunfey. "Hey...Jack!" You've listened to and supported so many of our mutual projects over the years, Global Citizens Circle and this book being two of the major ones. I found a memo you wrote to our brother Bud in 1985: "Ask Kay and Eleanor to write the book about Mother." It only took me thirty-plus years. Thanks for not giving up on me, Jack. Know that your family leadership, astuteness, and support, have made such a difference in our lives.

Eileen Dunfey Robinson. You stand by me. You offered your place as a hideaway for me to write. You've been my personal cheerleader, spirited and spiritual, sending thoughtful notes to spur me on throughout the process when "life" interrupted my writing for months at a time. You believed I could finish the project even when I was certain I could not.

Jim Freiburger. You "took on" the whole Dunfey clan when you married me. Everyone could/can count on you, and we all do. You've listened to and lived many of the stories in this book for more than fifty years. Some of those stories would not have become reality without your caring involvement. You've been my loving dependable touchstone in family matters and beyond. Above all, you've made our impossible dream, possible.

Joel Dunfey Freiburger. Your Nanna Dunfey inspired you to start writing at age eight, and you've been my inspiration to do the same at almost ten times that age. How often I tried to give up, but not with you as my "encourager-in chief." I wish I could have collected all your morning calls, texts, emails, timely humor and advice. I could have published another book: *Words of Wisdom for a Mother and Other Unlikely Authors.* Thank you for being the writer you are. Thank you for being the son you are.

Maria Catherine Eisl. Even with the countless demands of being the mother of three active sons; teaching, volunteering, and making your home the "Grand Central" of gathering places, you made time to record and transcribe the memories Jack shared with you. Those details got me started and kept me at this project. Spending time with all of you also helped me "escape" when words failed me. I would not have had many of the stories in this saga were it not for you. A daughter makes such a difference.

Because several of my brothers married when I was still quite young, a half dozen or so of their children have felt more like "younger siblings" than nieces and nephews. I'm grateful to them for responding when I "pointed at" each of them: Walter, Patrick, Dan, Ruthie, Tish, and Gail, for responding to my urgent calls for photographs for "the project."

Rick Dunfey. "Hey…Rick!" You're the one who reminded me how often your dad, Roy Francis, spoke about my father's using that "Hey there…" call. I listened. You warned me about the many plots there'd have to be in this saga. I didn't listen. Thanks for advice I took and some that I didn't take. Most of all, thank you and your colleagues—"Hey there…" Anne Gram and Kenan Woods at Dunfey Publishing—for the many hours you spent designing and proofreading GCC publications. Their work has been a great resource for this book, as was your timely assistance, Mary Elizabeth Bartholomew.

Will Dunfey. A genealogist. Every family needs one, a storyteller *par excellance*. Your tours of Lowell's Acre and Pawtucketville, along with your extensive research on deep and interest in the history of our family taught me so much. Your generosity of time and information were a great support.

Keith Dunfey. I thank your mother, Audrey, for her exhaustive collection of every possible photo and news item (and there are scores) about the family. Thank you for preserving that precious store of memories and for always finding just the item I was needing when I made my "Hey…Keith!" call. You are our family's "connector-in-chief." So many cousins are getting to know one another again because of you, at reunions and on the family website.

Michael "Mike" Dunfey. It seems your Grandfather Dunfey's "Hey…" call found a slight variation when you and your cousin, Ruthie Dunfey, worked at the C Street, Hampton Beach restaurant. It became the "Drop one for Benny," call. Thank you for your enthusiasm in sharing such memories when your generation replaced us behind the counter. I needed those.

Many, beyond the family, responded when I pointed to them:

Katharine Webster. You coaxed and cajoled me to take on the "impossible" task of writing this story. You translated that nudge by spending your own time, in addition to the series of interviews, to record/transcribe stories so I would have some tangible notes to tap into. That helped so much!

Frank Lewis. I reached all the way "across the Pond" to point at you in County Kerry for feedback. You teased more than one story out of me. Radio host that you are, you knew how to "wake up" an underlying story with your questions.

Beverly Hodsdon, founder, president of Joyce Design Solutions, thank you for your remarkable organization and creative skills. I had access to all publications we designed together, and many photos in this book were preserved because of your work.

Loring Mills. Thank you for your help at critical moments with stories and visuals of Hampton, NH. Thank you to the Tuck Museum, Hampton, NH, for its rich resources.

Don West: You were there from the early years of Global Citizens Circle, and your photographs told our story in ways words could not.

Paul and Liz Fitzgerald for your invaluable video: "Dunfey Family History."

Andrew Petkun. You provided superb visuals, some of which are in this book, of GCC's first South Africa delegation when we honored Graça Machel and Adelaide Tambo. Priceless.

Rye NH library staff. I won't shout "Hey..." because it's the library's quiet space that I've appreciated. I started and finished this saga there with the warm support of staff, especially, you, Pam Brown. I'm so grateful.

Peter E. Randall Publisher. You and your team provided the knowledge, thoroughness and support I needed, Deidre. Kate Crichton, you are an amazing image archivist. Thank goodness for your cool, calm professionalism and talent. Zak Johnson, you lent your keen, professional eye to the manuscript in such an efficient way that I began to believe I might actually complete this journey; and Martha de Lyra Barker, I am amazed at your ability to listen, and then deliver in such timely fashion. Tim Holtz, I valued the way you moved this book from proof to final PDF with expertise, adaptability, and efficiency.

My eleven siblings. When we were no longer within the "Hey...Dunfey" reach to point when we needed one another, our parents' lessons inspired us to keep connected in any way possible despite the distance. From "way out west" in Ohio during the Great Depression; from the "Round Robins" and letters to and from WWII outposts; from convents in Japan, Honolulu, San Francisco, and New England; to countless memos to and from hotel offices; updates via tape recorders and phone calls—and now emails and texts—we have never stopped communicating. Were it not for those family ties, I, as the youngest of the clan, would never have had the personal relationship with each of you that made the writing of this book not only possible, but more significantly, a genuine labor of love and gratitude.

Chronology: From clams to corporations

"A clam up the ladder of success"
Larry Bonko's 1983 headline in the Norfolk, Virginia, *Ledger-Star*

That headline aptly describes the evolution of the Dunfey Family business. Although turkey sandwiches were the original menu item at Dunfey's Luncheonette in the Acre section of Lowell, Massachusetts in the 1920s, it was, indeed, "pushing clams" at Hampton Beach, New Hampshire starting in 1946, that turned the first profit for LeRoy W. Dunfey and Sons. The author describes the seacoast clam stand as "no bigger than a phone booth," a metaphor that is not as obvious in a cellphone era as it was in 1983 when the Dunfeys secured the Pavillion Tower in Virginia Beach.

Twenty-five thousand dollars to buy a fried-clam stand miles north on the Atlantic coast in 1946 was a universe away from the amount the Hong Kong investors paid for Omni Hotels in 1988. The worldwide odyssey of a small New England company, Dunfey Family Hotels, happened in an unlikely way and from unlikely roots:

1920–1950: LeRoy "Roy" Dunfey opens a variety store in the Acre section of Lowell, Massachusetts, an immigrant enclave. Soon Dunfey's is a luncheonette thanks to the homemade roast turkey sandwiches delivered by Catherine "Kate" Dunfey while the couple also make and deliver a dozen kids in two dozen years! (see chapter 3)

1946: Three Dunfey sons return from WWII. LeRoy's practical sense (his sons would need jobs) and entrepreneurial spirit encourage him to buy a fried clam stand at Hampton Beach, NH, and build a "real" restaurant, also featuring clams, in the empty lot next to the original luncheonette in Lowell, 353 and 375 Broadway Street. Its drive-in car hop service was a first in the area. (see chapter 11)

1948: Thanks to the G.I. Bill making college education possible, the Dunfeys purchase a small block of buildings consisting of Hamm's Market and the College Pharmacy in the town of Durham, home of the University of New Hampshire. Transformed from pharmacy to restaurant (preserving its counter) over Christmas vacation at UNH, the Dunfeys went on to open one of the first (if not the first) "speedy launderettes" in the region and later replaced the market with one of the first (if not the first) major student supply stores in a college town, Town and Campus. (see chapter 12)

1950–1: Major fire in the center of Hampton Beach requires new construction on the C Street block. The inferno challenges our family to make a whole new commitment to Hampton Beach. Developer Paul Hobbs accepts the Dunfey bid for a lease on his new building. This C Street location is prime real estate and also launches the Dunfeys into the real estate and then, insurance businesses, because, according to Walter, "No one else would insure us!" (see chapter 13)

1954: The purchase of Lamie's Tavern in the center of Hampton, New Hampshire, launches the move (almost by accident) into innkeeping. From a varied assortment of entrepreneurial ventures, the family now make Lamie's its home office and hub, with *Come as you Are*, its message. (see chapters 15, 16).

"Let us make sure that each guest feels the same personal warmth they'd expect in our own home."
—*Catherine A. Dunfey*

1959: The takeover of the bankrupt Carpenter Hotel, Manchester, New Hampshire. Added bar/dining concept on twelfth floor: "Top of the Town." The hotel is a gathering spot for political campaign hopefuls each Primary season. (see chapters 21, 22)

1960: A move to Maine and purchase of the Portland property comprised of the Eastland Hotel (six hundred rooms) connected on certain floors to the Congress Square Hotel (two hundred rooms, many of which had permanent residents). At the time, it was the largest commercial hotel (as distinguished from resort

Carpenter Motor Hotel
Manchester, N.H.

Eastland Motor Hotel
Portland, Maine

hotels) north of Boston. Developed "Top of the East" piano bar and the first Polynesian restaurant, "The Hawaiian Hut" in Maine. Later, Dunfey would build and operate the first round hotel in the northeast, in South Portland. (see chapter 21)

1962: Opening of the Wayfarer Inn, Bedford, New Hampshire, site of historic John Goffe's Mill and first property—complete with authentically designed covered-bridge for pedestrians, the first hotel built by Dunfey Family Hotels with award winning architectural design of Donald Jasinski.

It becomes one of the Sheraton franchise properties along with 18 other properties making Dunfey the largest New England franchise owner.

The Wayfarer also becomes a center of action for the first-in-the-nation presidential primaries after the 1966 Convention Center complex is completed; connecting the ballroom, private event spaces, and Brookside

rooms to the main restaurant, bar and inn by way of the covered pedestrian bridge. Major networks set up shop with correspondents using the covered bridge and waterfall as a scenic winter New England backdrop for reporting the evening news.

Dunfey brings the first major department store to Maine and New Hampshire: Jordan Marsh (now Macy's). (see chapters 22, 23)

1958–1968: Jerry Dunfey is marketing and advertising director, "with no budget," Jerry adds. The for building and expanding a New England hotel company with some distinctive traits was:

1) Take over rundown, bankrupt, downtown hotels.

2) Go public with your success: advertising supplements in *The Boston Globe, Boston Herald*, and the *Private Line*, the company's own newsletter circulated regularly; create the "Wayfarers Club" and the "Wayfarers Table," for traveling salesmen to network.

3) Reach to Jamaica to introduce new tastes in food, music and service to the northeast, starting with the "Jolly Boys Jamaica Calypso Band"; musicians, Baba and Patsy Motta; and French dining service thanks to professional Jamaican servers. "Waiter exchanges" were developed so that Dunfey and Jamaican staff worked the off-seasons at each other's properties.

4) Recognize and advance qualified women and minorities to management jobs with a career potential. (see chapter 23)

1968: Acquisition of the Parker House, saving the oldest continuously operating hotel in the nation from bankruptcy. (see chapters 26, 27)

1970: First hotel to acquire "air rights" over the Mass Turnpike/Newton—opened as Howard Johnson's.

1971: Priorities turn to refurbishing the Parker House and to the national scene for which greater capital would be required. In 1971, the Dunfeys transfer 100 percent ownership to Aetna Life Insurance of Hartford, CT. Holdings, at that time consist of eighteen hotels and motor inns which the Dunfeys would continue to run and operate. Dunfey saves Royal Coach motor hotel chain for Aetna. Aetna supplies much needed capital for Dunfey Corporation.

With personal and business financials more stabilized, the company direction turns to socially responsible investing and eventually Working Assets/ Citizens Funds, founded by Sophia Collier.

After the Parker House comes the acquisition of Gene Tamburi's Yankee Drummer restaurant in Auburn, MA; the Yankee Pedlar near Holyoke, Massachusetts; and Tobacco Valley in

Windsor, Connecticut. Dunfey creates a "little bit of Ireland" with The "Drummer Boy" motif and its shades of green then popularized in all the Dunfey Taverns, a natural theme for the Dunfeys, whose dad was a drummer, whose home base was Lamie's Tavern, and whose ethnicity was Irish.

Newsweek

Reprinted from the issue of April 14, 1969

Dunfey family: From clams to Parker House rolls   Dan Bernstein

HOTELS:

The Dunfey Touch

For the last ten years a third-generation Irish family has been poking about the New England countryside, buying up one hotel after another. The Dunfey Family—the corporate name of five blarneyful brothers and their 74-year-old mother—now has a chain of eleven profitmakers and this year expects to gross $15 million.

But it is their latest acquisition that has moved the Dunfeys into the big time—that of Boston's famed Parker House, founded in 1854 and the oldest continuously operating hotel in the U.S. Close to the Bay State's gilt-domed capitol, the Parker House in palmier days was a politician's retreat, and it is no doubt fitting that its new owners should be as deeply immersed in New England politics as in commercial hospitality.

The Dunfeys have always been close to the Kennedy clan, with whom they shared common roots in Irish South Boston. Vice president William L. Dunfey, 43, worked for two years for John F Kennedy before 1960 and took an active role in Robert F. Kennedy's later campaigns. Robert J. Dunfey, 41, the treasurer, served as Maine Gov. Kenneth Curtis's campaign manager; Walter, 37,

director of operations, was on the campaign staff of New Hampshire Gov. John W King, and Gerald, 33, the company's vice president for marketing, has also dabbled in politics.

Only brother John, 45, who is president and chief executive officer, has kept his nose pretty much to the grindstone and sees to it that business—generally—comes first. At their annual Christmas meetings, when the family divvies up the pot, individual Dunfeys are docked for the time they have spent on politics during the past twelve months. "I'm still wounded," sighs Bill Dunfey, "from the years I spent with Jack."

The Dunfeys all worked as children in their late father's grocery and luncheonette in industrial Lowell, Mass., operating on a 5 a.m.-to-2 a.m. schedule. (There were twelve Dunfey children altogether; three older brothers branched out on their own and four sisters became nuns.) But it was not until 1946, when Jack, Bill and Bob came back from World War II, that the present Dunfey dynasty really got going. The three young men started a hole-in-the-wall, fried-clam stand at Hampton Beach, a robust resort on New Hampshire's brief strip of sea-

coast. Within four years, using profits and bank loans, they had branched out into a pizza parlor, a penny arcade, one big restaurant and three little ones.

H.Q.: The turning point came in 1954, when they took a deep breath and bought Lamie's Tavern, an oldtime Hampton landmark that had been the halfway point between Boston and northern New England resorts until a superhighway bypassed it. They added a 32-room motel and gave it their now distinctive touch: early American furniture, big fireplaces, ship pictures, dark oak tables and paneled rooms fit for a whaling captain. Lamie's helped boost their take to $500,000 and still remains the headquarters of all the family interests. Mrs. Dunfey, soft-voiced and grayhaired, lives there in an apartment next to son Jack's office, and there the whole family meets every two weeks to talk things over.

They have had a lot to talk over in recent years. Since 1959 they have bought up ten more hotels, starting with the old Carpenter Hotel in Manchester, N.H., where Jack Kennedy, soon afterward, opened his campaign for the Presidency, an event commemorated by a plaque in the lobby. Others, from Portland, Maine, to Hartford, Conn., were acquired from the Sheraton chain (the Dunfeys have kept the Sheraton franchise because of the chain's referral system, but ownership of the various properties is strictly theirs) Always they have added their own distinctive touches, such as a "publick table" where businessmen traveling alone can get acquainted.

But none of these acquisitions could compare in prestige with their latest purchase, the Parker House. The once-elegant establishment—where Longfellow and Emerson used to hold their "Saturday Club" meetings—had become, as Jack Dunfey puts it, "a tired old downtown hotel that just didn't keep up with the times." The Dunfeys bought it for $6 million, plus debts, back payrolls and taxes, and started pumping $2 million into its renovation. Last week, as a sign of the new regime, the Parker House reopened its newly furbished dining room. The Dunfeys had changed quite a lot of things. But not the well-known Parker House rolls.

1971: The Dunfey Family Corporation expands from a regional to a national company, acquiring Royal Coach Motor Inns in Houston, Dallas, Anaheim, San Mateo, Atlanta, and later—"our biggest apple"—New York City's Berkshire Place.

1974 (April 3): The *Hampton Union* front page headline: "Hampton to be Center of Dunfey Operations." Jack Dunfey, founder and CEO, explains: "We are very pleased about this development as we made our start in the hotel industry with the purchase of Lamie's Tavern twenty years ago, and it is apparent that all our people working here in the home office want to continue their careers in the seacoast area."

My sister, Mary, and me,
Hampton, NH. 1983

1976 : With Bob, Bud, Walter, Jerry, and then, Roy, as trusted equals, Jack navigated and negotiated each of the company's later permutations. Under his leadership and with Jerry's marketing initiative, the hotel family would "go Irish."

"We are now international innkeepers," Jack reported, and the company, starting with the Parker House, advertised its welcome in a popular Irish phrase: *Céad Míle Fáilte:* A Hundred, Thousand Welcomes!

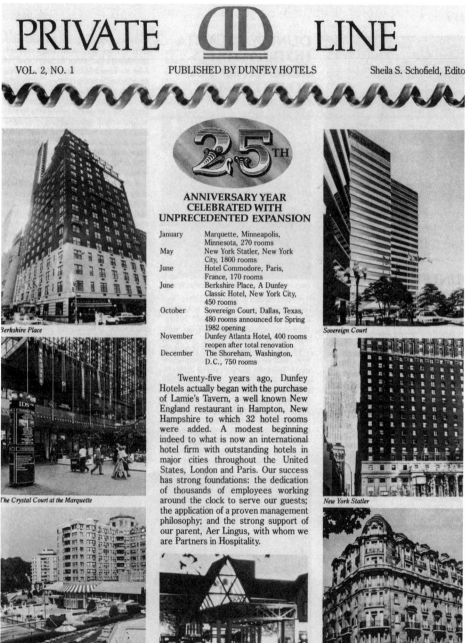

PRIVATE ⅅⅅ LINE

VOL. 2, NO. 1   PUBLISHED BY DUNFEY HOTELS   Sheila S. Schofield, Editor

25ᵀᴴ

ANNIVERSARY YEAR CELEBRATED WITH UNPRECEDENTED EXPANSION

January	Marquette, Minneapolis, Minnesota, 270 rooms
May	New York Statler, New York City, 1800 rooms
June	Hotel Commodore, Paris, France, 170 rooms
June	Berkshire Place, A Dunfey Classic Hotel, New York City, 450 rooms
October	Sovereign Court, Dallas, Texas, 480 rooms announced for Spring 1982 opening
November	Dunfey Atlanta Hotel, 400 rooms reopen after total renovation
December	The Shoreham, Washington, D.C., 750 rooms

Twenty-five years ago, Dunfey Hotels actually began with the purchase of Lamie's Tavern, a well known New England restaurant in Hampton, New Hampshire to which 32 hotel rooms were added. A modest beginning indeed to what is now an international hotel firm with outstanding hotels in major cities throughout the United States, London and Paris. Our success has strong foundations: the dedication of thousands of employees working around the clock to serve our guests; the application of a proven management philosophy; and the strong support of our parent, Aer Lingus, with whom we are Partners in Hospitality.

Berkshire Place

The Crystal Court at the Marquette

Sovereign Court

New York Statler

1979

1976: Bud Dunfey puts it this way: "In 1971, Aetna Life and Casualty adopted us. In 1976, we adopted Irish Airlines." The Dunfey Family Corporation moves on to new international parents, Aer Lingus (Irish Airlines, Dublin, Ireland) which would own the business for the next thirteen years.

1976–1988: With ongoing assistance from Fred Jervis, Bud's University of New Hampshire professor and longtime adviser, the company inaugurates new era of leadership and marketing, hiring Jon Canas in 1977 (more from Jon Canas and about Fred Jervis below). Founders Bob, Walter, and Jerry continue as consultants until 1988. Founders Jack and Bud continue as members of the board of directors until the sale in August 1988.

1984: With purchase of the Omni Hotel chain, the Dunfey name begins to be phased out with the introduction of Omni on all hotels.

1988: Hong Kong Holding Companies announces their acquisition of Omni Hotels.

Bud summarizes his chronology written on June 28, 1988:

> It started with clams. In 1946 when I was discharged from the Marine Corps, my father purchased Hayward's Fried Clam Stand, adjacent to the Ashworth Hotel on Ocean Boulevard, Hampton Beach, New Hampshire. Two young men from Lowell, Massachusetts, Paul McGauun and Jim Cote, who peeled potatoes, washed dishes and short-order cooked with us at the re-named Dunfey's Fried Clam Stand, would still be active with the 12,000 room Omni Hotel chain forty-two years later, Paul McGaunn as senior vice president, operations support; and Jim Cote, director of engineering and energy.

2018: The Omni Parker House continues to move forward with the leadership of John Murtha, general manager since 2007. With Ruth Dwyer, Parker House executive assistant for twenty-two years, and Susan B. Wilson, Parker House historian, **the hotel preserves and enriches its classic tradition.**

Embracing Transition

Jack's vision and strategy were never as evident as in the way he, and my other brothers, orchestrated the smooth transfer of his own position as president and CEO of the family business after almost forty years. Jon Canas, who joined the company in 1976 as vice president and director of sales and marketing, remembers well his introductions to the Dunfey Hotel Corporation and the foreboding winter storm that morning on New Hampshire's I-93: "I was tempted to make a U-turn and abandon this strange idea…After all, I had a very significant job as VP at Sheraton headquarters with international responsibilities taking me from Bangkok to Brussels, from Africa to the Middle East."

He had never heard of the small New Hampshire-based company until he received what he terms, "an intriguing phone call." Wanting to move in his career toward operations and general management, that phone call might just open the door, he thought—at least until that blizzard.

Canas, however, remembers many specifics beyond the weather that day. First, he met Pat Ford, director of operations, whom Canas recalls as "full of questions." He remembers especially his meeting with the Dunfey brothers Jack, Bud, and Walter: "I felt at ease with the three (very different) brothers." Then he learned there were yet another three brothers, Roy, Bob, and Jerry, also involved in the business.

Jack outlined two points according to Canas: "First, the path of operations management and the possibility of his becoming Jack's successor as CEO of the company; and second, the promise that the brothers, and their siblings, would not aspire to run the company, but would be as supportive as possible as long as, of course, results improved…"

Some people questioned the likelihood that the Dunfeys, and Jack in particular, would or could ultimately delegate the company's leadership. But Canas continued to assume increasing responsibilities during the following decade as the Dunfey Hotel Corporation evolved to Omni International Hotels. All the while he worked in close partnership with Jack, the six brothers and key corporate players such as Stephen Lewy, treasurer; Bill McClelland, controller; Jim Stamas, CAO; Bill Sheehan, CFO; Roger Cline, VP development, and others, in particular the talented management team at each hotel.

As promised, Jon Canas became CEO of Omni (International Hotels in 1988) and Jack stepped aside. In 2017, he reflected on those years: "During my tenure with the Dunfey brothers, I experienced nothing else but support and their being true to their word. I greatly appreciated the non-political atmosphere of the company they had created."

Dunfey alumnus, David Colella, then general manager of Boston's Copley Plaza Hotel, hosts a reunion of more than fifty Dunfey corporate alums. Thanks to Skip Stearns' communications, alumni continue to gather at the Exeter Inn in New Hampshire, a property of Hay Creek Hospitality. Dunfey alumnus, Norman MacLeod, is its founder, president and CEO.

Dunfey Alumni Reunion in 2005.

Fred Jervis, longtime corporate and family adviser; founder of the Center for Constructive Change; adviser to hundreds of Dunfey employees; director, Global Citizens Circle pictured here with his wife and partner, Janis Williams.

Listening, Engaging; Leading and then moving on…

The most gifted and visionary adviser in the evolution of the company the Dunfey family created was Fred Jervis. And to recognize Fred is to recognize Jan Williams, the nurse who cared for Fred after he lost his eyesight in WWII; the woman who became Fred's "eyes" and complemented his talents with her compassionate organizational ability. There is just no way to do justice to the impact they had on our family and business for more than a half a century. That extraordinary relationship began with the help of the GI Bill and a teacher/student connection at the University of New Hampshire in 1948—Fred, the professor of psychology and my brother, Bud, the student. And Fred was worth listening to.

When the Dunfey family hotels were beginning to see results: growing profits and opportunities, Fred kept the focus on the right priorities
at every crucial juncture of the journey. Long before the corporate world
would put a name to it, Fred showed us what genuine social responsibility
means: respect for employees, inclusion of women and minorities, consciousness that we must not forget our roots and values, conviction that
we must not pick up the ladder after we climb up. Jack shared with me
the invaluable guidance Fred's helping us walk the talk of corporate social
responsibility in philanthropy provided: identifying and financially supporting small start-ups, worthy causes and individuals. Bud, according to
Jerry, "was good in suggesting we talk one-on-one with Fred when things
might be going off kilter; an awkwardness when one of us did not have a
real interest in an issue or cause that others were promoting."

Fred continually "nudged" us from success—to significance.

It was his inspiration that helped initiate New England Circle/now
Global Citizens Circle, whose mission from the outset was to gather people, diverse in age and economic status, ethnic and racial background, to
engage in civil dialogue on critical issues—dialogue that would lead to
action—constructive change—in our communities, local, national and
global. We see Fred's influence even in the crafting of the 1974 mission
statement which echoes that of the "Center for Constructive Change." He
and Jan, as co-directors, were an integral part of every phase of GCC.

Jerry reminded me that Fred's reach went into other realms, as well,
including judicial and religious leaders like our brother, Richard Dunfey,
chief justice of NH's Superior Court; Boston's first African American
federal judge, David Nelson, and Msgr. Philip Kenney whom many
called, "the conscience of New Hampshire."

Fred facilitated major brainstorming sessions with anti-apartheid activists such as journalist, Donald Woods (whose story is told in the film, *Cry
Freedom*); Fred helped the participants to envision a post-apartheid South
Africa. Jerry recalls, "No one but Fred thought would happen in the time
frame it did!" Fred also helped Walter and Bob convene political leaders such
as Tip O'Neill in seeking a path to peace in Northern Ireland; he contributed
to the Panama Canal negotiations between the US and President Noriega.

Fred Jervis lost his eyesight as a soldier in World War II. With and
through his nurse, Janice Williams, who cared for him after he was
wounded and then became his life partner, he gained vision and insight
beyond any 20/20 measure. With that vision, Fred Jervis influenced many
lives, especially the Dunfeys'.

Global Citizens Circle: From epilogue to prologue

Design by McKayla Dunfey

WHAT ARE CIRCLES?

Circles are highly interactive, moderated conversations. Concerned individuals of diverse backgrounds and opinions add unique perspectives to each program. Questions welcome. Follow up encouraged. Respectful dialogue builds trust. Trust brings change.

1992: Where, oh where, will civil dialogue go?

> Sometimes you get what you don't even realize you need. Before
> the invitation [to be a Circle discussion leader], I had never heard
> of New England Circle [now GCC]...
>
> My mind kept going, "They gather to talk to one another?"
> Could it really be that there is a tradition being built for over a
> quarter century now, where people are invited to come together
> from their different places to talk and listen? I was so moved by
> the evening. The introductions of guests were incredible—pull-
> ing so many people together from so many places
>
> > *—Bernice Johnson Reagon, founder,*
> > *Sweet Honey and the Rock 1998*

Bernice Johnson Reagon

Now we wondered if that tradition would endure. The Dunfeys were no
longer in the hotel business. Six siblings had died in the previous two years,
and the Circle—which had evolved with success in intangible ways but
with no strategic plan or endowment—seemed destined for demise. We
finally acknowledged that providing programs free of charge in order to
assure diverse, intergenerational participation is *not* a plan for longevity.

Some people felt the Circle's unique format and style could not be sustained beyond the Dunfey family itself. Most funders and grant makers
are not interested in supporting "conversation," with legitimate reason.

Measurable outcomes are important. Often, however, focusing on the short term overlooks the time it takes to build inclusive, trusting relationships; and it's people who trust each other who make change—not simply programs.

1994: Life-Line

Enter as partners and sponsors: Pam McDermott and Tom O'Neill. They had experienced many Circles, and we shared hope about peace in Northern Ireland at a time when the three-decade strife was inching toward a peace process. Since "Bloody Sunday" in 1972, GCC and the O'Neill family had built trust among Protestant and Catholic communities. McDermott O'Neill Associates partnered with the Circle for two years. That partnership, along with the scholarships/sponsorships from individuals such as Zev and Pearl Hack, as well as Jeryl and Steve Oristaglio, and socially responsible companies such as Stonyfield Farm (Meg and Gary Hirshberg) and Pax World Funds (Joe Keefe), provided a life-line to GCC.

Beyond the McDermott-O'Neill two-year partnership, long time dedicated board members like Bill McNally, Tito Jackson, Carolyn Benthien, Frieda Garcia, and Lois Roach, kept on, guided by Randy Benthien offering his expertise as facilitator *pro bono*, to shape a future for the organization. The outcome led to the Circle's "holding on," by co-sponsoring programs with other area non-profits. Southern New Hampshire University then invited us to archive GCC materials. Christopher Cooper, SNHU archivist; Xinyi Zhang, graduate intern; and honors student, Melanie Friese were all involved in that process. (www.academicarchive.snhu.edu).

2015: An exciting thing happened on our way to...

An exciting thing did happen on our way to completing the Global Citizens Circle archiving project. In Martin O'Brien, a longstanding leader in Northern Irish justice and peace initiatives, we found a new partner. He is a member of GCC's international advisory board and had been involved with the Circle and the Dunfey family for over twenty-five years. His recently established Social Change Initiative, an international not-for-profit based in Belfast and committed to improving the effectiveness of activism for social change, shared many of the Circle's goals and values.

Because of the Social Change Initiative's global partnering with GCC, and GCC's twenty-five year involvement, Southern New Hampshire University's Paul LeBlanc, and Patricia Lynott, president of its University College, Global Citizens Circle was invited to return in 2017 and make our campus office GCC's home.

1974–2016: Dunfeys and more Dunfeys

> "Five Dunfey brothers founded New England Circle (Global Citizens Circle) in the early 70s. In 2016, three Dunfey women ushered in a new era of the non-profit."
>
> —*Jerry Dunfey, founder*

There are three key players who are important in the next chapter of GCC's life. Eleanor Dunfey-Freiburger, professor at SNHU for thirty years, has volunteered for GCC in behind-the-scenes' and leadership roles for thirty-five of the Circle's forty-year history. Nadine Hack, CEO of beCause Global Consulting, has worked pro bono as senior advisor on Circle initiatives for thirty years. Theo Spanos Dunfey, graduate, Brown University and Tufts School of Diplomacy, has been part time managing director as well as volunteer for twenty years. She is now full-time president of GCC.

Bernice Johnson Reagon had mused: "Could it really be that there is a tradition being built for over a quarter century now (1998), where people are invited to come together from their different places to talk and listen?" In 2018, our answer could now be a wholehearted *Yes.* The chronology of programs reveals years of such gatherings and it is the stories of its participants—some well-known, others not familiar—that strengthen our resolve to "stay at it." The website offers information on the history and can be accessed at globalcitizenscircle.org.

Listen to each one's story. They are all the same, and they are all unique.
Archbishop Tutu uttered these words when opening a session of the Truth and Reconciliation Hearings that Jerry Dunfey, Rodney Ellis and I attended in June, 1996, Worcester County, South Africa.

Grown from each inspiring story, a new era of Global Citizens Circle has dawned. GCC's epilogue has become prologue. Within the context of the story of ordinary mill workers who lived extraordinarily well, it seems natural to conclude this saga of Kate and Roy Dunfey with a few of GCC's many stories.

1) From Phnom Penh to Johannesburg "Children of war—making peace"

We were moved listening to "children of war" from around the world. It was at this Circle that Harry Belafonte and Judith Thompson introduced us to kids—all under fifteen. We heard, for the first time, Arn Chorn, who hid with other children in the jungle of Cambodia's Killing Fields. He had been spared earlier by playing the traditional flute his uncle gave him and taught him because, he said, "The flute will save your life." His uncle meant that the soldiers—many only young men as well—would want to hear their cherished traditional music. Arn's family were victims of Cambodia's brutal Khmer Rouge regimen. According to Arn's account, Reverend Pond, on a mission from New Hampshire, accidentally "stepped on me." Shocked by his "discovery," says Arn, "he took it as a sign that he should save me." The minister adopted Arn, who arrived at Logan Airport on a freezing February day, reflecting that, after surviving in the jungle, he thought he'd "die of the cold" in New England's winter.

In 1998, Arn Chorn Pond, author of *Never Fall Down*, is a longtime GCC advisory board member. He stood among diverse participants and dignitaries from around the world, including President Mandela. Arn played his flute in tribute to GCC's Award recipient, Graça Machel, for her work with child soldiers and authoring the United Nations study, "The Impact of Armed Conflict on Children." That poignant Circle brought many to tears, including the soon-to-be South Africa's first lady. From Cambodia to South Africa, peacemakers continue the struggle.

2) From Jerusalem to Boston, "Israeli-Palestinian Bereaved Parents Forum"

"What unifies us in 'The Parents Circle' is the sorrow, the painful experience, and both of us, Israelis and Palestinians, all of the differences between us disappear because we both suffer. I know there is NO WAY to accomplish peace without negotiation and dialogue. Our hope is to get there someday to spare other families the sorrow..."

—*Dr. Rihab Essawi, The Bereaved Parents Forum*

We were moved by Israeli and Palestinian parents who **expressed** their loss of a child to violence. They shared more than their unspeakable grief. New York Times columnist, Anthony Lewis drew out stories of the parents traveling together to hospitals in Jerusalem and Palestine to donate blood—blending it to symbolize the same life force circulates in all of us as human beings. The Parents Circle now has more than 600 Israeli-Palestinian members. The organization fosters dialogue between Israelis and Palestinians who are brought together by their bereavement and holds out hope that individual reconciliations will someday repair the rift between two nations. The struggle is not over.

3) From Belfast to Washington, DC, "Trauma and Forgiveness"

Who could not be moved at a Circle in 1993, listening to young Alan McBride of the Shankill Community in Northern Ireland describe how his wife was food shopping when a gunman burst into the shop and killed her. The couple's baby daughter survived. Alan later came to DC during the Northern Ireland meetings sponsored by the American Ireland Fund and Global Citizens Circle. Initially, he remained outside, joining protesters against the violence in Northern Ireland.

Fast forward to 2016, where, in sitting his Belfast office of WAVE Trauma Center with co-founder, Nancy Peake, Alan confided that, in the early nineties, while his righteous rage did not diminish, he began to see that he needed to accept the repeated invitation to go *into* the gatherings where his voice could be heard. He did. He accepted the invitation to participate in the dialogue: "You listened to the impassioned sharing of my story, and you continued to work with all of us toward peace." Now, Alan and Nancy Peake oversee WAVE's five centers across Northern Ireland serving hundreds of victims of violence. It now serves the needs of a new generation who inherited trauma resulting from thirty-five years of "The Troubles." Along with those lingering effects, communities also face the challenges of forming a new government at a time when Brexit adds another complicating layer to considerations. While others spend time and words in their commentaries about the original Good Friday Agreement, signed twenty years ago, dedicated seasoned community leaders and activists, like

Monica McWilliams, May Blood, Martin O'Brien, Jackie Redpath, and others not as well-known, forge ahead to "make the evidence change."

4) From Soweto to Boston, "South Africa's Struggles"

Left to right: Johnny Makatini, ANC; Jack Dunfey; Oliver Tambo, founder, ANC; Ted Kennedy, Jr., delegate, 1985 fact-finding mission to South Africa; Frank Ferrari, president, African American Institute.

There was a hush in the room in a 1985 Circle with President in Exile African National Congress (ANC), Oliver Tambo; Johnny Makatini, head of foreign affairs (ANC); and Thabo Mbeki (known more, at the time, as the son of Govan Mbeki (imprisoned with Nelson Mandela). Thabo Mbeki would later become the president of South Africa.

In a quiet, respectful tone directed to the president, a young South African took the microphone in the back of the room: "I have known your voice since I was a young child. My father played the many tapes you secretly sent to us with updates on the struggle and encouragement." Oliver Tambo, in exile, communicated to all his brothers and sisters in South Africa's liberation movement. Now, in the Press Room at the Parker House, Zweleke Sisulu spoke, already having suffered lengthy imprisonments for his activism for a free press and media workers rights. His role models were his parents, the anti-apartheid heroes, Albertina (a nurse and activist considered the "Mother of the Nation") and Walter Sisulu (still, in 1985, imprisoned with Nelson Mandela). He shared that his parents had played those tapes continually in their home.

Zweleke expressed his awe: "I now have the great honor to meet, in person, the hero who belongs to that voice."

5) From North to South: USA, "Freedom Summer 1994"

Like all the other compelling stories shared at Circles, the 1994 Freedom Summer campaign's thirtieth anniversary served as yet another call to "changing evidence" of blatant racism in our country. Carolyn Goodman, a Manhattan clinical psychologist, became a nationally prominent civil rights advocate after her twenty-one-year-old son, Andrew, and fellow volunteers James Chaney and Mickey Schwerner, joined the Freedom Summer campaign to register African-Americans to vote. On June 21, 1964, the three civil rights workers were murdered by the Ku Klux Klan in Mississippi. The Circle on the thirtieth anniversary of Freedom Summer was one of GCC's largest dinner gatherings, with two hundred in attendance. Marian Wright Edelman, the first recipient (1987) of a GCC award honoring Catherine and LeRoy Dunfey, moderated. Each discussion leader served as a table facilitator: Kath Delaney, civil rights advocate; Robert Coles, child psychiatrist, civil rights activist, and author; Randall Robinson, African-American lawyer, author and activist, founder of TransAfrica; Jeana Brown, native of Four Corners, Dorchester, founder of Black Women's Network at Yale and Boston's field director, Freedom Summer '94; Rev. Eugene Rivers, former gang member, minister and co-founder of the Ten-Point Coalition.

2017 and beyond...

Global Citizens Circle and **Social Change Initiative** co-host

Activism That Works!

Circle discussion leaders who will facilitate a dialogue among *all* participants – local and
international, onsite and online via YouTube livestream and Twitter include:

Monica McWilliams, signatory to Northern Ireland's Good Friday Peace Accords, who helped with
Colombia and Syria peace negotiations;

Opal Tometi, SCI Fellow, Nigerian-American Executive Director Black Alliance for Just Immigration,
who co-founded Black Lives Matter

Phumeza Mlungwana, SCI Fellow former General Secretary, South Africa Social Justice Coalition

Heeten Kanti Kalan, Director of Climate Action Fund at the New World Foundation

Special Guests of Honor
Archbishop Emeritus Desmond and Leah Tutu

Wednesday, November 29, 2017
Isivivana Centre, 14:00 – 20:00
Khayelitsha, South Africa

Together with the Social Change Initiative (SCI) in Belfast, and Southern
New Hampshire University (SNHU), Global Citizens Circle re-launched
with a weeklong series of programs in the Khayelitsha Township outside of

Cape Town, South Africa. The "hub" event around which all the other programs were built, culminated with the twentieth anniversary of GCC's first delegation visit to South Africa in 1998 when we honored First Lady Graça Machel in Johannesburg, and Adelaide Tambo, member of Parliament, in Cape Town.

In November, 2017, we honored Archbishop Desmond Tutu and his wife Leah for 'starting early and staying at it"—their lifetime of tireless advocacy and leadership.

One hundred-twenty five participants, including twenty SCI fellows from around the world, along with Vice-President of Global Affairs at SNHU, Chrystina Russell, students and other South African activists participated. Each of the three discussion leaders, (see program cover above- Isivivana) shared a personal story about facing an overwhelming and disheartening crisis, and the steps they took to persist despite the odds. In their own stories, participants expressed their frustrations, questions, anger, as well as, admirable determination.

We were reminded, once again, this time in a South African township, that we must "listen to each story." One student expressed the pain and fear that echo so many others'. And, as Archbishop Tutu says, her story is also "unique."

November 24—December 3, 2017
Township of Khayelitsha, South Africa
"This is some kind of magic," my table partner whispered to me.

The afternoon discussion had been facilitated by Heeten Kalan, longtime GCC participant, and led by three seasoned activists (see program cover above). Now, in dinner conversations, the 125 participants had introduced themselves. The initial round of follow up reflections mixed with the coriander, curry aromas. And then, one South African teen at my table who had introduced herself as having "the most difficult name to pronounce," seemed to find a way to express something much more difficult than her name: her anguish about the challenges of growing up in a township: "We do not understand what is happening to ourselves as we grow; our parents do not understand." She gave examples of confusion exacerbated by violence. "If I had not found this place [The Equal Education Centre at Isivivana where our programs were being held], I don't know what would have happened to me."

Her words spun a story of being swept from one dwelling to another, from one school to the next. We were impressed by her ability to convey her experiences with passion and clarity but with no trace of self-pity. Just sheer honesty. Her street-smarts had educated her far more than any formal learning, but her formal learning at the Equal Education Centre in the second largest township of South Africa, was helping her find the way to express herself.

"I came here today discouraged. I have wanted to start a group to talk honestly about being a teenager, but it has seemed impossible. Then I listened to those amazing ladies at this afternoon's discussion and I said, 'I can do it. I can start my program, and I will.'"

At twelve other African-design-covered tables across the room, students, entrepreneurs, Belfast Northern Ireland's SCI fellows from nine countries, GCC delegates, SNHU leaders, philanthropists, and not-for-profit activists, listened and shared stories of dreams and setbacks. We all asked questions of one another and listened to one another. By dinner's end, we knew what our follow-up to this week of connections could and must be in the long term.

Thanks to social media, we would not have to leave these amazing emerging leaders with only fleeting "good feelings." We are setting up online follow-up for mentoring and making connections; we can link these students, discussion leaders and others to a host of people and organizations in South Africa and beyond who are doing similar work, and they can help us understand a new generation's purpose and promise. This "magical experience" was only a beginning. There is no magic involved in translating dialogues and dreams into long-term personal links that can sustain those who have "started early." We encourage them to "stay at it" by staying with them on the journey. Their elder role models have done just that—despite disheartening setbacks.

Above all, we know there is no "magic" in that most fundamental of human needs—to be invited, included, and remembered. GCC begins anew in whatever corner of the world we find ourselves around a table: listening, leading, responding with hope—and action.

> We learned from experience that Circle participants do indeed translate their energy and enthusiasm into action
> —*President Jimmy and Rosalyn Carter, GCC discussion leaders,*
> *1986*

> Hope is believing—in spite of the evidence—and then working to make the evidence change.
> —*Jim Wallis, social justice icon and founder,* Sojourners magazine.

Monica McWilliams, professor; founder, Northern Ireland
Women's Coalition; international human rights leader, greets
Archbishop Desmond and Leah Tutu, after the presentation of
the Global Citizens award by Martin O'Brien (right), founder and
director, Social Change Initiative.

Global Citizens Circle continues to recognize ordinary people living
extraordinarily courageous lives. Our awards are made in honor of our parents, Catherine and LeRoy Dunfey, and are inscribed with this tribute:

> These awards have been earned in schools, prison cells, courts,
> protest marches, boardrooms and newsrooms, at kitchen tables
> and in neighborhood lanes. We honor courageous and compas-
> sionate members of our human family. They started early and
> stay at it. Their courage gives us hope.

"The potential for hope is only a sentence away."
              —*Benjamin Zander, conductor, Boston Philharmonic Orchestra,*
                                Global Citizens Circle, July 10, 2018.

Kate and Roy Dunfey's life lessons reflect the Maestro's conviction. A hundred years ago, my parents spoke many a sentence of hope around a large
dinner table and over a small luncheonette counter in the Acre section of
Lowell, Massachusetts. Their counter culture served and sustained their
twelve children. Now, our expanded family of global citizens—each with
a unique story—continues conversations that can lead to hope in our local
and global communities. It is my parents' priceless legacy.

A Circle of Global Citizens Since 1974

A Parker House tradition revived after 150 years with new issues for dialogue and action. Bob Dunfey welcomes Richard Goodwin, President Kennedy's speechwriter, as the first discussion leader of New England Circle at the Parker House. 1974

Kay Dunfey with GCC's second discussion leader Henry Steele Commager, respected historian and scholar of the issue of impeachment. Commager is known as a life-long crusader for civil rights. He asked to return to the Circle because of the "diversity, intelligence, and participation of the guests." Bob Healy, *Boston Globe* columnist, joins in the exchange.

Time to listen; time to question. New Hampshire's Senator Warren Rudman and hearing Rev. Charles Stith's, ambassador to Tanzania.

GCC's Tenth Anniversary Circle: "Nuclear Age" participants
Left to right: James Rouse, civic activist, urban planner; Inga
Thorsson, Swedish leader in disarmament and development; George
Kistiakowsky, Ukrainian-American physical chemist. He joined the
Manhattan Project; Bud Dunfey, moderating. Not pictured: Evelyn
Handler, president, Brandeis University; and John Kenneth Galbraith,
economist and GCC Advisory Board chair.

"Global AIDS and the Human Right to Health," had been scheduled for
September 11, 2001. Its urgency led us to re-schedule it as soon as pos-
sible after that tragedy. The program was dedicated to Jonathan Mann,
American physician who was an administrator for the World Health
Organization, and spearheaded early AIDS research and the Human
Right to Health. Facilitator Janet Wu (not pictured) facilitated the con-
versation with Sandra L. Thurman, Ochoru Otunnu and Eric Sawyer.

Known for "starting early and staying at it," Gloria Steinem, co-founder in 1972 of *Ms. Magazine.* A journalist and social/political activist, she is nationally recognized a leader and a spokeswoman for the American feminist movement and equal rights.

In this 1975 "New Politics" Circle, it looks like "new hairstyles" might be sub-topic. Co-discussion leaders, Georgia State Senator Julian Bond and U.S.Senator William Cohen, Republican from Maine with host, Bob Dunfey. 1975

"Transforming the process: Women at the Peace Table." An issue that continues to call for our action. Left to right: Steve Curwood, PBS executive producer and host, "Living on Earth"; Luz Mendez, feminist writer, journalist, poet, actress; and Swanee Hunt, chair, Women Waging Peace and former ambassador to Austria, founder, Hunt Alternatives. 2003

Dedicating the Martin Luther King, Jr. Room on the Parker House mezzanine in 1977. Left to right: brothers, Jerry, Walter, Jack and Bob join Coretta Scott King in the unveiling.

"Americans for SALT" (Strategic Arms Limitations—Treaty signed, 1972). The Circle, held at Dunfey's Hyannis Hotel brought Catherine Dunfey and Rose Kennedy together once again, in their respective sons' pursuit of this urgent cause. Senator Ted Kennedy and Senator Henry Cabot Lodge.

Eyes on the Prize producer, Henry Hampton, with students after being presented with the Global Citizens Circle award in memory of Catherine and LeRoy Dunfey. Left to right: Brian Brady, NHC (SNHU); Joel and Maria Freiburger, Trinity High School, Manchester, NH; Tim Mills, Manchester Central High School.

Circle issue, "The Brady Bill": Sarah Brady became a gun control activist after her husband, James, White House press secretary, was permanently disabled when shot in the 1981 attempt to assassinate President Reagan. Pictured on left is long-time WBZ reporter, Charlie Austin and, on Sarah's right, Pete Shields, co-discussion leader and founder of the National Council to Control Handguns. 1989

Eugene Lee, sixth grade student, participating in a Circle with facilitator, Susan Weld, and discussion leader, Wei Jingsheng, Chinese human rights activist and democracy fighter and author of *The Courage to Stand Alone: Letters from Prison and Other Writings*. Paul Nelson, president, Aquinas College, Grand Rapids, Michigan, listens thoughtfully. 1999

Child survivor of Cambodia's Killing Fields, Arn Chorn Pond receiving the Global Citizen award. Left to right: Lew Felstein, GCC director; Sean O'Kane, general manager, Center of NH Holiday Inn, co-sponsor; Sharon Cohen, Reebox, co-sponsor; Kerry Kennedy Cuomo, moderator; Arn Chorn Pond; Jerry, Bob, Eleanor and Jack Dunfey, Global Citizens Circle. 2001

"Liberal vs. Conservative," is the theme for a discussion between New Hampshire Governor John Sununu (left) and Congressman Barney Frank. Their different opinions on issues were punctuated with humor, a key factor advancing the conversation with participants. 1986

Towering physically over us as he towered intellectually during his long career as an economist, John Kenneth Galbraith celebrated his 91st birthday with his wife, Kitty, at a Global Citizens Circle.

We had no trouble listing a trait of Galbraith for every letter of the alphabet. The baker had the challenge of fitting each one on the cake though.

1974–1994 CIRCLES: INTERNATIONAL AFFAIRS • WORLD PEACE

Edward Markey, "Nuclear Proliferation"

"*In 1983, I was joined by John Kenneth Galbraith and Dr. Helen Caldicott, the founder of the American anti-nuclear movement, at a New England Circle on the politics of proliferation. With the world precariously perched on the tightrope of mutually assured destruction and faced with an administration that was committed to nuclear brinkmanship, we gathered to align ourselves in defiance against one of the most important concerns of our species.*

We gathered for twenty years to challenge these issues and our mission is not yet complete. NewEngland Circle has served an indispensable role in confronting the crucial issues of our time. Ever ahead of the curve and prescient in their ability to focus our attention, the Dunfey family has created a common ground from which progressive ideals have flowed. New England Circle has served as the seminal force for progressive ideals as well as the preeminent voice of humanistic concerns ranging from racial desegregation to nuclear non-proliferation."

—*Edward J. Markey*
U.S. Congress, Massachusetts
Circle Discussion Leader, 1983

Bob Dunfey introducing Texas congressman, Mickey Leland, Circle co-discussion leader addressing, "Drugs Circle the Americas" in 1988 with Clara Lopez Obregon, a Harvard-trained economist, and in 2014, the alternative democratic pol's nominee for President of Colombia. Months after the Circle, Mickey was leading his third delegation to deliver essential supplies to famine-stricken Ethiopia. The plane crashed, killing the congressman, his congressional staff of talented, dedicated young leaders; USAID staff and American and Ethiopian supporters. Mickey championed causes of the poor and disempowered. His efforts, vision, and heart could not be confined to the boundaries of his congressional district or one nation. Mickey, a true global citizen, whose first child is my brother, Jerry's godson.

For 30 years, Texas legislator, Rodney Ellis has been a GCC participant and global advisor, making his own mark while carrying on Leland's legacy especially in the Texas Legislative Internship Program. "I was inspired to create TLIP in 1990 because my mentor, the late Congressman Mickey Leland, stressed the importance of using one's individual success to provide opportunities for others."

Civil Rights icon, Congressman John Lewis, with Tito Jackson and Eleanor after being presented the Global Citizen Award in Washington, DC, 2003, for "starting early and staying at it." He personifies Jim Wallis' definition of hope: "believing in spite of the evidence— and then working to make the evidence change."

As Jerry describes the courage of Wendy Woods and her husband, Donald, she accepts the Global Citizens Award from Archbishop Tutu in 2001. Donald, journalist and anti-apartheid activist died just months before the Circle in Belfast, Northern Ireland. Twenty years earlier, the family had to find refuge outside South Africa after the youngest of their five children received a"gift" in the mail—a poisoned T-shirt designed to maim or kill the wearer through absorption of poison into the bloodstream. It had been sent by security police to the five-year-old daughter of Donald Woods, the author of Biko (1988 film "Cry Freedom.") The burns did heal and served to deepen the Woods' family commitment to destroy the corrupt system that spawned such evil. In accepting the GCC award, Wendy read one of Donald Woods' classic editorials answering an apartheid leader's cynical question: Who-would-even-rejoice-at-the-overthrow-of-apartheid? Donald's response—after cataloging a plethora of world communities from remote villages and major cities, "rejoicing," concluded: "The whole bloody world will rejoice!"

Hubie Jones, GCC director and professor, J.W. McCormack Institute, UMass, Boston; Pat McGonagle, president, Plan Sponsor Compliance Systems; Bill Forry, editor-in-chief, *The Reporter Newspapers*, Boston; and Linda Dorcena, Neighborhood Development, City of Boston.

"I (Governor Shaheen) recognize that one party, one group of people, doesn't have all of the answers on any given issue and that we are really better decision makers if we get more people involved in the process—if we try to get a broader perspective on the issues." Following a spirited conversation, the first woman governor of New Hampshire listens to Harlan Jones, executive director, Citizens for Safety, Boston.

GCC honors First Lady Hillary Clinton for her decades of work with children when her book, *It Takes a Village*, was published. Pictured here receiving the Global Citizens award is Maria Freiburger, teacher, Jackson Mississippi. In my remarks, I "had" to mention that, as the twelfth child of my parents, and with their almost a hundred grand and great-grandchildren, Kate and Roy Dunfey must have thought it was their sole responsibility to "populate" the village!

Global Citizens Circle honored founder and director of Yakar Center for Social Concern, Benjamin Pogrund, journalist, with the GCC award for Justice and Reconciliation, in Jerusalem. South African born Pogrund was with the *Rand Daily Mail* in Johannesburg for 26 years, reporting on Black politics and apartheid. Pogrund and Ata Khalil Qaymari, general director of Almasdar for Translation and Press Services and project facilitator for workshops in conflict resolution, peace and reconciliation engaged participants in a challenging dialogue. Left to right: Eleanor Dunfey, Nadine Hack, Ata Zaymari, Benjamin Pogrund. Jerry Dunfey, Zev and Pearl Hack.

Theo Spanos Dunfey presents the Global Citizens Award to Yhitzak Frankenthal, left, and Mubarek Awad (right). Awad, a Palestinian-American psychologist, founder of the Palestinian Center for the Study of Nonviolence in Jerusalem, was deported by the Israeli Supreme court in 1988 after being jailed for organizing activities involving nonviolent civil disobedience. He has since formed Nonviolence International, which works with various movements and organizations across the globe. After his son, a soldier, Arik, was killed by Palestinians in 1994, Frankenthal founded a bereaved families forum, The Parents Circle, an organization fostering dialogue between Israelis and Palestinians who are brought together by their loss of a relative. It holds out hope that individual reconciliations will someday repair the rift between two nations. The struggle is not over.

Global peacemakers gather in Atlanta to honor Coretta Scott King. Presenting
the Global Citizen Circle award are Left to right: Maria Freiburger, Jerry Dunfey,
Archbishop Tutu; honoree, Mrs. King; John Hume, and Ambassador Andrew
Young. Mrs. King had presented John Hume the Martin Luther King award earlier
at the Ebenezer Baptist Church.

Elma Lewis, known as the "Grande Dame of Roxbury" and a true cultural icon,
enjoys Harry Belafonte's teasing as he presents the "Matriarch of Roxbury" with
the Global Citizens Circle award in 2001. Elma founded the National Center for
Afro-American Artists in 1968, eighteen years after opening the Elma Lewis School
of Fine Arts in Roxbury. Elma was at the forefront of civil rights action as well as
one of the first ever MacArthur Award Fellows. Above all, Elma was a no-nonsense
mentor and, all teasing aside, Harry honored her for that inestimable gift.

Global Citizens Circle Transition Team

Global Citizens Circle's mission remains the same: convening intergenerational, diverse, concerned people for civil dialogue that can lead to constructive change in our local and global communities. Circles remain free of charge to participants. We count on the transition team's generosity of time and talent and thank them for making GCC's re-founding a reality:

Nadine Hack, GCC senior global advisor; CEO, beCause Global Consulting

Theo Spanos Dunfey, GCC president and executive director

Eleanor Dunfey-Freiburger, GCC co-chair; professor emerita, SNHU

Elizabeth Tamposi, GCC co-chair; former assistant secretary of state, George H.W. Bush administration

Jonathan Marston, GCC treasurer; partner, Williams Marston LLC, Boston and New York City

Rodney Ellis, GCC director; commissioner, Harris County, Texas; Texas State senator, 1990-2017

Peter Dunfey, GCC business manager

Jerilyn Asher, GCC global advisor; co-founder and executive vice-president, JIBO, Inc. president, The Rainmaker Group

Heeten Kanti Kalan, GCC director; New World Foundation and South Africa Development Fund

Mack Wilbourn, GCC global advisor; president, Mack II, Inc. Atlanta, GA

Janet Breslin-Smith, GCC global advisor; president, Crosswinds Strategic Consulting; historian, National War College Alumni Association, Washington, DC

Lilleye Ramos-Spooner, GCC advisor, community activist and longtime advocate for families living with HIV/AIDS.

Catherine Rielly, GCC global advisor; executive director, Rubia, Inc. USA, Afghanistan, Mali

Deb Krizmanich, GCC consultant; founder and CEO, Powernoodle, Inc

Sara Mears, GCC website design

A new generation of organizers, social media specialists and interns:

Melanie Friese, SNHU, class of 2018; University of New Hampshire graduate student in education

Carey Dunfey, master's in city planning from the MIT department of urban studies and planning

Mia Dunfey, University of Vermont alumna; City Year Corps, Miami, FL

McKayla Dunfey, Harvard University graduate student in urban planning.

Mei Seva, Hampshire College, class of 2018

Meaghan Blaisdell, SNHU School of Education, class of 2018

Please visit us at globalcitizenscircle.org for more information.

About the Author

Born the youngest of twelve children in Lowell, Massachusetts, Eleanor Dunfey grew up working with her siblings in the family's luncheonette and clam stand, which eventually grew into Omni Hotels International. She joined the order of Notre Dame de Namur, serving as a nun for thirteen years. She earned her master of arts degree at the University of San Francisco and was dean of women at Emmanuel College in Boston.

Now professor emerita at Southern New Hampshire University (SNHU), she was the university's first endowed chair of business ethics and civic engagement. Eleanor was a recipient of the university's excellence in teaching award and taught in its Malaysia program in 2001.

For more than thirty years, Eleanor has co-chaired Global Citizens Circle, a non-profit educational forum founded by her family in 1974. Its mission is to convene diverse groups of concerned individuals for civil dialogue that can lead to constructive action on critical issues in our communities, nation, and world.

The recipient of honorary degrees from Southern New Hampshire University in 2014 and Franklin Pierce University in 2008, Eleanor is married to SNHU Professor Emeritus James Freiburger Ph.D. They have two adult children and five grandchildren.

from Ballyferriter to Boston;
back to Ballyferriter,
Belfast, and beyond…